In Them Days

A Scrapbook of Friends and Happenings

and..

An Alternative Enterprise

by

J. D. Bramley

Don Bramley.

First Published by J. D. Bramley, 2003

Home Farm, Sherburn-in-Elmet, Leeds LS25 6AD
Yorkshire, UK

www.in-them-days.co.uk

Copyright © J. D. Bramley, 2003

Typeset by Barbara Wilson

Printed in England by North Wolds Printers Ltd.,
Pocklington, York.

ISBN 0-9546225-0-2

CONTENTS

Page

INTRODUCTION

CHAPTER 1 - Reminiscences from the Milford Messenger
Memories are made of This 1
Farming - The Good Old Days 3
Keep Right on to the End of the Road 6
Friends or Foes 9
Young Farmers 12

CHAPTER 2 - Jim Bramley's Cycling Adventures
Bike Ride to Brighton 14
One Man on a Bike to Switzerland 16
Trip into Scotland 19

CHAPTER 3 - Dick Pearson's Stories
Building the farmstead 1939 21
Dick Pearson and His Load of Hay 23

CHAPTER 4 - Sherburn People and Memories
Old John Thornton 31
My Friend Eddy 33
Dolly Battersby's Wonderful Sherburn 40
Claude Kendrew and His Sherburn Memories 53
The Windmill 65
The Cinema, Joe Mills and Harold Mills 67
Red Red Robin 72

CHAPTER 5 - South Milford
Alec Jackson 73
Vic Williams 76
Bowers Row - Where's That 79
Alf Burnley 81
Bob Cockerham 83
George Watkinson 86
Guy Wilson 92
The Belles of Saint Mary's 96
Interview with Dennis Hick 98

CHAPTER 6 - Monk Fryston
Old John - Mr J. J. Foster 103
Monk Fryston 106
The Life of Arthur (Warren) 115

CHAPTER 7 - Fairburn
Fairburn Memories 125
Icy Coolly 139
Jim Bellwood and the Pollum Fire 141

CHAPTER 8 - The War
Wartime Escapades of Flight Sergeant Sid Dudley 1480232 146
Harry Rawling and the Railway of Death 161
The One that Got Away 167
Nurse Metcalfe 170

CHAPTER 9 - Sport
This Sporting Life 173
I Was There 176
Warv Up and Gee Back 178
The First Win of the 1997 Season 180
September Cricket 182

CHAPTER 10 - Writers
J. L. Carr 183
Frank Muir and J. L. Carr 186
A.G. Street 188

CHAPTER 11 - Miscellaneous
1932 and All That 190
Every Village Should Have One 191
Signing In 192
Grandpa Walker 194
The Last Roundup 197

INTRODUCTION

It will take some explaining as to how I come to be trying to write a book. My father and sister were the bookworms of this family, Father spending between 2/6 and 7/6 on his Tuesday Corn Exchange days for second-hand ones. Sister Kay would infuriate my mother by reading whilst dusting or washing up. Kay's daughter Joanna started a magazine called Storm, which printed stories from Eastern Bloc countries.

In 1945 I was packed off to Drax Grammar School at the other side of Selby, now a twenty-five minute drive away, but then, to an eleven-year-old, the back of beyond. There I mainly discovered rugby which has been more than just a game - nearly a religion. The battles fought for fun over ten or fourteen years at Selby, the friends made and their sons too, the high temples of Twickers, Cardiff and Dublin visited have all been a major part of my life. At Drax I enjoyed drawing, history, geography and English - not the best subjects for a potential farmer. An ex-Hessle prop Harry Hopper and bachelor R.E.F. Maloney were my favourite teachers. Both later became good friends and Spike Maloney was a kindly headmaster who eventually left £59,000 to school music in his will. What he would say if he knew I had succeeded him in supplying quotes for the Menu at the Old Draxonian's Annual Dinner I don't know!

The Young Farmers was another golden road I went along at school and later 'til old age of twenty-six at Church Fenton. Fathers and interested worthies kept an eye on us at meetings. It was a great grounding in how things should be run, and in all my travels, except for the WI, I found nothing to beat it. Reports were given, minutes taken, speakers introduced properly (most of the time), questions asked and thanks proposed and seconded. We organised our own meetings, matches, rallies, parties and balls at the Riley Smith Hall Tadcaster and Harrogate. Later on with our fathers' cars and more worldly, we would retire with the speaker to the Half Moon. Ted Whitaker's wife would spoil us with juicy pork pie, chutney and introduced us to serviettes! Young Farmers also got me to Norway with on-going contacts and life-long friendships! Labour was short on farms in the fifties. All our men seemed to go off to Avery's for an easier life and more money. I had had only a week off at Scarborough in the three years since leaving school, so when particulars came round of an exchange visit I signed up and father didn't object too much. He couldn't really as in his young days he had biked to Brighton, Aberdeen, round Ireland and across France to Germany, Switzerland and Italy. He also raced at Roundhay Park as the Flying Farmer and did over fourteen thousand miles one year - more than I do in the car.

It was a two-night mini cruise in those days from Newcastle to Oslo on Fred Olsen ships, with a stop off for an hour at Christiansand on the second afternoon. I was very impressed with the welcome we were getting. Flags were flying at every house and holiday cabin, bands were marching through the town, and the loaded tables back on the ship were specially decorated. It turned out it was Mai 17th, their Independence Day from Denmark in 1814. Many years later I was presented with a full size flag and had to buy a flag post, which needed to be extended to look right. I proudly fly it for visitors, birthdays and of course every Mai 17th. We arrived home after an eye opening time, to a wet miserable coronation in June '53, with the house full of ancient aunties and friends crowding round the just bought black and white television. For me Stanley Matthews was more magical on it, helping Blackpool win the FA cup. I have been to Norway and Lier Valley thirteen times since by various routes, and twice skiing. I have hitch hiked and sailed up the Hardanger and Sogne ffiords with pal George Woodall, and hitched by myself via Hull, Rotterdam, Amsterdam, Copenhagen and Stockholm to Oslo.

I married Pat Walker in September '64 and took her there on honeymoon - I had to! Part of the time we stayed three nights in a log cabin (with flag) on a lake, and came home by train over and through the mountains to Bergen. We are proud of our now grownup children Suzanna, Karen and Martin James and our four grandchildren, the last arriving in June and July 2003. I was fortunate to be born into a farming family with lots of farming uncles and grandparents at the time, sadly not so now. Pat's father was a buyer of Irish Cattle and her grandmother was the eldest of the famous Makin family of Fairburn. Consequently, son Martin has enough farming genes in him to see Home Farm (between Sherburn and South Milford) celebrate four generations (with two on the bench) and a hundred years here since 1906. Vast changes have taken place and I have mixed feelings at the, still probable, building of many houses on our best land. Subsidizing this book could be one bonus from that.

I think I started taking slide photos on my third Young Farmers exchange trip in the winter of '57. My pal Phil Batty got me going, and his chemist friend, Ken Rutter at Adel, sold us films and equipment with a bit knocked off. His wife Bunty supplied the supper!

Later, after I had initially been conned into showing my pictures to Young Farmer's clubs, Phil became my map-reader and supplier of information. This turned out to be a great happening for me, as I had dried up talking about pea growing at a public speaking competition. Describing my pictures in the dark wasn't a problem, and amazingly I have had a lot of pleasure doing it for over forty years. The late Bob Sutton, the late Eddy Edmunds, and now Peter Watkinson (son of George) have turned hundreds of old photos and postcards, which people have kindly lent me, into slides. Besides Norway we now have shows on Sherburn (two nights), South Milford, Barkston Saxton and Fenton, 'This England', 'This Yorkshire', 'Milford Cricket Club', 'Selby Rugby Union', 'Old and Present Farming', 'Gardens' and my favourite 'The Good Old Days at Monk Fryston Hall'.

Taking pictures is my kind of drug and during this summer a box of thirty-six slides usually comes back in the post every three or four weeks, and matching them to these articles has been quite a pleasant task. I started writing as cricket correspondent for the Milford Messenger Parish Magazine in 1989. I collect cricket books especially Cardus, Kilburn and Swanton, and set my sights high. I sometimes borrowed bits from them but no one noticed. I also collect John Arlott but his poems rarely match my needs. No one else would do it, but I quite enjoyed putting articles together and seeing them in print with my initials at the bottom. I was asked to carry on in the winter months, so I started transcribing interesting chats on tape of local characters (with permission) that I'd done over the last twenty-five years.

When I started Somme and Ypres veterans were still around but sadly now my World War Two friends are beginning to get thin on the ground. I come home from these sessions on a high, knowing that if everything has worked I have events and situations recorded that many of their own children don't know of, and aren't interested in, until it is too late.

It has been fun so far bringing everything together for this book, but it has taken longer than expected. There are many people to thank. Firstly, all those who gave a night up to talk to me, if we weren't friends before, I feel we are now. I can't take any credit for my father's cycling bits or Dick Pearson's contributions, though they are good examples of village education with minimum facilities, but enquiring minds, lots of reading and a sense of adventure. These are random selections of pieces in not much sort of order, and I apologise to those who may be disappointed not to find themselves here. Maybe next time!

I would like to thank Barbara Rigby, in the early non-technology days, for making out my writing, correcting spellings and making some sort of sense for the Messenger articles and since she retired, Pat's old tennis colleague Barbara Wilson has taken over and has the same problems, but she puts them on a disc to simplify things for present editors. She also 'enjoys' mixing and matching the photos in after Peter has 'moused' out defects and stored them on his computer for future use, and maybe on his websites.

All this really started because of a tragic accident. In 1967 Leif Sylling came from Norway to work and live with us for nearly a year. He was brother of the 1964 World Ploughing Champion and was the perfect lodger and babysitter. Sadly in December 1973 he broke his back in the sea whilst on holiday and has been in a wheelchair ever since and lives on his own. To try to help and be positive we sent him tapes of the families activities, school concerts, carol services, holidays, recitations and singa-longs etc. I think it did us more good than him! At first Leif recorded back on the same tape, (to save money), until we realised we were rubbing out the history of our three children growing up, so it was a good excuse to go and bring some back. It had usually rained for a week when I dated them and set the scene. Prices were always bad and have got worse since! Now if I want cheering up I have half an hour on the 'phone with him, and I've yet to hear a complaint.

This book, if it ever appears, is dedicated to Leif, and also to someone who always gently sidestepped me when I tried to fix him up for a chat. I think he's the only one to resist me, so I know very little about him! I do know that he must have suffered greatly as a prisoner in Japan, and when he died recently he took his horrors with him. I'm very proud of this picture I took of him. His name is George Mytum. J.D.B.

Leif Styling

George Mytum

FOREWORD

It is said that everyone has one book in them and in Don Bramley's case, I think there might well be several. When he gave me the manuscript of 'In Them Days' to read, I considered it a privilege. 'When he then asked me to write the foreword, I realised the full significance of the Yorkshire saying 'Tha gets nowt for nowt.' Why Don should bestow such honour on me, I have no idea, for I have no particular qualifications for the job, but such is his personality that when he asks one for a favour, it is just about impossible to say 'no'. (And who is not partial to a little flattery anyway?)

Our friendship now extends into its fourth decade. It began through our association with the South Milford Cricket Club of which he became Chairman and I was invited to be their President in the early Seventies. I still hold that position - (I suspect because no one else is daft enough to take on the job of making the main speech at our Annual Dinner) - and Don has graduated ' ever upwards to the role of elder statesman and with his son, Martin, still does an enormous amount of unsung work behind the scenes.

He is a man of many parts, - farmers local historian, photographer, sports buff (especially cricket and rugby - both codes), part-time barber's shop singer and much else, and above all, a family man.

He has a deep interest in people and in the historical and sociological content of the environment in which he lives. More than that, he has the patience and the foresight to record all of this for posterity and therefore for the enjoyment of others.

This book is a collection of memories, faithfully recorded and graphically presented. Most of us observe but do not record, perhaps out of laziness or lack of confidence in our ability to do so. Thus, we deprive others of the chance to share our enjoyment.

Don Bramley has that ability and confidence and there is much warmth and love of tradition in what he has assembled here. This book could well have been entitled 'Harvest Time of Memories' and like me I hope you will thoroughly enjoy reaping the harvest.

Ken Hammill 14.04.03

The Moving Finger writes; and, having writ,

Moves on: nor all thy Piety nor Wit

Shall lure it back to cancel half a Line,

Nor all thy Tears wash out a Word of it.

Rubáiyát of Omar Kháyyám

CHAPTER 1

REMINISCENCES FROM THE MILFORD MESSENGER

MEMORIES ARE MADE OF THIS

"A quote from today's (8.2.98) supplement on the over fifties caught my eye as I felt I qualified for part of it, if not all! - worldly cares evaporate to leave a spiritual essence - with grandchildren."

Earlier a combination of all three had granddaughter Billie-Giorgia, daughter Karen and potential godmother Suzanna attending family service at Hambleton Church with a christening in mind. In this day and age this pleases me. All three of our children have been christened and confirmed and are used to church, but sadly I am the only attendee, and still waiting to see the light.

Sherburn church from Kirkgate in the sunshine

We are surrounded by wonderful historic churches, that all struggle for survival with ageing helpers, thin attendances and financial worries. Sherburn is my treasure and local one, but like Benny Hemsworth I have interest and friends at Milford, Monk Fryston and Saxton, where after an outlay of thousands of pounds on restoring their three bells and stonework after a lightning strike, the bells remain silent and the church nowhere near full. Alas, I read in the Hambleton, Birkin, Haddlesey and Hirst magazine today that January's total givings came to £743 and their monthly outgoings £2305! Shops, schools, pubs, cricket clubs and churches have or could all eventually disappear from village life because of indifference, if young blood doesn't begin to take an interest in their running and finance and so on.

None of this came to mind as we sat in Hambleton's cosy brick built church amongst the Brownies, Guides, a brass quartet and one or two familiar faces. My thoughts were partially back to a breezy day in September '62 when the church was full and resounded to 'Cym Rhonda' at our wedding with Reverend Lowry in charge and my prospective wife one of his Sunday School teachers. It is all a long time ago and the memories of events and long gone Aunts and Uncles have to be jogged by a black and white album, colour slides and a short jumbled cine film now converted to video like the rest. The best man, who shall be nameless, did his duties adequately but didn't impress my mother-in-law with at least one of his jokes. One ten-year-old bridesmaid (in royal blue) from Sussex now lives in Headingley. Her tearful three-year-old assistant, who competed with the bride for camera attention, later published her own magazine for writers from Eastern Bloc Countries and now has her own bundle of fun in London. The very amateur cameraman, Milford fish man, councillor, Young Farmers' leader and my laid-back badminton partner was Harry Butterfield.

Sherburn butcher Walter Wainwright had left Hambleton for Sherburn with his family in 1906, the same year as my father, aged three, arrived from Fairburn, and they remained friends for the rest of their lives.

Uncle George was head of Knottingley School and a first class soccer referee. He had my autograph book a whole season and only managed to get a Chesterfield goalie and the Aston Villa team signed on a programme. At his Christmas parties he was niggardly with his drinks and heating. Ladies attended in layers of woollies and whenever he or Auntie Dolly left the room at least two would jump up to try to mend the fire. Two farming brothers from Bolton Percy, one from Burton Salmon and their wives are all gone now but still having fun on film.

Sherburn council chairman and picture house owner Harold Mills was always full of fun. He could play anything on our piano as long as I could whistle it. Losing both legs later didn't seem to dampen his spirits, and he was never short of argumentative visitors.

These and many more memories came to mind as I walked out of the church door and down to the gate, carrying the next generation. The bride will never forget the trouble the wind caused with her veil. Mysteriously the car wouldn't start but was pushed off successfully by half the Selby pack to go to the posh 'Owl Country Club'.

Back to the present day and calling on the way home at Hambleton's ever open, surviving butcher's shop, to stock up and enjoy Mr. Thompson's banter. The pencil and mental arithmetic still rule there and whilst we discussed the beef trade, Karen added up her purchases and he accepted her maths. That doesn't happen in a supermarket! A most satisfying morning and much more enjoyable than even the Sunday papers.

J.D.B.

Mr. Thompson's Last Day in the shop

With customers and his Grandson, bottom right

The Old Village Shop

Where are the days of my youth,
And that door which just opened so wide?
And the bell that jingled its welcoming notes
As I squeezed through to gaze round inside?

Where is that nice Mr. Thompson
Witti his flat cap, glasses and grin?
And where are the little paper bag things
That he wrapped all my liquorish sticks in?

Where are the big sacks of flour
Or the butter cut up just for you?
Half a pound for young Mrs. Walker
A quarter for old May would do.

Where are the jars on the shelves,
Their contents so tempting to spy?
The humbugs and sherbets peardrops and mints
Whatever my tuppence could buy.

Where are the hams and the tripe,
The ox-tails and trotters and brawn?
And where is the lad on the wobberly bike
Who'd deliver them later that morn?

They've gone like the days of my youth,
The old village shop is closed down.
And Barretts have built upon where it once stood,
Alas there's a Tesco's in town!

Compimed by Margaret Barr with twenty-four hours notice, 10-04-2003. Names slightly altered

FARMING – THE GOOD OLD DAYS

When I left school in 1950, we still had a horse, a cow, kept hens and fattened three geese for Christmas. Jack Bradley came to kill two pigs in the garage on Saturday mornings for home consumption.

In those far off 'good old days' all our corn was cut with a binder. It was stooked, led home, stacked, and the straw stacked again after threshing. In the winter it was used to bed Irish cattle being fattened for beef. The 3ft of muck (manure) was carted out in the spring and spread on the land for potatoes. All this was done by hand!

Haytime casuals - Jim Bellwood(foreman), Walter Wainwright(retired butcher), Frank Downing, Geo Reynolds(ex headmaster), Jim Bramley(boss), Walter Bramley(retired farmer), Peter Hiley(pupil and son of Selby doctor)

To help with the haytime and harvest, father's cousin, Uncle Wally, travelled from Pontefract every day to be stand forker in the field. He was a bit rough and never got tired. His favourite saying was, "Tread them down, they'll be reight!" Later on after a good tea at eight or nine o'clock they would reminisce in a fog of St Bruno and Digger smoke. In the days before television I had nothing to do but listen. Farming, Fairburn, 1st World war, pea pulling, threshing days and cattle buying in the West of Ireland were subjects they never exhausted. Neither of them would have reached fifty then, but to me with their tales of long ago, they seemed positively ancient. Time rolls on and it is my time to look back and act the sage and recount the days when men were men and I was a lad! Our record account books go back to 1896, so it is easy to look up 50-51. Half our present acreage was worked with one more man than now. Harold Barnett, Jack Cawkill, Reg Lincoln, Sam Snowling and Ray (Cosh) Liddle were paid between £5 and £6 a week each. I started at £2 with nothing for overtime! The working day was 7.30am to 5pm with one hour for dinner (lunch) and no stops for drinkings except in haytime and harvest. Five or six women worked on and off most of the year through. Potatoes were planted, picked and sorted by hand. Then they were stored outside in long pies covered with straw and soil. A very simple tool called a hicking stick - a piece of wood with a man at either end - was used to get the 1cwt sacks to the lorry!

Potato sorting - Mesdames White, Lewis, Lincoln, Midgley, Dyson and Spencer

Singling and hoeing sugar beet was a most boring job for everyone for three or four weeks in June. When Jim Bellwood joined us, time went quicker, as we listened annually to his version of World War II and his happy times in the Home Guard. In autumn it was women's work to pull, knock the soil and chop the tops off the beet. Our job was to fork it into trailers and then again into railway wagons at South Milford station. Nowadays a contractor's six-row machine could take the same acreage up in one day and we don't even have to get off the tractor to take the pin out of the backboard!

Hoeing Gang 1960's

We didn't own a sprayer or a baler in those days, so thistles were scythed, docks pulled by hand and all root crops were side hoed many times. The scent of new mown hay didn't compensate for sweat lost and blisters gained. The loose hay was forked into cocks to dry and for safety from rain. When fit, it was led home and stacked in a big stack and, if my memory is correct, usually in gale force winds. Reg Lincoln was the horseman and before safety officers had been thought of he would use a lethal thing called a hay spade to cut a flap one foot thick and four or five feet square. He then proceeded to get this flap on to his back, come down the ladder, and totter up the yard to his stable. He would do this all winter until the stack slowly disappeared. Threshing days were most exciting for youngsters especially in the days before rat poison!! However, after the first hour or two chaff carrying or stacking straw in the dust, the glory began to fade. Thick bread and dripping and fat bacon, hot sweet tea, and listening to Bob Cockerham and his assistant Bill Marshall at drinking time, are among happier memories.

I could go on, but back in 1974 I taped Mr Walter Wainwright and he talked of Sherburn and its farms in 1906, when he first came to live here. He was the last of four generations of butcher farmers going back to 1824. His shop was where Jackson's now is, and he lived at Low Street Farm, which is now Qualter's.

1954 - The Last Harvest at Low Street Farm
Geoff Marklew, Harry Jackson, Walter Wainwright and Jack Stead

To show how times really have changed and for the interest of a few old timers and friends, I record here Walter's Farms in and around Sherburn in 1906.

Sherburn Cross towards Cawood

- Mrs Simpson -White Swan with farm.
- Ambler   -Sherburn Grange.
- E. Sykes   -Ash Row.
- Mr Penty   - Common Farm.
- Mrs Rainbow -Wheatsheaf.

Finkle Hill

- Mrs Wainwright - Butchers shop and farm.
- Paver.
- Lupton
- J. Wheldrick.
- John Atkinson -Stream Farm.

Low Street to South Milford

- Joe Wheldrick.
- F. Bramley.

- Harry Lewis.
- Henry Mason
- Mr. J. Sissons.

Kirkgate

- W. Wainwright - Hall Garth Farm.
- J. Jakeman.
- G. Hill.
- W. Foster
- J. Foster.
- W. Rowley.
- A. Jackson.
- Mr Thurogood.
- Mr G. Hall. - Church Farm
- Mr. W. Dennison.
- Mr. A. Dennison
- John Steel - (bottom of Sherburn Hill).

Going back to these 'good old days' might reduce unemployment figures somewhat, but who would want to, and how many would survive? Safety Officers would have a field day!! J.D.B.

Threshing Gang Home Farm Low Street pre 1906 - James Bramley and Daughters Hetty and Milly
'The Sails of the Mill go Round and Round'

Kirkgate showing Forester's Arms, site of Henry's Garage (now Henry's Mews) and beyond the last farm in Sherburn
in the Wainwright Family for a Hundred Years

5

KEEP RIGHT ON TO THE END OF THE ROAD

I have realised for some time that tempus was fugiting, and becoming a grandfather exactly two weeks ago on January 8th 1998 only exaggerated the fact - but I can see the compensations!!

So today, with elder daughter Suzanna to look after me, I ventured off to Leeds - on the train. Once this was nearly a weekly occurrence, then either on by tram or bus up to Headingley or to the pictures at the 'Majestic' or 'Odeon', and once or twice to the library to borrow jazz records. Leeds has grown beyond and away from me, and the car and York are more preferred and treasured!

It is two years since I last travelled on a train, and maybe five since I last went to Leeds, so my memories and thoughts become razor sharp on these rare occasions. A whole book should be written about Milford Station, our starting point, and now not even a shadow of its former glory.

South Milford station as it used to be

No Fred Milner porter, no Messrs Todd, Durance and Terry station masters. No Ernest Harrison or Harry Lunt bagging coal from the bunkers or George Harrison's men, Charlie and Teddy Farrar, or ours loading beet or waiting for the pickup to shunt wagons in. No signalman or box to signal from - just an occasional recorded voice and two plastic, decrepit shelters on either platform to huddle in.

Time was when it buzzed with staff and we loaded beet and corn and collected cattle pulp, seed potatoes, coal, and hired corn sacks to fill with sixteen stones of wheat or barley. In earlier days my trunk went off to school from there, carried down on his shoulders by a giant Romanian prisoner of war. There were fires in the waiting rooms and the biggest in the office in which I got my ticket, and waited and pulled rank whilst ordinary travellers got theirs through the glass cubbyhole.

South Milford station now

The diesel train came on time, was clean and fast and we soon passed familiar sights, except Micklefield pit, which is now like a Scottish sheep pasture with little to eat. The rows of grim cottages remain, with one having a glass extension on the front which must have cost more than the whole lot did way back. At the other side is the football pitch and what looks like a deserted cricket field on which I got one of my only two 50's!! I opened with the Red Bear landlady's son, Stuart Kirkup, and he had his fifty whilst I got to seven!

There are tanks still on the scene at Barnbow and still a lot of cattle in a big muddy field on the left. Crossgates hasn't changed basically since courting days except it's tattier and littered. I assume the 'Ritz' is no more?

We got into Leeds station fairly quickly without much swaying and clanking over points as before, and disembarked at the farthest platform in the open air. No leather strap to struggle with to open the window and then the door handle on the outside. Except for the lines the station is hardly recognisable, but seems much improved. Leeds on a wet Thursday is, as it always was, miserable, but there are lots of places without shopping to escape into.

The brilliant Corn Exchange was first stop for a coffee, and that was the only transaction I saw happen! Father used to take his corn samples on a Tuesday for merchants to bid for, and with two friends and a packet of second-hand books, would meet mother and us at Collinson's for a fish tea, fancy cakes, and a string orchestra!! About twenty black desks with each merchant's name on are still to be seen but sadly photos of them in action are only on show at the toilet entrance - which costs 10p (2/-)!!

We split up after this slice of history, me to the Art Gallery and Suzanna to Marks and Spencer's, which sums up the generation gap, but I knew I would enjoy her efforts later. The huge painting of the Sogn fjord is always my first stop, and it was good to see Mr. Grimshaw didn't find a lot of sun in Leeds either!

I had already pointed Dysons out to Suzanna, from where our engagement ring was purchased. The clock, unlike the one in Selby, is still there! Also I was more than pleased when she preferred Whitlocks for lunch instead of MacDonalds, Pizza Hut, and various salad bars she had thought of before. Amongst all the changes that have taken place, and the huge crane hovering above a future Debenhams, it was very reassuring to find Whitlocks exactly as over thirty years ago when I spent the rest of my money! - Friendly crowd, good beer, glowing coal fire and white tablecloths, and nothing nouveau or Italian in sight.

To crown the day I bought a CD of early Ella Fitzgerald for the little one as an investment. There are twenty-five songs with various swing bands. Most of them I'd never heard of, and all good. I will write on it, 'May your tastes and standards never drop below this'. It's wishful thinking, but I know I'll enjoy it!!

A P.S. and bonus to this story came with buying a paperback book of Leeds memories and poems by 94-year-old Sam Wood at Austicks. I wrote to him via his publisher to tell him how much I had enjoyed it and to ask permission to put one or two of his poems in the 'Messenger'. Seemingly quicker than return of post, he was on the phone for a lengthy chat regardless of cost, and permission granted! He is one of a decreasing band of stalwarts who clearly remembers the First War and everything that has happened in his life since. Being partially sighted has not bothered him and over the years he has had three books of Old Leeds published and has raised over £7000 for charity by his efforts.

He used to lead the singsong on his accordion in his local, and still goes there, but sadly knows no one, as his old friends have all gone before! Close up magic was always a big interest, and he's busy passing on his secrets to numerous grandchildren and great grandchildren. His books are read both in junior schools and to elderly people in rehabilitation centres. One little girl was upset, when neither teacher nor classmates believed that her grandfather was the Sam Wood on the cover. He has sent his poems to all sorts of people, including Princess Di, Prince Charles, and the Duke of Edinburgh, and tells me he has had some wonderful words of appreciation. He had his own show on Radio Leeds, has appeared on TV many times and good old Alf Roberts is related, but he can't have had a lot of time to watch him.

His lively cheerfulness and telling me that I'm 'nobut a lad' has helped to balance my new found dotage!

J.D.B.

IT'S GREAT FUN BEING A GRANDAD

It's great fun being a grandad, I've been one for quite
a few years, I'll never forget all the pleasure I've had,
sharing their laughter, drying their tears.

Fun I have had in good measure,
When the dear little darlings were small,
Each moment my mem'ry will treasure,
Till the time they grow up and walk tall.

Delightful days by the sea,
A tiny-tot holding my hand,
Punch and Judy, jugs of tea,
Being 'buried alive' in the sand.

Trampolines, Dodgems, see-saws and swings,
I've been on 'em all and done other daft things,
I've sat on a donkey with one tiny-tot,
The donkey went 'Hee-haw', but go it would not.

I've gone searching for sea-shells, that was great fun,
Then dozed off to sleep in the blazing-hot sun,
I've woke up with the tide almost reaching my toes,
And three mischievous faces right under my nose.

I've had my mouth stuffed with iced lollies,
And candy-floss,
I've been lumbered with deck-chairs and dollies,
Without getting cranky or cross.

Grandads have lots of time to spend,
Doing things grandchildren like,
Nearly ev'ry weekend they'd bring something to
mend
An engine, a doll, or a bike.

I've enjoyed all their nice birthday parties,
With lots of cream-cakes and red jelly,
I've sat with my mouth full of 'Smarties',
Watching 'Blue Peter' on telly.

Before their bedtime at eight on the dot,
They'd bring me my hat and my brolly,
Then I'd kiss them 'Goodnight', the whole sticky lot,
Three kids, two dolls, and a 'Golly'.

Sam Wood - A Meander Down Memory Lane

FRIENDS OR FOES

With the passing of Laddie Lucas, another of the Battle of Britain fighter pilots in March, the Few are certainly the Few.

On Saturday 9th May veterans' next of kin and friends of 578 Squadron from all over the world will gather, probably for their last time, to attend a special service at Selby Abbey at 11 a.m. to dedicate a Book of Remembrance. Afterwards they will return to Burn airfield for a buffet lunch.

The Squadron only operated from Burn between January '44 and March '45 when it was disbanded. During that time their Halifax Mk III aircraft flew two thousand seven hundred and twenty-one sorties on a hundred and sixty targets dropping nine thousand six hundred and seventy-six tons of bombs. Two hundred and nineteen members of the aircrew were killed and seventy-nine taken prisoner. Forty-five aircraft were lost on active service and many medals, including a VC, were awarded in that short time. I wouldn't have known anything of this if I hadn't borrowed a book called 'Based at Burn' which I read in a week, and I'm still dodging the searchlights, landing as near home as possible, and like Deirdre have no liking for prison! It is the Association's hope that local people will join in the events and I'm sure youngsters attending and showing interest would really make their day.

Goodbye Burn till next time - Hugh Cawdron with banner

OLD AIRFIELD

I lie here still beside the hill,
Abandoned long to nature's will,
My buildings down, my people gone,
My only sounds the wild birds' song.

But my mighty birds will rise no more,
No more I hear the merlins roar,
And never now my bosom feels,
The pounding of their giant wheels

From the ageless hill their voices cast,
Thunderous echoes from the past,
And still in lonely reverie,
Their great dark wings sweep down on me.

Laughter, sorrow, hope and pain,
I shall never know these things again,
Emotions that I came to know,
Of strange young men so long ago.

Who know, as evening shadows meet,
Are they still with me a phantom fleet,
And do my ghosts still stride unseen,
Across my face so wide and green.

And in the future should structures tall
Bury me beyond recall,
I shall still remember them,
My metal birds and long dead men.

Now weeds grow high, obscure the sky,
O remember me when you pass by,
For beneath this tangled leafy screen,
I was your home, your friend, 'Silksheen'.

Walter Scott, ex 630 Squadron Royal Air Force.

Another group of people getting fewer are the ex prisoners of war and displaced persons who stayed on here when it was all over. Many of them Latvians, Lithuanians and Roumanians who had to fight for Hitler without choice or desire. The three who worked for us all went back when the time came but only one went home.

Karl Bauer had been a bank manager in Aalen in Germany and could speak reasonable English. He was short, wore glasses, and was fussy, but got on with father who had cycled through Germany to Switzerland in the '20's and admired most of the things he had seen. But Karl was no farm man and stuck the fork in his foot on the first day of harvest. Nevertheless he was a trier and later was better suited as camp organiser at Riccall.

Big Michael was Roumanian and I have no idea how long he was with us, but I do know his spoken English never improved. It was still zero when he left. At home he had been a butcher farmer. He was a giant and had a look of Joe Bugner. He could fork sheaves all day long in harvest from wagon to stack and never tire. We still have an extra long fork used to pitch through the end doors at the top of the barn. No one has used it since! Later in the war he came in for Christmas dinner and then on to Castleford v Featherstone. He couldn't go in his prisoner's clothes and it was quite a pantomime fitting him out in the biggest of father's.

However, Otto was our favourite as he was younger, laughed more, was a good footballer and stayed longer. I still have a sad, moving letter of thanks written in strange English on his way home. We also have skillfully made jewellery boxes, pencil cases, and those pecking hens on a table tennis bat that they all seemed to make in their camp workshops.

Karl must have been a big admirer of my ten-year-old sister as he had a crayon portrait done from a small polyphoto. The accompanying letter to my parents adds interest and I quote, 'When I am considering a portrait, I am trying to find in it beside the external beauty, the mental values and the traits of that personality. So this picture may also depart from the photo I have in my possession. The artist has been putting into this picture what he has been told about this girl, clever and graceful far more developed than her age. Will you please see this what is called Mother's Darling!'

Neither Michael nor Otto dared to go home to Russian occupied Roumania for many years. Otto lived in a nice flat in the centre of Munich, sent all his money to his elderly mother and only saw her at the end of her life. Sadly Big Michael lost patience and was shot trying to swim a river to get back to his family and farm!

Karl Bauer   *Otto Hann and Jutta*

In July 1960 with friend Geo Woodall we camped round Europe in a Hillman Husky and slept in seven countries in ten days. We had planned to meet Karl at his bank, which we found closed and being renovated, We retired to a bar opposite and tried to explain our problems to the locals. As we struggled to do so I noticed a little man come in and begin to have his empty bottles refilled. I realised who it was and we both came up behind him and tapped him on the shoulder in a sort of Gestapo role reversal. There were roars of laughter as we marched out, towering above him and back to a welcome shower, delicious bread and sausage and to drink his beer. His son was a doctor, but one Christmas no letter arrived and we never did know of his end.

Later on we ventured into Munich on a busy Sunday night, and managed to find Otto and family high in his comfortable flat near the station and the famous Hoffbrau Ha Ous where we drank beer from huge steins. He went and bought me one, explaining that many tourists were caught at the door trying to steal them. I didn't like admitting that I already had one under my coat for a friend, but carrying his helped me past the doorman nicely.

Otto had a little daughter called Jutta who sent sketches of our goings on every Christmas - wedding, first baby, second, etc. In 1974 they arrived for a week's stay and my parents had a great time showing them Yorkshire. He signed our Visitors Book, 'Back in England again a free man after 25 years' and Jutta supplied the illustration! He was pleased to see his old Nissen hut home at Richard Buckle's poultry farm still in use, but had mixed feelings about the chickens in it, and round the corner nettles smothered his old flowerbed.

Otto died of cancer in January '95. Luckily I had persuaded Sherburn adventurer Brian Lockey to call on him and deliver presents, in a spare moment on his Oktoberfest golfing trip. Only Brian would have persevered in finding him, sadly very ill. He cheered up considerably whilst telling of Sherburn in wartime and the happy days he had had as a prisoner.

It's a funny Old World!J.D.B.

EVERYONE SANG

Everyone suddenly burst out singing,
And I was filled with such delight
As prisoned birds must find in freedom
Winging wildly across the white
Orchards and dark green fields, on; on; and out of sight.

Everyone's voice was suddenly lifted.
And beauty came like the setting sun.
My heart was shaken with tears; and horror
Drifted away.... O but everyone
Was a bird; and the song was wordless; the singing will never be done.

Siegfried Sassoon 1886 - 1967

Jutta's Sketch of visit to Home Farm

BID TIME RETURN or THE END OF AN ERA

It was a sad evening on Monday 11th January 1993 for the past and present members of Church Fenton Young Farmers Club who met to discuss its closure. With over £2000 in the bank and only seven lonely and unhappy members, over fifty years of youthful activities came to an end in the area.

The decline in the number of farmers, workers and connected families, and other things competing for young people's time were given as the main reasons. Unlike youth clubs with paid leaders in charge, Young Farmers Clubs are self-financing and run by the members themselves. Clubs elect their own committees. Fortnightly meeting are (were) run efficiently with minutes taken, read and a vote given to the speaker. Countless Young Farmers chairmen have admired the abilities of their secretaries and progressed into lifelong partnerships!

To help recruitment in my time meetings were held in all surrounding villages, but it was about as successful as the efforts of modern-day members and led to much confusion. When I joined from school in the early '50's most meetings were semi-educational as not so many people went on to college or university. Public speaking competitions were taken seriously at regional and county levels. 'Should fox hunting be abolished?' was as keenly debated then as today. Drama competitions and carol singing for charity came later.

Church Fenton YFC and friends - trip to Bibby's, Liverpool, 1958

Christmas party time was worth the subscription. Each club put on a party and invited three or four of its favourite neighbours and hopefully enjoyed their hospitality at Knaresborough, Wetherby, Tadcaster, Leeds, Selby or Pontefract in return. Our mothers provided cakes and sandwiches, and dancing and games took place. St Mary's schoolroom never took much filling, but with Mr. Harry Butterfield in charge, fun was guaranteed. Being in the wholesale fish trade, he always enjoyed being the caller of a sort of fishy musical chairs (and the wind changes). We also ran our own Annual Ball at Tadcaster, with a live band, proper dancing, a buffet supper and evening dress!!!

The County Ball was similar and held at the Royal Hall in Harrogate. Summer programmes traditionally started at the Maltings at Milford or a Tadcaster brewery. After that it was farm walks with good suppers, factories and Sunday bus trips. The big event was the County Rally held at the Yorkshire Show Ground, with sports in the main ring and a dance in the Stockmans dining hall to finish off with. Practice nights were held for weeks before to get the right people for the various events.

One evening in Mr. George Harrison's field, we had to back a tractor and trailer through a course of stakes and ropes. Mr. Butterfield was the judge and Mr. Batty timekeeper. I went round clear and twice as fast as anyone else. I was not amused when not selected and less still when the reason given was dangerous driving - but I daren't complain.

Another year I was knocked out of beef judging at Regional, but was told I could judge poultry at County. So three hen-haters went to visit Mr. Geoff Hall of Mill Farm for advice. He told us that Mr. Butterfield had asked him to supply two pens to be judged at the Rally. He didn't take much persuading to show us them, and later to put them in order. Unfortunately there were four docile white wine dots and four fighting game birds. He warned us not to handle the cock and showed us scars to emphasise the point. At the showground Mr. Butterfield had been sent off in disgrace to try to catch some commercial egg-laying hens as per programme, at a nearby farm. He returned empty-handed and we had to judge the wine dots. Embarrassment forbids me to name the winner - but every point counted in those days!

Many local and foreign exchange visits have taken place over the years and lasting friendships made. A school friend from Nottingham won a three-month trip to Australia by boat and via the Suez Canal.

Not having had a holiday in two years since leaving school, I risked my father's wrath and put my name forward for a West Riding exchange to Norway in May 1953, and I didn't know at the time that it was to be the first of thirteen visits!! After a great time, leaving the sunshine, apple blossom and blue-eyed blondes to return to dull, wet Yorkshire and a room full of ancient (50 year-old) relatives watching the Coronation on our new television was a tremendous anti-climax!

Norwegians being shown round Farnley Hall by Major Horton Fawkes

It was hectic too when the Norwegians came back here - three times. Visits and bus trips by day and parties and dances somewhere every night was the norm. County Chairman for twelve years up to 1958 was Major Le G.G.W. Horton Fawkes O.B.E., M.A., D.L. Born in Somerset, he had been a classics master at Harrow for many years until taking on his estates at Farnley Hall near Otley and becoming, in our opinion, the perfect squire and gentleman. I think the Young Farmers' motto is 'Good Farmers, Good Countrymen, Good Citizens'. The Major limited his to Punctuality, Public Speaking and Good Manners. He was an expert at all three and never gave up trying to encourage us uncouth youths to do likewise! A Sunday afternoon at Farnley Hall in 1954 was an unforgettable experience for the Norwegians and their hosts with the Major and his family, and his Turner paintings!

Regional Tug-of-War Team 1956

I could go on but sadly fashions and times change and all this has come to an end in this area. My own three horses were taken to the water but didn't stay to drink. Will they have better memories than I to look back on? I doubt it! The successors of that first Coronation T.V. have a lot to answer for!!   J.D.B.

CHAPTER 2

JIM BRAMLEY'S CYCLING ADVENTURES

BIKE RIDE

This month's sport is an account I have found of my father's solo holiday tour to Brighton in 1923 on his bike.

He never talked much of his early exploits. In his later years he seemed to be always reading of other people's travels in the second-hand books he bought. Various folk have told me of the special racing bike he ordered from Granville Lunn and I do know that for four or five of his unmarried, prime years he did clock up between 11,000 and 14,000 miles annually!! Touring Italy and Switzerland was his most adventurous trip, and he was lucky in Ireland in 1925 to find ' that the bridges that had been blown up had now been rebuilt.'

I don't think he would be best pleased at my telling his story, but with present educational problems and breakdown of discipline, these well written pages with no spelling mistakes are a great tribute to Mr. J.T.S. Potts and his two assistants and the old fashioned methods of that time.

I don't know at what age he left school, as he doesn't appear on the payroll of any of our account books!! One thing is certain. He would be delighted that his Hungate School is at last being sympathetically renovated, and will be part of the doctors' practice, and the pride of the village again in due course.

Speeding down the motorway with fixed concentration, we don't realise how much more we would see and learn doing it peacefully on a bike - especially in 1923!!

Jim Bramley

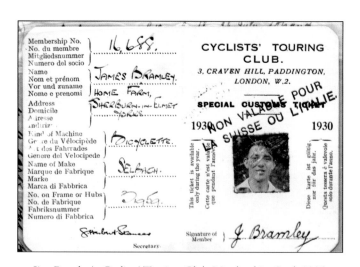

Jim Bramley's Cyclists' Touring Club Membership Card 1930

Account of Holiday Tour 1923

Set off on Bank Holiday Monday August 6th. Dullish morning but hot afterwards. Made for Doncaster and Bawtry. When through Bawtry, Notts is entered. Went on to Retford where I had dinner. The country passed through from Doncaster up to Retford is very flat and seems poor land. I now left the G.N.R. (Great North Road) and made across through Lincs. for Lincoln. Here the land is more undulating and more pleasing scenery. The road runs alongside the river Witham for a mile or two where many anglers were busy. Lincoln can be seen some miles away and seems to stand well up. I passed through the large racecourse and into the town. Streets are pretty narrow.

Made for Sleaford. From Lincoln to Sleaford the road is very straight and in perfect condition and always up and down. Here the fields are very large, many being 100 and more acres. They are chiefly fenced by stone walls just round here. Very large clover stacks were to be seen but none get thatched down; they just get a few wires thrown across them and weighted. Crops around here were bad except thistles and docks and other weeds. Reached Sleaford about five and put in at the White Hart Hotel. Walked about at night until I was tired and had seen everything. Nice walks down riverbank where one could get to Boston, 15 miles away. Got to bed about 9.30pm after about 72 miles ride.

Tuesday

Had breakfast with a Leicester man and started at 9.10am. Went through Folkingham to Bourne. Harvest here was well ahead. The farm wagons are very large and clumsy affairs. Many steam plough sets working about here. When through Bourne the country is very flat, for here we are among the fens. I reached Peterboro' at 12.30pm (34 miles) having had head winds. Suburbs have grand avenues of trees on the streets. Noticed that in Lincs. there seems to be a larger percentage of clean-shaven men than elsewhere. Was now in Huntingdonshire and ready for some dinner but could not find any. Here are many large brickyards about. I now joined the G.N.R. again, which down here is a perfect road as far as surface goes. Found some dinner at last (1.30pm) at Stilton; this is where a famous cheese used to be made. Reached Huntingdon at 3pm. It is an old town with narrow streets and fine river views down the Ouse. Had tea at Royston, 20 miles to the south. Quite half the houses here have thatched roofs and many are only wooden walls. The model village at Papworth is exceptional however with its flower garden to every cottage forming a blaze of colours. Much hillier this way on.

Wednesday

Went on to Buntingford then to Bishops Stortford, where I stayed the night. Got in at 8pm after a 92 miler. It had been a grand sunny day with cooling breezes. I had been through 5 counties, viz. Lincs., Northants., Hunts., Cambs., and Herts. And was now on the borders of Essex. Much wheat seems to be grown this way on.

Started again next morning at 9.10am in champion form and weather perfect. Had to leave main roads now to cross the Thames at Tilbury Docks. Reached there about noon having passed over rough roads. Tilbury side is known as 'World's End' and everything in motor car shape must go miles back to London to get across. Just in time to catch boat, and was charged 7d. The River Thames was full of shipping, and flags of many nations were to be seen. It is from a quarter to half a mile wide or so here. Gravesend lies on the other side and here I had some dinner (1.30pm). I then struck out for Tunbridge and Brighton. The sun now hot which made it hard work even with coat and waistcoat off. It was now very hilly and slow going across the North Downs. Miles of long hills and wind unfavourable. Reached Tunbridge Wells for tea and had the best feed for some time. This part of Kent seems to be very thickly wooded, and plenty of rough country about. Had passed by large areas of orchards and a few hop gardens. Although turned 5 o'clock I decided to get to the coast, 31 miles farther. Not so hilly after Sussex is entered and on the down slope till the South Downs are reached. These hills are very steep on the sides and flatter on top. In places they rise up to nearly 1,000 feet, straight out of the plain. They are generally bare except for down grass and sheep. In places however the tops are cultivated. Up here one can see miles and miles of the surrounding country. Reached Lewis at 7.10pm and found it a very hilly town but did not stay. The road runs down a valley alongside a railway to Brighton with the Downs on either side like huge walls. Got to Brighton at 8pm which I found was full but at last I got a bed in a cellar at a cafe. Had a run round afterwards but did not get to the sea until next morning. It is a fine town with plenty about worth seeing. Went in Aquarium etc. Sea was very calm and morning very hot, and no breeze. Could have had a day in France if I had known in time. (14/6d Day to Dieppe)

Thursday

Left at 1.30pm and made for Horsham and by good riding got on to Shalford for tea. Was in Surrey now and roughish country. I then made cross country towards Chertsey but got lost once or twice. Large areas of heath land about here on which six main roads meet in one place. Put in at the Vines at Chertsey at 8pm, after a scorching hot day.

Friday

Started out at 9am having rested well. Planned day's route to Buckingham and north towards Leicester. Went through Staines and Windsor and re-crossed the River Thames here which is not very wide now. Saw Windsor Castle and Park Gardens etc., which are surrounded by a big wall. The scenery here is fine especially where the river runs with the road as it does in places. All sorts of punts and boats on river, whose banks are clothed with woods and shrubs generally, whilst gardens come right to the water's edge. Went through Middlesex and Bucks. These are full of woods and parks. Fine scenery around Amersham. Crossed the Chiltern Hills about noon. They are only slight rises and the road runs through a pleasant valley towards Aylesbury, along with the railway. Had dinner at Gr. Missenden. Aylesbury I found to be a nice sized town with a square in the centre. Monument of John Hampdon at one end. Flatter country to Buckingham and Towcester, where I had tea. Towards Daventry however it is very undulated in long sweeping hills. At Weedon there is a large cavalry barrack. Got to Daventry about 8pm and put in at the 'Bear' where I had a good time. Came across two C.J.C. men who had been north and were making for London. Landlord a real man. Got to bed about 11pm.

Saturday

Could not get away until 10.10am. Went through Rugby, Leicester, Notts. Still up and down through Northants., Warwick and S. Notts. Had dinner in Leicester and made for Nottingham. Much cricket in evidence all up this way. Reached Trent-Bridge about 4pm and had tea. Lancashire C.C. happened to be there but had not time to see them. Found Nottingham to be a big town. Large areas are laid out as sports fields on the south side of town. Went forward to Mansfield through some fine country including parts of Sherwood Forest. Market night at Mansfield and plenty of life. Stayed there the night

Sunday

Started about 9am and kept up a hot pace for miles. Grand scenery through the Dukeries. Flatter to Worksop again. Reached Doncaster at 1pm and had some dinner at Wentbridge at 2pm. Then dodged about a bit and got home again by 4pm. Total run well over 500 miles. Cost at about 1 penny per mile for everything.　　　　31.8.23

ONE MAN ON A BIKE

I have come across another of father's biking diaries from the days before Calcaria travel, and when computers going down didn't matter! In 1929 he averaged seven hundred and twenty miles a month, did thirty-two century rides, and in July to get fit for harvest, he recorded nineteen hundred and ten miles mostly around Switzerland and Italy on his own. It might be an exhausting read in these driving and flying days, but one or two, like me, might feel slightly envious. He was twenty-six at the time and a product of Sherburn School! J.D.B.

Saturday 20th July

Hot sunny day - Started on tour to Continent at noon. Got to Hull and sailed on D. of C. for Zeebrugge at six. Perfect night and sea very smooth. Full boat.

Sunday 21st July

Hot sunny day - Zeebrugge at seven and caught train for Brussels where spent an hour and then got through train to Basle via Namur, Luxemburg and Strassburg. Very hot and dead tired at Basle with journey. Reached Basle at midnight and put in at Hotel Hofer for night.

Monday 22nd July

Hot and Sunny - Left Basle at eight still feeling train effects and made along the Rhine for lunch. Very hot but beautiful scenery. Rhine looking very blue and roads fairly good and not much traffic. Every garden full of bright coloured flowers. Got down to Zurich, fairly large manufacturing town, and followed Lakeside out to Rapperswill and Utnach. R. very old picturesque place with very narrow streets. Along Lake Zurich side got first view of snow-capped mountains to south. Stayed the night at Weeson on Lake surrounded by mountains.

Tuesday 23rd July

Very Hot Day - Climbed out to Moire Wallenstadte Ragatz where had dinner of raw bacon a few miles away. Fine scenery and harder work. Left main road and entered on narrow winding mountain road to Kloster Platts, Dorfi etc. Main industry in these parts is lumbering. Climbed the Fluela Pass after six and reached the Hospice on top just before dark after a hard walk and push. Very rough country on top the col reaching 2392 metres and the Mt. Weisshorn over 3000. Got a room with a Swiss M. C. and a climber. Good do.

Wednesday 24th July

Very Hot Day - Good run down the Fluela but very dangerous hairpin bends down to Zerneth. Climb out again over the Offen Pass 2148 m. and dropped down the long fall to Santa Maria where had lunch at Hotel Stelvio.
Climbed up to the Stelvio Col in afternoon reaching the top about 6pm after walking nearly all way. Stelvio is highest road in Europe, the Col being 2843 metres. Dropped down other side onto Italy over amazing loops and twists, tunnels and bad roads, finishing at Bormio where stayed night at Hotel Bormio. Very dirty wild town with rough inhabitants.

Thursday 25th July

Hot Sunny Day - Made out to Tirano and Sondria where had lunch. Very pleasant country, much lower but awful bad road. Downhill last 30 miles. Then round Lake Como where had tea. Very heavy storm at 6 o'clock for an hour, but got down to Lecco and across to Como for night, Hotel des Postes. After two days of bad roads the stretch from Lecco to Como was good tarmac.

Friday 26th July

Thunder and Rainy - Crossed into Switzerland again to Lugano, in heavy storm. Lake Lugano very beautiful and peaceful. Bad roads again now. Had lunch at Bellizono and made up to Biasco and St Gothard.
Strong wind in afternoon followed by heavy thunderstorms and hard struggle up, through beautiful gorge to Ariolo where had tea.
Still raining very heavily. I took train through the St. Gothard tunnel and put in at Andermat for night.

Saturday 27th July

Sunny - Crossed over the Furka Pass, 2436m., reaching the snowline. Very cold. Swiss army on manoeuvres going up. Much winding on decent and very dangerous. Cut back tyre very badly but patched it satisfactory. Had long drop down to Brieg where had dinner and made good progress to Sion finishing at Martigny for night.
The river Rhone starts from the glacier near Furka and is followed by road all way down. The water is a peculiar light green colour and flows very fast.

Sunday 28th July

Hot and Sunny - Made out round Lake Geneva to Lausanne visiting the famous castle of Chillon en route. Came across a CTC lad near L. who accompanied me all day to the French border. Had lunch at Lausanne and then proceeded over pleasant country lanes to Orbe having tea in the last village in Suisse and having said au revoir to friend got over into France crossing the Jura Mountains to Pontaslier for night at Hotel St. Pierre. The views today were not very extensive owing to hazier conditions.

Monday 29th July

Rain on and off all day – Got away to Bessacon and Gray for dinner and then via Langres to Chaumont for night. Very hard going all day – head wind, in cape, and up long drags. Typical French countryside.

Tuesday 30th July

Better day – Went via Joinville to St Dizier for dinner, Chalons for tea, Rheims for night.
Uninteresting plains this way and roads of the Routiere National type. Land very open and of a very chalky type. Corn crops on the main very short.
Rheims has been rebuilt on a very extensive scale with wide boulevards and open spaces. Had much difficulty in finding the centre of town. Only saw the cathedral from a distance.

Wednesday 31st July

Dull and Rain – Took train at Rheims for the coast at 9.

1st change	Charleville	4th change	Brussels
2nd change	Givet	5th change	Bruges
3rd change	Namur		

Finished at Blankenberg at 11 pm, weary, lame and far from home and utterly fed up with the trains and Belgian railway system. Got in at Hotel Sedan.
Had intended to get across France via the battlefields to Lille, Ostend etc.

Thursday 1st August

Very strong winds and rain – At Blankenberg for the day. Plenty of English in and no language difficulty whatever.
Visited Zeebrugge Museum etc.

Friday 2nd August

Dull – Had a ride to Bruge to kill time in morning.

Climbed the famous bell tower and saw most of the places of interest.
Back to Blankenberg for dinner and having tea at Zeebrugge got on boat at 6.30 for home. Sea roughish. Pinched a bunk and had a fair night with plenty of company.

Saturday 3rd August

Rainy day – Reached Hull at 7 and got up to Rutherfords (Beverley) for breakfast, getting home for dinner after exactly a fortnight away.
Went to Sherburn Sports in afternoon but a poor do.

Sunday 4th August

Heavy rain in morning – In bed until nearly ten (a record) and at home all day.

Chief reflections on tour in retrospect are:
1. Solo touring in many ways more preferable to party touring,
2. A low gear of 63 much too big for passes and a free wheel useless. About 45 – 50 ample for climbing.
3. Made a big mistake when took train for Rheims in not going via Lille therefore missing to me - new country.
4. During tour being under impression that boat sailed Thursday. One day wasted in Blankenburg instead of being spent in Suisse.

Following in father's footsteps in luxury - Lucerne 1957

Ancient methods in Austria

Flailing onion seed in Germany

Turnout near Boulogne

TRIP INTO SCOTLAND

(Related by Dick Pearson)

We go back to the time of the cycling days now Don. After your father died and you brought those magazines to me, amongst them was a CTC handbook with notes in written by your father. Now these notes related to a tour of Scotland, and of course he had my name in this and Harry Booth's, the three of us. I had completely forgotten about this tour. I can remember things that happened on this tour but I couldn't have told anybody whom I was with at the time, but this refreshed my mind and I could go right through the tour again then.

This was a tour up into Scotland. We didn't bother with tents, and we didn't bother with bed and breakfast. If we could manage, if the weather was anything like, we had sleeping bags. These were made out of ex-First World War ground sheets. These were strong gabardine stuff, and they had a rubber surface at one side. Of course the rubber was on the outside and the gabardine on the inside, and they were made up into sleeping bags, open down about halfway and one flap had big lace holes in, and the other side had loops on. You threaded them up and laced them, and a flap covered the face. There was space so that if you took any clothes off, you could put them in there to act as a pillow. Very often you had a loaf of bread in there as well.

It was rather funny that we had a way that if it was fine, we used to ride right up to dusk, to lamp time. If we were lucky and we'd just drop on a field where there were milk cows or cattle of any sort, they naturally were all laid down by the time we arrived, and we prepared our sleeping bags and got everything ready. They were always laid down at the hedge that was most sheltered of course, and when we were ready we used to move one of them, get down where it had been laid, and then you had under-floor heating. Apart from that you got an early start, which was very difficult when you were young, because you used to oversleep sometimes. We always got an early start when we did this, because when it was dark the cattle didn't bother you at night, but of course they were up as soon as the sun was up, and they'd come around wondering what was in these bags. Of course with their rough tongues licking on the bags, they used to turn you over face down on to the dewy grass, so that was a good way of waking you up so you got a fair good start in a morning!

I remember from Aberdeen we cut across by Keith to Inverness, and we were going to have an afternoon and evening at Inverness. Well, we had the afternoon, but it was miserable, hazing most of the time. Then it came on to rain very fast, and we were just outside the Royal Station Hotel. So we dived into the porchway of the hotel to get away from the pouring rain. It was coming down like stair rods. Well it seemed to keep coming. We'd put our bikes up at a pub. There was a shed; well it was a CTC place. We had our bikes there. I had a small bag with me with some stuff in. Well it didn't look as if it was going to clear up, and I was so fagged out with sleeping in sleeping bags - it never seemed to bother Jim, but it did me - and I said, 'Well I'm going to turn in and have bed and breakfast here.' I remember Jim saying, 'Aye and he'll know about it when he gets t'bill!' 'Well,' I said, 'it doesn't matter what it costs, I'm going in here.' They decided they would go back to the place where we had the bikes, so we arranged for a time in the morning to meet, and get set off. Well I had a jolly good night's sleep that night, and a breakfast next morning, which was a bit more civilised than we'd had with the old billy can and the lid for frying, and all this sort of thing. I got my gear together and went to the reception for my bill. Well, I did get a shock! He was right was Jim, it was eleven shillings! Now that might not sound much, but you see bed and breakfast varied from about two shillings to two and nine and three shillings. Usually if it was over two and three, we went somewhere else. At the same time, to got from Leeds Wellington Street station to Belfast, and come back on the same boat at night, back to Leeds, the excursion fare was eleven and sixpence. That gives you some idea comparing the two.

Anyway we set off and went down the side of Loch Ness, Fort Augustus, down the Caledonian Canal and out to Oban. Why I don't know, because you've got to come back so far before you set off down again. So we came right away down and over the Clyde at Erskine Ferry. There was no bridge at that time, just a ferry. Well, as we approached the ferry, before we could see it, there was a bend in the road, and we heard the bell going. We knew that the ferry was ready for starting off, so we had a final sprint, round this bend, down a slope and they were just about to raise the gangplank, and we ran down this slope and straight onto the ferry. I'd think they wondered what was coming! We paid at the other side. We got down into the Lake District, and at Keswick we were undecided whether to go down the Lake District and come back by Kendal, Skipton, Settle and that way, or whether to come over Stainmore to Scotch Corner and down t'A1. We tossed up for it, and of course it was Scotch Corner, but when we got just out of Penrith a strong east wind started. It was a head on wind, and you nearly stood on the pedals against it, so we turned down Wenseleydale as far as Leyburn. It appears we'd gone through Bedale and were making for the A1, because we'd had a tea at Bedale according to Jim's notes -two and threepence.

We must have crossed straight across the A1 and gone to Thirsk. Why I don't know! It wouldn't be my idea. Maybe Jim hadn't had enough riding, I don't know, but because we'd had some tea there, I know we were there. That was down in the notes; it was at the Golden Fleece I think. Anyway we came back as far as Boroughbridge and we hadn't long down the A1 it appears according to this note, because we'd called to have some refreshment at the Green Tree Inn at Little Ouseburn. So we must have come back to Tad that way, but remember that was from Saturday dinnertime, to Sunday the following week!

Map Showing Route Followed

Approximately 936 Miles

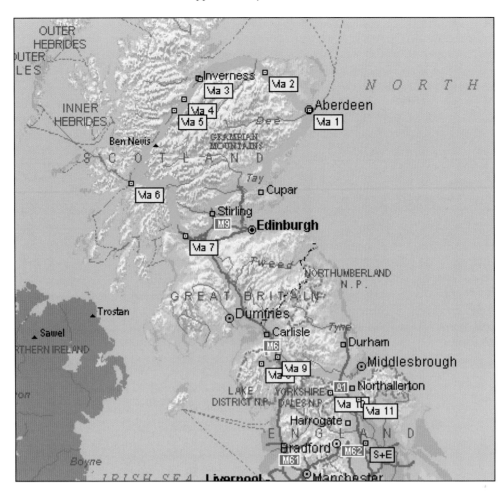

Key

Via 1	Aberdeen	Via 7	Erskine
Via 2	Keith	Via 8	Keswick
Via 3	Inverness	Via 9	Penrith
Via 4	Loch Ness	Via 10	Leyburn
Via 5	Fort Augustus	Via 11	Thirsk
Via 6	Oban		

CHAPTER 3

DICK PEARSON'S STORIES

BUILDING THE FARMSTEAD 1939

When your father bought the house, I didn't know at that time that it was only part of a master plan that he had in mind. It was a few weeks later, I was over at your house, and we were looking round the house, and talking about various things. He said, 'What do you think to it?' and I said, 'It's a grand house. I'll tell you this, you won't spend that amount of money better, I don't care how long you live.' He says, 'No I don't suppose I shall, but it's only part of my main plan is this.' I says, 'Oh?' 'Oh yes' he says, 'I intend pulling t'old buildings down in Sherburn and building a new farmstead here.' I was a bit surprised at that, 'cos I've no need for anyone to tell me what this was going to entail. I also knew, knowing Jim as well as what I did, that if he'd got to t'stage of telling me his plan, that it had gone beyond the point of a pipe dream.

A week or two later he came over to Saxton to see if I was available for a week or two just to get him set off. So that weekend I went over just to discuss things and see what things were like. Perhaps it would be on a Sunday, I dare say it would be. I was a bit surprised at the siting of the buildings right at the far side of the field. So I said to Jim, 'Why right over here with all t'buildings?' 'Well,' he said, 'If tha wants to know that tha'd better go and ask t'wife. I'd nowt to do with that.' So of course I put two and two together, knowing Winifred, I knew she wasn't a townie, and she knew where she wanted t'farm. She didn't want Jim stepping out of t'foldyard into t'back door, so it appeared that whatever his original plan was, where he was going to have it, he had to abide by this amendment. There was no doubt about that.

So when we started, the first job was to dismantle the barns up at Sherburn, because these were going to be used to build the fold yard, and this was his priority number one, the first building he wanted up. When we went down on to the site, of course he'd done a lot of work in the meantime, he'd got a lot of buildings pulled down, no end of work he'd got done. When I looked at the site he'd already got pegged out what he wanted for the fold area. I measured it over and I said, 'Well them two roofs that we have will only cover two-thirds of it, so I suggest we put them both together at t'north side of t'site, and make a new range of buildings down this side.' 'Oh.' He says, 'I want an open yard.' 'Well,' I said, 'Nowadays most of t'yards are covered in altogether.' 'Well,' he says, 'they can do as they like, but I like t'bullocks to get some rain on their backs.' Well I couldn't argue with that point, because I knew nothing about it. I was a joiner. So I says, 'We'll have t'open side at t'south end then.' 'No,' he says, 'I'll tell tha what I'd planned Dick. I'd planned to have a shed down each side, and t'space between. That'll stop t'wind.' I says, 'Aye but it won't stop t'wind from t'east and t'west.' So he says. 'Well look here,' and he had his drawing, 'I intend putting a range of buildings down each side, east and west, that'll break t'wind.' Of course that was right enough.

When t'job started, we had a week of, ...oh we dismantled a barn and got it down onto the new site,... and the first week it was grand working. It was dry, really pleasant. Over the weekend it rained a lot, and Monday morning, well it was like a quagmire. We were up to the neck in mud, digging t'holes and one thing and another. It got round to dinnertime, and we used to go over to t'house for our dinners, well I got a brush and started to do some boot cleaning. I couldn't help but smile at Jim. I don't know whether his were clean or not, but as we walked across t' field he says, 'Well there's one thing about having a grass field between, when t'grass is wet, it washes your boots.'

Jim Bramley still building walls years later

21

Anyway when we got to t'house Jim opened t'door, and when I saw t'scullery floor, you could have eaten your dinner off it. I knew that, I knew how house proud she was. I took my boots off, and your mother gave me a pair of slippers to put on. When we went into t'kitchen your dad was already sat down eating his dinner, his book propped up against t'milk jug, which was t'usual performance for him at mealtimes. Your mother looked at me with a look of.. Well I don't know whether it was hopelessness or disgust.... shook her head a bit, and sat down. Then she happened to look up from t'table at his feet. She says, 'Have you seen your boots?' Well I thought he'd say something, but he didn't say owt, he continued reading and eating, and nothing was said for about five minutes. There was a stony silence then he says, 'Dick.' I says, 'What?' He says, 'What would it cost to build a shed fourteen foot by ten, and about seven foot to t'eaves with a floor in?' 'Well,' I says, 'off-hand I don't know, but going by Sutcliffe's prices, their ready-made huts, it would be about fifty or sixty pounds I should say.' 'Well,' he says, 'I want one,' and without looking he nodded towards t'window, 'I want one over that hedge in t'field.' Of course when you looked out of t'window, there was t'drive, and t'hedge, and t'field at t'other side. I says, 'Are you going to keep hens?' He says, 'Hens be damned, I want it to live in!' 'Live in?' I says. 'Aye we might as well live in there, then she can keep t'house, as a show piece.' Your mother looked at me and smiled. I'd think she'd heard this before.

Home Farm across the field in 1953 plus four hen huts

Anyway when we were walking back across t'field – it so happened that about this time I was going to get married – Jim says, 'Tha's getting wed then?' I says, 'Aye.' 'Well,' he says, 'I'll give thee a bit of good advice. Never argue wi' t'women because, you'll never get t'last word in, unless tha says 'Yes darling you're right.' I says, 'Oh, but mind you, I could understand her playing war with you at dinnertime.' He says, 'Aye, but tha didn't make it any better taking thy boots off!!'

Recent view of Home Farm with new straw shed

DICK PEARSON AND HIS LOAD OF HAY

(Related to Don Bramley in 1982)

Dick Pearson left school at fourteen, served his time, and became a skilled joiner. He worked for many years for Mr Cec. Lund of Saxton, before launching out on his own. At one time he lived in Holy Tree House, the former home of Geo. MacCaulay of Yorkshire fast bowling fame.

He had a passion for history and was a knowledge box at our local meetings. Once at a talk on the Battle of Marston Moor, he almost came to blows with the speaker. In the pub afterwards he had a fund of good stories and his own pet theories, which often took too long in the telling. Five ninety-minute tapes in 1982 kept him out of mischief for a few nights. Now and again, on a long car journey, they bring back good memories of Dick, his times and his various escapades.

The Load of Hay is one of his best! J.D.B.

Storyteller Dick Pearson

This is the story of a load of hay that Don mentioned earlier. The year was 1946, the year after the war finished. It may have been 1947, I'm not really sure. I had to do some work for Hall's at Towton. Now first of all I think it would be better if I explain who these people were and the characters that I mention in the story because without getting some idea of these people the story hasn't much meaning. You miss the humour of this story otherwise, so I'll start with the father and mother of this generation I'm speaking about.

They moved from Copmanthorpe to Towton in 1924 and they were Mr and Mrs Arthur Hall. Mr Arthur Hall bred shire horses but he was an expert with hackneys. Now he bred one of the finest hackneys that was ever bred in this country, 'Copmanthorpe Performer'. This horse was sold at an enormous price to an American, to go to the American stud for the hackneys. It died on the boat, on the trip over but then, that is nothing to do with this story but I was just giving you some idea of the background of this generation that I'm going to talk about. They hadn't just jumped into the bloodstock and horse business; it was bred in these people.

The Racing Halls - Tom, Sam and Charlie

Now the generation I am talking about was Arthur, the old man's sons and daughters. There were three sons and two daughters. So if you take the first son, the eldest, he was called William Arthur but he was never known as William Arthur, because with his father being William Arthur they used to get confused so he was always called Charlie. Now he was what you could call a nature's gentleman. He was, well they all were very nice people. Charlie was always very gentlemanly, always very smart wherever he went and he, at the time that I first knew them, stabled hunters for the various hunts and members of the Bramham Moor. He also had horses of his own and he used to do point to point jumping, but they went out of that into racing and he was always interested in the steeplechase horses.

But Tom, the second son wasn't. He liked the flat racing and he had a licence as a trainer for the flat, and both lots of horses were trained down at Towton because the brothers worked there together. Now Tom was the only boy that was married in the family. At this time of the story he'd be about forty-three or four. He'd married a lady called Agnes Stoker. Now her father was the landlord of the Rockingham Arms at Towton and his family, the Stokers, actually owned the pub, a brewery with it, and other pubs at one time but like a lot more families they'd come down in life. Anyway she was Tom's wife.

The only other that was married in the family was Mary, the eldest daughter and she'd married a chap called Ronald Tessyman, a nice, quiet chap, a little bit on the gentlemanly side. Mary and Tom were very much alike in character and were the only two that were alike in the family. The youngest daughter, she married a solicitor and was living at Whitby. He was called Peter White and it's rather ironic that I'm telling this story because there's not one of this generation living today.

Anyway Tom had three daughters at this time. Jean was the eldest, maybe eighteen or nineteen, Anne was seventeen or eighteen and Sally was only about seven or eight years of age. She was the youngest. By the way, Sally is one of the only lady trainers that is training today on the actual place that this story concerns, up at Middleham.

Tom Hall in traditional overcoat talks to Harry Peacock (with cigarette)

Well now, there's Tom, he was a character. He didn't care how he looked when he walked about. Anyone would have taken him for a tramp at times. He always had this same old slouch hat on, and when he got up in a morning it didn't matter whose coat it was on the peg, he'd put it on, and a pair of shoes. If one of the lads had happened to leave their best Sunday shoes in the kitchen on the floor, if his feet would go in them, he'd wear them, and he'd never lace the laces up. He'd go up the gallops when it was wet in them. This was the sort of chap he was, and when he came back he'd sit in a chair and put his feet up and a lad would have to take them off and bring his slippers and put them on. These people didn't do anything physical at all. Even old Tessyman, the brother-in-law, he wasn't too keen on a lot of hard work, but Charlie and Tom, they were like gentlemen, they didn't do a thing. They didn't do anything physical, in fact Tom would sit down and tell a lad to bring this, that and the other and he wouldn't do a thing. But from the business side, the racing side, they were experts. They were really first class. I would say that Tommy was one of the best judges of bloodstock there was in the country at that time. He was highly respected, they both were, the whole family were, by the racing fraternity. So don't get me wrong, because he was a bit on the sloven side when he went about, didn't mean that he was no good. Oh no, not at all, and Agnes had a job with him I can tell you because she had to get him dressed up for the race meetings or he would have gone as he was. She used to go dressed up as if she was going to Ascot every time, even if it was just a Wetherby meeting, and so this was the position. She did all the business, well her and Jean between them. She ran Tommy's side of the business. She was Chancellor of the Exchequer and everything else. She had to do all the booking, all the entries, all the correspondence, everything. So Tom didn't do anything on that side. If it wasn't to do directly with the horses he didn't want anything to do with it, so she had to keep a very tight rein on Tom, had Agnes. She had a very high-pitched voice. You could hear her all over if she got a bit excited, and apart from the tight rein she had to keep on him, she nearly needed a gag bit at times as well.

Well, Tom being a trainer for the flat horses, they had at that time, quite a lot of horses at Towton, and I don't know how many Tom trained, but he always complained about the gallops down there not being suitable for the flat season. I think what happened was that during the flat season in the summer the gallops got far too hard and bad going and it was laming horses on them. So they were cut up in the winter and became very bad in the summer when they got hard and a bit clayey, and he was always on about this. Well Tom had one very, very good patron and this lady, they called her Mrs Gaskin. Now her husband was a medical man, I think he was a specialist but she was a woman with money of her own. She wasn't dependent on her husband because she was actually the founder of Batchelor peas. She was a very fine woman, a good-looking woman, tall and much older than Tom of course, so her connection with Tom had nothing to do apart from the business. But she took a great fancy to Tom, more like a mother would of her son, not in any other way, and being a wealthy woman of course he seemed as if he couldn't do anything wrong for Mrs Gaskin. He had four or five horses of hers down at Towton. So I think she'd heard these complaints about the gallops or maybe some of her horses had been lamed, I don't know. But at this time Noel Murless, a well-known trainer up at Middleham, left to go down to Newmarket. Well, the racing establishment up there came on to the market and Mrs Gaskin bought this and put Tommy on to it. So that's the connection between Middleham and the Halls and the story.

Well, before they could move up there, I had five months altogether doing work in and about the house, various things, repairs and decorating for them to go in. But I was up there nearly a month before they moved up. I lodged at the Commercial in Middleham and I had to go up and down with a taxi night and morning to their place, because it was about a mile and a half or a mile and a quarter to it from Middleham up Coverdale because this was in Coverdale, not Wensleydale. Now it was up the fell side as you leave Middleham and go up Coverdale; going west, it was away on your right-hand side up the fell side. It was the farthest establishment on that side. There were three - Ashgill, Thorngill and Brecongill. Thorngill and Ashgill were run by the Armstrong families. Anyway, this was Brecongill what they went on to and after I got things so that they could move in, they moved up.

Modern sign indicating township of Middleham

Well, they hadn't been up there above a fortnight, and Tommy always has a hankering to go home at the weekend, back down to Towton, more or less so he could swing a free leg. I think this was the idea because she watched him did Agnes. Anyway I used to go and Ron Tessyman, the brother-in-law was the driver of the wagon, their wagon, and he used to take things up. He used to come up on a Friday with something, whether it was feed or some things they were moving up to the house, stop overnight and next morning he used to bring me back down again. The same thing happened on the Monday. Well, this particular week I went out and Ron was in the yard and he had the engine running. I jumped into the cab and I said, 'Right Ron, off we go.' 'Just a minute.' He says, 'Tommy's coming with us.' I says, 'Where's he going?' He says, 'He's going down to Towton.' Well I says, 'That's a bit unusual isn't it? How's he got himself down there?' He says, 'Well, I don't know. There must be some business or other he has to go down for or you know he wouldn't be going down,' I says, 'No, well that's what I thought. Where is he?' He says, 'He's in there and I've just left him. He's arguing with Agnes about the small amount of money she's giving him to go down for t'weekend. But whether he gets ought or nought he'll borrow off Charlie whilst he's down there if he can't get it off her.'

So Tommy came. He didn't seem very pleased but anyway he brightened up before we got to Bedale, and when we got out at Towton he says to me, 'Don't be late on Monday morning.' I says, 'Why do you want to be off in good time?' He says, 'Aye.' I says, 'Well what time, what do you call good time?' He says, 'Well don't be any later then eight.' I says, 'I never am. That's my starting time. I shall be here at eight.' He says, 'All right then.' So I turned up about five or ten minutes to eight on Monday morning. I saw that the wagon was loaded up with an enormous load of baled hay and it was all roped, all ready for off. Anyway I asked a lad where t'governor was and he said, 'He's down at t'far end of t'gallops.' I says, 'Oh, he would be.' Anyway I went round to Ron's, he lived not far off and he was just finishing his breakfast and Mary, Ron's wife, Tom's sister, she was just exactly like Tom. I don't know whether she had an annual clean-up or a bi-annual clean-up but she was a happy-go-lucky lass and a right grand sort. She liked a bit of fun and nothing seemed to worry her, but there was Ron sat at one end of the table and they had a little lad, Richard. He would be about four at this time and he was sat at the other end. Ron got up to come and says, 'Well I'm ready Dick. We'll go. If he wants to be off he ought to have been here.' The lad was shouting to his mother, 'I want to sit where me dad's been sat.' She says, 'Well you can sit where your dad's been sat. Nobody's stopping you.' He got up and stood on t'chair and walked over t'table with all t'pots on it and sat in his dad's chair. Well, I thought she'd have gone off the top but she never took a bit of notice. It must have been a regular practice. Anyway that's just a little bit of background but it shows Mary and Tommy were very much of a nature.

When we got there, Tom had got back. He came out of the house and got in and away. When we got to Wetherby, of course there was no by-pass then, when we got opposite the street to the market, the cattle market, it was market day and Tommy said, 'Stop Ron. I want to be out. I want to see a fellow here.' So he went and before he went Ron said to him, 'Well I've got to call at Teesdale and Metcalfe's so come round there when you're ready.' So Tom says, 'Right,' and off he went. Ron went into Teesdale's and says, 'I'd stop in Dick if I were you because you don't know when he'll come back and he'll wonder where we are.' So I says, 'Aye.' But before Ron had got into t'place hardly, Tom turned up. He says, 'Where is he?' I says, 'Well he's just gone in there.' He says, 'Well, when he comes, out tell him to come down to Linton.' Then he was off. So when Ron came out I said, 'Tommy's been.' He says, 'Well where is he?' I says, 'Well he's gone. He went that fast I couldn't ask him where, but he says we've got to go down to Linton.' He says, 'There's no need to ask where. I know where he'll be at Linton. What he's done is he's met up with Crosby Welburn at t'market here and they'll be at t'pub down there, at t'Windmill.' He says, 'Crosby lives at t'Windmill.' I didn't know whether he was married or divorced but he must have been living down there with t'landlady. I don't think he was married but that's another story.

We got down there to t'Windmill and I looked at my watch and it was about twenty minutes past eleven by the time we got down there. So I said to Ron, 'If he gets in here he'll not go while closing time.' He says, 'Well he'll cop it when he gets home with Agnes if he does.' I says, 'Well I dare say he'll cop it in any case but I can tell you this...' Oh, we went in and had a drink but I said to Ron, 'I'm not stopping with this party else they'll be drinking all day.' I said, 'I'm going for my dinner.' He said, 'Where are you going for your dinner?' I said, 'I'm going to my brother's.' My brother was stud groom for Major Ackroyd at Linton Springs so it wasn't that far to walk. So I said, 'I'm going there. What about coming wi' me?' 'Oh, no I'd better not come,' he says, 'He might decide to go.' I said 'He'll not decide to go. I'm going and I'll not be coming back here while closing time to-night, never mind this afternoon's closing time, because I know Tommy.' He said, 'Oh well...' I said, 'Well if you do go before I come back tell him I'll be up to-morrow. I'll come up on t'bus so you can take me case with you.' So I went, and I rang up from me brother's to t'pub to see if they were still there before I walked back. Oh, yes they were still there, so I landed back about twenty minutes past ten and when I went in t'same crowd were there, t'place was full. There were Crosby Welburn and his brother Gunner and there was a fellow called Tom Fox and George Winter and George Winter's brother, Adam. There were a lot. They were all horsey folks. T'place were full.

When we went in there was a seat between Tommy and another chap, so I sat on this seat and I couldn't help but smile. Tommy turned to me and says, 'Has tha' been to t'toilet?' Well I thought, I'm not going to explain where I've been or owt because he's that far gone so I says, 'Oh yes. Aye.' He says, 'I thought I'd missed you.' Anyway it went on did this 'til maybe five minutes to twelve when someone came in. I don't know who it was or whether they were staying there or what, but they were very wet and Tommy jumped up in alarm. I thought somebody must have shot at him or something and he says, 'Is it raining?' This chap says, 'It is raining. It's just come on bad.' So he went to Crosby did Tom and he says. ' Has tha got a sheet, a wagon sheet?' Crosby says, 'Aye. There's one in t'shed I think.' He turned to a man did Crosby, maybe his right-hand man, I don't know and told him to go and get it. Well they got it and they put t'yard lights on and we went out. T'fellow was coming across t'yard wi' t'sheet and he threw it on to t'cab. Well of course at that time they had a bonnet and a cab had t'wagons, they weren't flat at t'front like they are now.

Well t'funny thing about it was, Tommy of all folks jumped onto t'bonnet and up onto t'cab and onto t'sheet and climbed up t'load and got onto t'top of t'load and was shouting for t'sheet to be thrown up to him. Well folks were saying, 'Thou needn't bother about a drop of rain on t'hay. It wain't hurt t'hay.' He didn't say nowt. He seemed to be really panicking. I couldn't understand it. Anyway he got the sheet and got it spread over each side and he was rolling it out and backing towards t'back of t'load. They'd got t'front ropes tied on, the sheet tied down at t'front . T'rain had nearly stopped and t'biggest part of 'em out of t'pub were outside looking on and laughing at Tommy opening t'sheet out at t'top. When he got near to t'back of t'load they were shouting, 'Hey up Tommy. Be careful. Tha'll go off t'end!' Well anyway it were too late. Tom slipped off t'back of t'load and he plummeted down, feet downwards and he was lucky. He stuck to the sheet but his feet stopped about six inches off the floor, and there he is hung on t'sheet down t'back of t'load. He didn't know where he was. He daren't look down and of course everybody was howling with laughing and standing round. And I'll tell you the air was blue with what Tommy was saying, telling 'em to get a ladder. Anyway somebody told him to look down and when he looked down of course he was only about six inches from the ground so he just let t'sheet go and landed on his feet. Anyway I thought this would break the party up and we would get off. I was hoping it would anyway. But Tommy had to have a double or two just to steady his nerves after that experience and it weren't one for the road, it was one to steady his nerves. Anyway they got going again and, I don't know, it was somewhere round about two o'clock before we did eventually get away.

Well we got on somewhere round about Allerton Park and Tommy was sat at the outside. I was sat in t'middle and he had t'window open at that side and his head hanging towards t'window. He was sleeping and all of a sudden he woke up and turned to me and said, 'Had I a hat on when I left yonder?' Well I couldn't have told him whether he had or not but

I said, 'Well you had one on when you left home this morning.' He says, 'Oh, it must have dropped off through t'window as I've been asleep.' He wanted Ron to turn round and go look for it. By gum, but Ron says, 'I'm not going back in t'dark trying to find a hat. 'Well,' he says, 'If I go home without it she'll think I'm drunk.' Well it tickled me did that. I didn't laugh out but...

Anyway we got as far as Bedale and Ron says, 'What's that in front of us?' There were some white marks across t'road. I says, 'I don't know.' Anyway, before we got to these we realised what it was because across a field there was a farm barn on fire, and it were the fire hoses that were across into a pond. I think it must have been a supplementary supply they had from this pond because we had to stop. There was a policeman and he wouldn't let us go over t'pipes and so Ron says, 'Well if we have to stop here while they clear them pipes we might as well go over and have a look at t'fire. So we went to this fire. Anyway they weren't long, in fact firemen followed us back to take these pipes off t'road. So we were off but Tom had never woke up. He was still asleep in t'cab, he knew nothing about this and before we got to Leyburn Ron says to me, 'There's two ways we could go to Brecongill. We could go straight on and through Leyburn, down to Wensley village, over the Ure, over the bridge and turn right to Hawes.' Two or three hundred yards up the road there was a road branched off to the left that went right up the side of the dale, Wensleydale, and on to the moor top where the gallops are for the horses. We would have had to go over the moor to the end of the gallops and then downhill into Coverdale and come in at the back entrance at Brecongill, at Tom's place. But Ron was doubting whether he could get up Wensley Bank with this big load. He said t'engine wasn't ower great but he says, 'I think we'll turn off left before we get to Leyburn and we'll go over t'Ure at Cover bridge, then turn right and go up to Middleham, right through Middleham and out over t'other end of the gallops, go up Coverdale and come up t'paddock towards the house.'

Now when we were discussing this, just before we got to Leyburn, Tom was asleep but he must have woken up and been listening, because he said, 'Look, tha goes up Wensley bank and straight though Leyburn.' Well it seemed a bit stupid that Ron couldn't have his own way about this, but anyway he insisted we went that way and Ron couldn't argue with this. After all Tom was the boss. So we went that way and when we got on to the top of the gallops, as soon as we started to come down Coverdale to the back of the house, he said to Ron, 'Tha could shut t'engine off and cruise down into t'yard.' Of course that's when we realised that the idea was that Agnes wouldn't hear us coming up the paddocks at the front. This was to creep in you see. I laughed. I didn't say anything but I laughed and it must have annoyed Tom a bit, but when we got into the yard we'd put our two cases off, Ron was stopping because it was hay time and he was going to help them. He was stopping that week and I say, 'Don't worry Tom, I can get into the house. I can get through the pantry window and open t'back door.' Of course with me laughing I think he must have still been annoyed because he says, 'Now look here, whose t'B..... boss around here?' I could have told him like, but that wouldn't have pleased him neither but anyway he says, 'I'm going to shout 'em, get 'em up,' he says and went round to t'front of the house. Of course, naturally Ron and I were listening for a real blast that Agnes would give him from t'bedroom window if he did knock 'em up.

Staircase at Brecongill

Anyway he must have chickened out when he got round there because he came back. When he'd been on his own he daren't shout. Anyway he says, 'Well t'dining room window's a bit of way open, tha can get through there Dick.' I couldn't see that made any difference to going through t'pantry window but anyway I went in and the dining room door opened into the front hall. I went in then into the back hall, and a staircase went up from there. It was a sort of dogleg stair that went up from the hall and halfway up on the quarter space landing, behind it was a lancet window. I thought there was somebody stood there and when I looked again there was. I didn't know whether it was the house keeper, Jean, or Agnes. But just as I got to the door to the kitchen she shouts, 'Where the hell have you been 'til this time?' Well I wasn't going to argue with Agnes, I thought I would leave that to Tom to sort out, and I bobbed through the door, shut the door, turned the light up - they had calor gas at that time, there was no electric - I turned the light up and went and opened the door and went out. Tom says, 'Is there anybody about then?' 'Well,' I says, 'T'missus is halfway down t'stairs.' He says, 'Go on!' I says, 'It's right, she was.' He sort of panicked and, as I said normally he wouldn't do anything, but he went and picked our cases up in his hands and started to walk into t'house and Ron and me followed him. He looked like our porter like, carrying t'cases in. He must have been in a state! Well when he got into t'kitchen and looked round and she wasn't there of course he didn't put t'cases down he just opened his hands and t'cases just dropped on t'floor.

I says, 'We're going to make a cup of tea, what about it Tom?' He says, 'Oh no, not for me. No,' he says, 'I'll get off.' So Ron says. 'Come on.' So we opened t'kitchen door to listen. He says, 'She won't half give him a rollicking when he gets upstairs.' We were listening for it but there wasn't a sound. She must have been awake t'biggest part of the night waiting and when she went back in knowing he was back home safe, she'd just dropped off.

27

Anyway I bet Tom didn't get into bed in case he disturbed her because t'next morning I was out at seven o'clock and when I crossed the stable yard there was a lad and I says, 'Where's the governor?' He says, 'He went up with the first string on to the moor.' I thought, 'Well he's been up in good time,' and so we didn't have breakfast until about a quarter to nine when Agnes got up. We usually had breakfast in the dining room, but dinner always in the kitchen and the lad's had theirs at a long table at the side. There were about fourteen lads in there at that time. Anyway I was doing a bit of work before breakfast and a young lad came in and said, 'T'governor wants to see you Mr Pearson.' I said, 'Oh, where is he?' He says, 'He's over in t'feed house across t'yard.' So I went out and of course when I got there, there was Ron having a right conversation with Tommy, sorting things out, and Tommy says, 'Now look Dick. She might interrogate us separately so let's all have t'same tale.' Now I wasn't reckoning on this but I didn't see how I could get out of it. So he had a tale about breaking down outside Boroughbridge. I can't remember all t'details but he had a real story made up. He must have sorted it out while he was out on t'gallops that morning, because by then I'd think he was sober enough to sort it out. Anyway it came to breakfast time and we went in. Agnes hadn't come down and Jean, t'eldest daughter, she was about nineteen, she knew he'd be in for it so she kept giving her dad a glance as much as to say, 'You're going to catch it when she does come down?' I thought t'same. Anyway she came down, she sat down at t'table – I thought she'd start as soon as she got through the door but she didn't – and we finished breakfast. I thought, 'Well what's happened?' Anyway then she started to ask us. Of course we left it to Tom to sort out between 'em. He told this story that he'd got made up and of course he wanted it substantiating with us like. Ron had to join in 'cos he was t'mechanic like and I just had to say it was right and all t'rest. I think with me saying that she thought there must be some truth in this so she seemed to calm down a bit and no more was said.

Horses going back home from The Gallops

Well when we went out Tom was congratulating himself on such a plausible story that it had beat her. Anyway nothing more was heard till dinnertime. We went in for our dinner at dinnertime and we got sat down at the table. We were at the table across the kitchen. It was an enormous kitchen. The long table where the lads were was on the far side and we were near the window. We were having our meal and nothing was said, she hardly spoke in fact, but Jean kept looking across at her father as much as to say 'You haven't finished yet.' I could see by the way she looked, and she looked at me with just a bit of a faint smile. I thought, 'Hello, there's something to come yet, goodness knows what it was.' But when we'd finished dinner Agnes started on about breaking down outside Boroughbridge and she had us repeating t'story all over again. Well whether we got it t'same as t'first time I don't know but it didn't matter because as soon as ever we'd finished telling t'story and us all saying it was right she stood up, and I can see her now, she stood up and put her hands on t'table and she looked straight at us all and she says, 'Well I'll tell you what, you're a lot of bloody liars, that's what you are.' She says, 'They rung up from t'Windmill at Linton and t'cleaner woman, she's told me that you'd left your hat there and I got to know from her what time you'd left.' Of course it made us look very small, and not only that, she motioned to Tom to go to t'hall doorway and he went with his head down, right hang dog, just as if he was going to a death sentence. Anyway I don't know what happened when they got at the other side of the door so that was the end of the story of THE LOAD OF HAY.

LOAD OF HAY - Postscript 1

Letter from Marie Hartley and Joan Ingilby

COLEHOUSE - ASKRIGG - LEYBURN - NORTH YORKSHIRE - DL8 3HH
TEL: (01969) 650253

Dear Mr Bramley,

Thank you for your letter, congratulations also for the story of The Load of Hay. Having read this, I was quite taken to Coverdale, Linton etc. The account tells the tale well. It is a bit too long in places, the editor of the 'Yorkshire Journal' said, but unlike her we think that you could cut it down without taking away from reality. We like the description of the kitchen and table for stable boys and events at the Windmill at Linton. Perhaps the beginning is a bit overloaded with relationships. But some weekly or monthly paper ought to take it. Have you many like this? What about a little booklet including a few?

We both know all the places you mention. I even know the Windmill, as we lived at Wetherby for twenty years, on the Linton side. We once had a maid from Linton - her mother, a real character, used to take a jug to the pub every night. I remember seeing a kingfisher in the river, on an island at Linton Bridge.

Yes we remember you coming one evening. We talked about old times. In the war we stayed as a family at Lennerton Lodge. I am put out that I cannot remember the name of the taxi driver who took us from the station to the farm. He was elderly with whiskers and wore a sort of top hat, but it had rounded corners. The Firns had a farm boy - Tommy Mytum. We went pea picking and were paid like the others. Alas, one old character drank too much at the Half Moon and drowned in a dyke.

The tale is so real, and bringing in race horses and stables has extra interest. We like the argument as to how to get to Brecongill. We suppose that Agnes is Mrs Hall. Cutting down would have to be carefully done.

We are both fairly well. Joan Ingilby's eyes are not too good, and nothing can be done because it is age-related. I very soon tire.

Thank you again for letting us read your story. By the way isn't Macaulay spelt thus? - I remember him at Scarborough cricket festivals.

Yours sincerely,

Marie Hartley & Joan Ingilby

Marie Hartley at Home

LOAD OF HAY - Postscript 2

Since the coming of Set-a-Side in 1994, most people deliver the very important forms to Northallerton in person, and for the last three years we have celebrated the relief by staying the night in various favourite places. Rosedale and Richmond were two good choices, and last week (16th April '99) ulterior motives took us to Middleham, home of many racing stables, and of course, Miss Sally Hall's Brecongill, a mile or two out of town.

Sally had given Dick's story nine out of ten for accuracy so we followed Tom's chosen route through Leyburn, Wensley, over the Ure and up the long steep Wensley bank, which would have tested the old lorry, and I couldn't fault any of that. The place was certainly off the beaten track, and I could excuse Tom his desire to get down to be with his mates at the Rockingham at Towton. A lady helper showed me into the house where Sally and her dog were recovering from 'flu. In the circumstances they were both pleased to see me, and I was taken on a tour of the large rooms covered with racing prints and pictures of past winners. The fourteen lads are no more - just four girl lads - so the huge Aga is having it easy in the echoing kitchen.

Dick had spent a whole year working there and his craftsmanship, especially his imitation panelling going up the stairs is surviving well. It is easy to imagine Agnes appearing over the banister at the top at the top when Dick had gained entry through the pantry window. In 1982 when Dick taped his story he thought all the main characters were dead, but Sally's mother Agnes, the ogre of the story, at ninety-five is still here and at the moment confined to bed, but at peace with everybody now.

I then photographed Sally outside the front door with her fifteen-year-old schoolgirl helper who had put the story on their computer. This young lady then took her favourite horse, the one I had lost three pounds on at Wetherby on Easter Monday, out of the box for me to snap them together. We toured the rest of the yard and I still enjoyed seeing a shed of fine cattle as much as anything. Very much conscious of my wife reading the Daily Mail in the car and worrying about me catching their 'flu, I nevertheless ventured back into the house to rummage through bags of old black and white photographs, sadly none dated or named for future researchers. Eventually we found the one Sally wanted of her father, exactly as Dick had described in scruffy overcoat talking to a fellow Middlehammer who had trained Dante, the famous Derby winner. (A phone call to local expert Alec Jackson informed me that Mr M D Peacock was the trainer, Billy Nevitt rode it, and an early Sherburn bookmaker Tad Aycaster suffered a major setback.)

Next morning at 6.30 we were woken by the clip clop of Mark Johnston's first string under our bedroom window, making their way to the gallops in the falling snow. After breakfast, and at a more respectable time, I walked past the castle and up out of town to the moor, where there was about an inch of wet snow on the grass. Horses from various stables were coming and going all the time and as they left the main road they cantered off up the hill in line astern, their hooves drumming astonishingly to the sound of skylarks and occasional curlews. There was no sun and my pictures, which could be of the U.S. cavalry, are a bit cold and don't quite evoke the magic of the occasion.

I hadn't got up soon enough to get to the point where they go flat out. That was a few hills further on and by 10.30 Deirdre Johnston was returning from her third trip, still chatting away and making a mad photographer's day with a nice smile and a cheery wave. You don't have to go as far as Greece or Hong Kong for a good day or two out!   J.D.B.

Sally Hall with York Birthday Club - June '99

CHAPTER 4

OLD JOHN THORNTON

One Saturday night in September, I watched a little of Elton John and his friends on television. The following Monday I attended a moving funeral service in Sherburn church for another John - 88 year old Mr. John Thornton, one of Sherburn's best loved characters. I couldn't help thinking that an hour or two spent with old John, as he has been affectionately known these past years, was worth months of Elton and all his friends put together.

One evening back in March 1980 I did just that and enjoyed filling two hour long tapes with his knowledge and reminiscences. Like his father and grandfather before him John was the local undertaker, joiner, wheelwright, blacksmith, engineer and much more besides. Like my father, he was taught at the Endowed Boys' School at Sherburn Cross by Mr J.T.S.Potts. Like him too he didn't want anyone tidying up as he knew where to look for things he needed. Once, as a last resort, I asked if he had a small cork for a petrol tank for our engine on the potato riddle. We picked our way across the yard into a gloomy, decrepit shed piled high either side with shavings from, I assumed, his coffin-making. There at the end he took the cork from a tobacco tin inside a biscuit tin in some old drawers. Brilliant!

Danger money to go in here

Later when his old blacksmith's shop had been replaced and was soon to come down, at great risk I explored its treasures (to some). A bundle of damp 1930's parish magazines and the hand made wooden templates for cart wheels were retrieved amongst other things. But amazingly, on pegs on the wall covered in grime were a bowler hat and a crutch.

Cottage in the lane where John was born

John was born, down Moor Lane in a cottage exactly where his petrol pumps now stand, in 1909, into a Sherburn of no gas, water or electricity services and very little traffic. He and his friends could play various games in The Lane itself with horses galloping down to their fields at the end of their day's work, their only danger. John made it quite clear that residents never called it Moor Lane - just The Lane. Nature study was a favourite subject at school with weekly summer walks along

31

the lanes with hedgerows covered with wild roses. Sunday's church hymns were rehearsed through the week and, with Mr. Potts a church warden, the male choir must have been at its all time peak.

A Cart made by John Thornton

With housing estates still twenty years away the village was well served by pubs and butcher's shops. Albert Bradley helped Mr. George Hill, Mr. Pullan, Mr. Billy Wheldrake, and Walter Wainwright do their slaughtering on their own premises. There was a butcher's shop, slaughterhouse and farm at the old 'Swan', which had four entrances and a boot scraper like a cross, which folk would sometimes get entangled with, said John. He could describe all the houses and occupants down The Lane and probably knew them all. Doctor Pickersgill's sister had retired from teaching but gave music lessons. Yeaman's garage, which disappeared recently, started with its founder working on the railway, living in a carriage, building his house and then the garage and helping at Thornton's in his spare time! In 1931 the Thorntons sold a new farm cart for £17.10s. When John explained that trees were cut down for threepence each for the planks and wheels, and the nuts, bolts and iron work were all made on the premises, there can't have been a lot of profit. Oak trees were used for the spokes, elm for the centre (or nave), ash for the rim (or felloe), each piece chalk marked and dated. Ten or a dozen wheel hoops were in the blacksmith's fire at once, and John could explain the process as if it had happened yesterday. On leaving school John spent two years at Micklefield pit before joining the family firm.

The 1920s and '30s were bad times and the Thornton labour force consisted of John's father, his brother George and his son Fred, and John himself. At the age of seventy, George and his son started making carts on their own and parted company. After his father died in 1950, John got planning permission for two petrol pumps and proceeded to build a new garage which he did himself, making all the angle irons and trusses, and buying a load of bricks as he could afford them - no 0% interest or hire purchase then!

At about twelve years John was in at the start of radio by becoming a crystal-set expert, and would sit up all hours listening to the only two stations, 2Lo and Daventry. His father had been a very early photographer. Sadly his glass slides of flax growing and steam threshing in the First World War were smashed up. Lads going off to that war visited Mr. Thornton for a portrait and, if they were lucky enough to come back, had him do their wedding photos too. John, of course, gave a hand with the processing and when Jack Habesh opened the Low Street Cinema John started as sweeper upper and progressed to spooling the films off and delivering them, on his bike, to South Milford station on a Saturday night to catch the last train to Leeds. An old Crossley engine turned the machinery at the cinema, but it had seen better days and tickets often had to be returned after serious breakdowns and a lot of stamping of feet.

In a lifetime of hard work and change, the burning of the mill and the rebuilding of the 'Swan', the building of the Highfields and Springfield Road housing estates must have been the most memorable. At the very end of his days the renovation of his old school by the doctors would have given him most pleasure.

A book could have been written about the life of John Thornton. I tried hard to get him to talk of his main gift in life as a caring funeral director, but he wouldn't be drawn. I haven't mentioned his friends in the Buffs and his long connection with the Wheatsheaf. Old John, but young in mind, was supposed to have retired back in 1980 and sons Alan and Ian are following on in the steps of previous generations and in the same quiet way as their father - a hard act to follow!

MY FRIEND EDDY

Eddy Edmonds was born in Castleford and settled in Sherburn. He was a pitman who got away to see the world in the war, became a mechanic at Sherburn Aero Club but finished working back at Micklefield pit. He was his own man, a free thinker who had many interests, one of which was photography and another nature. For many years he made my old postcards into slides and was a good assistant when showing them around the villages - a real raconteur and character!

Eddie and faithful friends

(We've been talking long enough, let's get down to basics. Where did your parents come from?)

Bolsover. Me Mother was a Hunt, and they started out in the Dukeries as young people, and then they followed their work. Now me dad, I find out later, was a chapel organist, so when the manager moved, he moved with him. We have a family bible that my sister has, and I thought we were born in caravans, as we were all born in different places. My mother looked like a gypsy and had hair like one, and to be honest I always thought we were from gypsies. T'managers were always Wesleyans or Methodists, and I could never understand while we were in such a destitute situation we had a beautiful carved organ in the front room. My sister got that.

With him being a good workman and an organist, when t'manager went he'd say, "Right, I've got a house for thee, and when he got to t'chapel, usually they were t'queen bee there, he had a ready made organist if they hadn't one. If they had he'd a spare. He couldn't lose out 'cause he was in a pit house. His last pit was at Glasshoughton and I was born at Powell Street, one of eighteen really, but TB, meningitis and pneumonia sorted us out. I got pneumonia and survived but two either side of me died.

It's difficult to believe a kid could be badly and no one'd come and see it because you owed 'em money. I've said, "If I mended your car and you didn't pay me do you think I'd keep doing it?"

The doctors emptied all the houses. I was born in 1920 and can vividly remember the '26 strike. We had lovely pictures on the walls, they all went; and china, they were like gypsies for china. My sisters all worked at Castleford Potteries until they went into service and always brought something home at Christmas time, but the doctors took it all for payment. It was merciless; there was nothing else to pay with.

When I started working in 1934 I'd three days at t'pit and three on t'dole. I worked at Glasshoughton but couldn't get down t'pit to start with. But for some unknown reason I'd a kinship for first aid. I could remember first aid but nothing from school. Even now I can quote the book word for word. Wheldale had a good team with a bloke called Tilotson. I went to work there and got straight in. Once I read it, it stuck, but not with anything else.

H3 Edition Circulation of Blood - the organ is concerned in the circulation of blood and the heart, the arteries, the capillaries and the veins. The heart is a muscular organ which acts like a pump. Page 43 - shock is a condition of sudden depression of the nervous system resulting from and occurring after every accident or sudden illness. Never forget it.

The science of first aid to the injured is based on the fundamental principals of practical medicine and surgery, a knowledge of which enables a trained person to give help and assistance, but I was winning all ours. At that time they didn't have mock-ups. It was the book and a doctor, so I scored a hundred percent all over.

I'll show you t'first things I won and into our bottom drawer (two cake dishes) and it was all about snakebites. - The bite of a venomous snake endangers life, and care must be taken to prevent the spread of venom around the body.

The next thing in our bottom drawer was a canteen of cutlery, which working men didn't have in those days. I've also got a medal from Lane Fox with my name on it. Only three of us turned up so I took the head and trunk and t'other two took the limbs, and we won it.

Mr Wildgoose went to manage Wheldale from Glasshoughton, and he set me on the following Monday and eventually, at eighteen, I was the youngest First Aider in the area. When the war came I joined the Home Guard 'cause I was mad about guns and wanted to join up, but Fred Tilotson said, "You're stopping here with us and help with the ambulance." Why I didn't go into the medical corps when I did join up I don't know. They wanted mechanics and that's what I became even though I hardly knew what a spanner was.

(We're moving too quickly. Schooldays, did you enjoy them?)

I did because we had a choir. Welbeck had a strong music tradition with a Welsh headmaster who'd come from Lock Lane who were always winning. We'd compete at Pontefract. Lane Fox had something to do with it, and we won the Wood Shield two or three times. I can nearly remember the songs we sang. We had a super soloist called MacFarlane and songs were arranged around him. With being trained at school for singing we were an asset. We'd compete at Pontefract Town Hall, and we'd no stage fright. We knew our parts and what to do. I was an alto. We took to singing like ducks to water. It was a great choir school, but I was never any good at lessons although I never caused any bother.

(Where did you get your nature interests from?)

That was inbred because you were expected to go and get a dinner. My mother was good with ferrets and nets and knitting. At ten or twelve you went with someone older and learned. There was some poaching but not to hurt anyone, commercially, just for dinner. We went for rabbits and were not too keen on birds - they weren't a meal.

Lambs, I've taken the odd lamb. Mother would burn the pelt on the fire a bit at a time. She'd put it in the oven and at two or three in the morning say, "Get them bairns up." We'd come downstairs, tuck in round the stewpot and go back to bed.

It's hard to describe what the house was like. Two bedrooms, seven or eight feet square, each filled with two three-quarter sized beds. Bare boards on the floor and to get into bed you'd climb over the bottom railings. Lasses, up to going into service, all slept in Mam and Dad's room. We had a big straw mattress and slept under a flock and overcoats and anything. No pillows - it was real poverty.

Meals were always out of the oven - all home baked, stews, and twice a week she'd do a stone of flour and a quarter of yeast in t'big yellow lined bowl. It was all graft! They'd washing to do with the peggy tub and rubbing board and all to dry in the house in winter. It's incredible how the women managed, the patching, mending, knitting and they'd even time to do lace work.

I can never remember my mother other than a drudge. She liked a gill of beer but that's what it had to be, a gill - and a pinch of snuff. They'd sit round like a group of old witches and they'd send me to Sweating's shop. He'd a wonderful knack of getting one oblong piece of paper to finish like a trumpet. He'd screw the bottom end for starters, make a spiral round his finger, and he'd this little measure, scrape the top with his knife, put it in, then fold the top. It was absolutely a work of art.

It was the time when every street had a midwife and someone to lay them out when they died. No one would die on their own, they had a vigil and took it in turns, someone had to be there. My mother was always in the thick of it. She was the midwife, and said when they were dead, and put pennies on their eyes. That was another nice thing, then they'd give them to the wife or one of the kids to keep. And they'd all bake. Ham was the thing. It was a posh funeral if there was ham.

So when I took the snuff home she'd open it all up and lay it in the middle. They'd all be round with shawls and caling, and keep leaning over sniff, sniffing till they saw it off. Another day they'd meet up at someone else's house. You don't get that now. Some people don't even know their neighbours never mind talk to them.

(When did your mother die? Did she go first?)

No, me Dad went first but I can hardly remember him. At three-year-old I can remember starting at Welbeck Street School, but sadly have no recollection of him whatsoever. Even now I can picture the schoolroom with the rocking horse, sandpit and shells - but nothing of me Dad, not a thing. I know he was strong on chapel, we all were. It was straight opposite Powell Street Chapel. I'd a brother who was a lay preacher. He was a fitter at Glasshoughton pit and he was on the circuit, going to different chapels and we used to go with him. He was with religion like I was with first aid. He really knew his bible and was always quoting from it. On a Sunday in t'room practising his sermon, we all had to listen and Mam 'd pick him up on it.

He put in for full time, and got on their short list with a bloke called Wilkinson, whose folk had t'co-op shop at the top of Glasshoughton Hill. But he got knocked back and said to one of the panel, "Where did he beat me?" and he said, "With thee background owd lad." So he said, "If that's religion, that's me out." He didn't swear about it, or go drinking. He still went to chapel but packed up preaching. Like he said, Wilkinson got it 'cause his Dad was manager of the Co-op, and that was a hell of a gap to being a miner's son.

It was all Colley's fruit people, Briggs' bricks, Sainters, Davisons. There was more business done in t'vestry than in t'shops. Then there was Clarke's potteries of course and Hartley's bricks. They were all chapel, and I do believe now, a lad like me, if I'd played me cards right I needn't have gone to t'pit. But I left school on t'Friday and me stepfather went into t'manager about me, and he said, "Bring him in on Monday." It was automatic and we didn't know different. But in hindsight I could have used chapel like they did.

(Your Mum then, you'd get a knock when she died.)

I got married when I was nineteen. We lived with in-laws, outlaws, best friends, neighbours. We were ten years before we got a house. When the war came I joined up and Doreen came back to Milford. I started going there in '38 on my bike when I was courting her. But me Mum would be sixty-five when she died and is buried at Castleford.

We lost a bairn under the old system, and now there'd be hell on. The treatment for infantile convulsions then was lukewarm and cold water. They found out later that killed them. Now it's out completely. So I said, "I'll go out for Doctor Crispin," and he wouldn't come. I went three or four times during the night and that bairn died. There was no comeback. The treatment now is just a flannel. They've altered a lot of things since then. Here's me, a trained man, and me own bairn died. It's difficult to believe today that a doctor could say, "No, I'm not coming."

EDDY EDMONDS - MINER

(There's opposition from the canary. How long have you had that?)

Not long, it's just coming to me now. I let it out and it sits on me knee, it's a miner's bird. Most miners in t'thirties 'ould either have a linnet or a canary. I'll cover it up.

(Did you take them down the pit in your days?)

Oh yes, but the lamp made them redundant. They call it the Garforth lamp and it's so sensitive. But in the latter days, the seventies and eighties they took a resuscitation chamber down with them and if the bird fell off its perch, they'd bring it round in the chamber, put it in the spare cage, and never use it again.

It was always a hit and miss job. They were just sensitive to gas and you held them in front on a stick, but when they dropped off it didn't tell you the depth of the gas, and that Garforth lamp registers to almost 0.5%.

(So the lamps were for gas not lighting?)

In the early days there was nothing electric, it was all candles of course, and like an idiot I borrowed all the files on the Micky explosion for our Freda for an exam. She had the choice of Hickson's explosion, Cas Market fire or Micky pit.

Some of the men weren't even getting paid. They used to go down on a Saturday afternoon to bare their coals and it's said it was a young lad that had gone somewhere to relieve himself of a natural thing. He'd taken his candle and there was some gas. How they knew that I wouldn't be sure. It went round the pit bottom twice, then up the shaft, and threw the cage into t'pit yard. On the Micky monument the youngest was fourteen or fifteen and the eldest over seventy.

There was no compulsory retirement then. We had a man called Rodgers who was eighty-two, which is hard to believe. He was a button man on a conveyor. There were men on t'face hand filling coal on wi' t'young 'uns at sixty-seven. It was always said that an old 'un 'ould kill a young 'un and that's true. There was a lad called Brian Docherty, lived at Leeds. He was a power pack with an old man at each side of him, and when the hydraulic supports came in they weighed twelve to thirteen stones each, and each man handled about ten to hold his stint up. Young Doc used to say. "You finish that bit of coal off and I'll chuck 'em all in." He finished up having a fifty-fifty operation, which luckily sorted him out. It's very difficult for a lad working at the side of an old man, and not wanting to help him.

(Were you on piecework?)

Well you had your own stint to fill, probably about nine yards of coal and a yard high, that were yours. A young lad could eat it. Gerry Broomhead was one of the best shovellers I've ever seen He could do it easily and in reality he should have said, "That's me finished, mine's on t'belt." But you got paid for the whole lot. You could have yours away but what was left affected your wage. Mr X had a bad name at Micky and they shouted from man to man, "Is there any coal left?" and it 'ould come back, "X's got a bit," and the answer was, "Aye, he allus 'as!" - and somebody 'ould move in and fill it off for him. If any was left they'd send t'afternoon men to shift it before they could cut it.

They'd cut underneath at night with a six-foot jib. Laurie Thornton was t'machine man. Dickery Render put chock lumps under the cut so it didn't settle to the floor, so when t'men went they'd put holes down to t'floor and fire it.

(What do you mean, fire it?)

With explosives and break it all up.

(So you could shovel it?)

Well to start with you'd to scrat it out by hand till you got room to shovel, and away you went. They always had a mind to safety, and as soon as they could they'd get a bar across and two uprights, and work underneath that. They were all fanatics for straight lines. You'd soon get told if yours was out of line. They were also scrupulously tidy. Gerry and a lad called Pearson always tidied up first thing. Everything that would stand was stood up, everything hung up and then they'd clean up - that's before they started! Immaculate.

Anything new that came to be tried out, they would be put on it. They were like the hallmark, and fortunately for me I was their fitter. I knew my job, but I'd to work under their rules, and they were dead strict. Nothing thrown on the floor, give themselves plenty of room, and Henry Malkin was a special bloke on their gearhead.

But back to Gerry and this manager Hague who'd come from Lofthouse. There was a managerial meeting and this chap said, "This pit we were at had a sauna bath, and it didn't cost a lot. All it was was extended steam pipes from t'boiler house." So Hague said, "We'll look into it and see if it's feasible for here." Now at t'next meeting Ernest Hardy, local bred and I admire him forever, was in the chair. He was brought up in Micky, had four brothers working in Micky, he was self-taught with a Maths Diploma from Selby Tech. Nobody could point a finger at him, he'd been so good as a workman. If he caught anybody asleep they couldn't turn round and say, "Well tha used to." Hague wasn't there and he was t'under-manager and so he was chairing the meeting. This bloke says, "Oh, Mr Hardy what's happened about this sauna bath?" "What bloody sauna bath?" So he explained the situation to him and he heard him out. Then Hardy said, "If anybody in this pit wants a sauna or sweat bath, they can go and get in t'stable 'ole with Gerry Broomhead!" 'Cause Gerry, all his ale used to come out on a Monday morning. He was like an old beast. He was a power pack and a hell of a fella. When I see him now I cringe!

(He could lay 'em down in his time as well couldn't he?)

Oh aye, but he never caused much bother. Only two or three years ago, he was going from t'Club to t'Swan, and this young lad about nineteen or twenty was putting his motorbike up on the curb. He didn't see Gerry and bumped into him. "Hey, what's tha laikin at?" said Gerry, "tha nearly knocked me ower." He said, "I'll knock thee ower if tha likes." Lad 'ad taken his helmet off and put it on t'bike, and before he knew it, he was on t'floor, and Gerry looked down on him and said, "I'll give thee a tip old lad. If you're going to talk to a bloke like me like that, leave thee tin hat on!!"

Another time he was playing dominoes in the Swan fairly recently, and one of t'lads put t'double six in Gerry's pocket out of t'sleepers. So next time they shuffled someone said, "Hey up, hang on there's only three sleepers. Where's t'other?" So they shifted t'table, searched all around, and Gerry put his hand in his pocket for a cig and said, "Oh hell," and pulled it out. This young lad said, "I knew you were cheating you old get," and bang, he was on t'floor too. He can't abide anyone taking advantage of him or calling him old.

George Baker lived over t'road, and when we all first retired, we used to go for a walk and call at t'Thack for a pint in summer, then Milford Club, then t'Bull or t'Swan and home. But old George was bothered about his health, not that he was a poorly fella, he was a natterer, and he wouldn't have one, he stayed outside. He must have read it didn't do you any good. Then he got cancer and Gerry and me 'ould go and see him nearly every day when he was downstairs, before we went off walking, and just before he died he said, "I've been thinking about all them times I refused that beer with you. It wouldn't have made any difference at all. I thought I was doing myself a bit of good and I could have murdered a pint!" So when I say to Gerry, "Why does tha get so much?" He says, "Tha was stood at side of t'bed with George Baker..!"

(Let's get back to Micky pit. Half of Sherburn and Milford must have worked there. How did they get there?)

On days, afternoons and nights a double-decker would leave Milford and by the time it got to Sherburn Church it was standing room only, and that was every shift. When they were starting with Selby Coalfield in the seventies, a chap wrote to the paper and said, "If we're not careful we'll have miners in Sherburn and Milford," and they invited him to show him there'd always been miners. The last used to get on at Newthorpe. There'd be at least sixty a shift. Gerry and me had an advantage. If we got up too late to catch t'bus at t'bottom, we'd catch it at t'Top End but forfeit a seat. I see Colin Skinner every day, and his dad had a great, bad, mucky old pipe and his bacca was foul. He'd get on at Joe Firn's, and he'd fog the bus up. He was a railway man that caught the train to Leeds at Micky. And Walking Stick Willy (Tomlinson), I never knew what principles were in a man until one day it had been really heavy snow. The bus was struggling, and Billy was walking in the fields with his bike over his shoulder. Later we asked him why he hadn't come on t'pit bus and he said, "When they had a meeting to decide about a pit bus, I didn't even go, so I don't see why I should take advantage of another man's foresight." That's true, he always biked. When Gerry and me worked on Saturday or Sunday, which was very rare, we had to walk it and went through t'willows, up t'line side and through Newthorpe.

Canaries, whippets, Bedlingtons, pigeons, choirs, brass bands, you don't have anything of that now. But I've some lasting memories, one when Micky choir came down the pit bottom with two or three bandsmen, and to hear carols sung down a pit is something unique from man to man.

I hear what they say about this manager at Selby - "Tha wants to get thi pit booits on and chuck thi jack booits away!" Look at their notice board. Throw a plastic can down, finish for good, sine die in t'coalfield - everything - will be instantly dismissed!

There was always a bit of give and take in my time. Ernest Hardy was supposed to be a bad boss but if you were a decent worker you had nothing to fear.

(Back to Gerry before we finish. You said his favourite to get them going in the Club was 'Your Cheating Heart'. What was the other? I've never heard of it.)

Go to sleep my little buckaroo
Don't you know from the acorn that the oak tree grew
And remember that your dad was once a kid like you
So go to sleep my little buckaroo.

(Well sung and thanks.)

EDDY EDMONDS – AT WAR AND PEACE

(When you signed up where did you go to train?)

I went to Leeds, then Padgate, Warrington, to get kitted out, then to Weston-Super-Mare for foot bashing and drilling, and I took to it like a duck to water. I loved the marching and the rifle range. I'd have made a good professional soldier. I loved the bullshit and the marching to bands.

I did a fitness course at Blackpool, there, of all places, I got sent to Church Fenton when they converted it to fighter command. The planes there were Avro Ansons, Blenheims, Beaufighters and Miles Magisters. Our CO was Beaverbrooke's son Max Aitkens. We called him 'Sexy Maxy'. I used to go up with a young lad in a Magister, doing what they called the Blackout Run round Leeds. He'd a short-wave radio to the ground, and if we saw a light it's amazing how quickly it went out.

I always had a good ploy. T'Admin officer was always frightened of rats, and I'd done a bit of rat clearance for t'Council at Cas. Pilot Officer Mustard was in charge and he welcomed me with open arms, and I was excused all duties. I did me own work but didn't have to go on fire duty or pickets. I had permits to keep a dog and a ferret. I did it on all the camps I went to. I could always get a rabbit, an occasional old hare, and a few mushrooms. I used to take them to Wardy at Milford. Also I was never rich, but never skint either, as there was always places for rabbits. They welcomed 'em in t'local pubs at half-a-crown apiece then. Meat was scarce and you couldn't move about at night.

Then I went overseas from there in 1941 and we were 8th Army Support in the Middle East. We went right through to Tripoli and were more or less redundant then. We were on submarine patrol. Gerry ran all his supplies through on barges, but they were like sitting ducks. We knocked hell out of 'em. I thought we were going home then. We got on a boat and they said, "We're going home t'long way round," and we finished up in Bombay and then into Burma, and I came home from there.

(Were you with the same Squadron all the time?)

In the Middle East we were with Australians, 459 Squadron, and we didn't get on so good with them. They were very anti-British and pro-American - I think they're switching back a bit now. They wanted a 100% Australian unit but they hadn't the tradesmen or the airframe fitters, so they sent us. We got us own back on 'em. A lot of us were Yorkshire lads from Cas. We reckoned to play them at rugby. They'd try to catch it, and we'd go straight into their guts with our heads. "Oh, you don't do that." "Sorry," and they were laid on t'ground writhing! But they were gamblers same as we was. Two up with two coins and t'dice. They were like t'Scotch, if you upset one, you upset 'em all. They were very clannish, and I didn't rate 'em a right lot. They'd a lot of mouth. They always had the best. If they'd a donkey, he'd be six 'os power. After a year or fourteen months we sort of came to terms with 'em. We wore 'em down.

I've got one of their 'Comfort for the Troops' tins upstairs. We were with 'em months before we were allowed one. I used to get a five-shilling postal order from Cas with a card saying 'to buy yourself something'. They got tins of all sorts, chocolates, and cigarettes.

I got one from a banker in America and I've still got that card. I was going to write but never did. Then there was a dead Italian laid in a right grotesque position. His top button was open, and this card was sticking out. It's fifty years since and I was going to get it translated and send it on, but I never have either.

Were you ever strafed?)

Often in the Middle East, you were the target and stuck out like a sore thumb. Funny thing about that, when we got there in '42 a bloke said, "You'd better dig a slit trench." "Why?" "'Cos you'll need one." We dug a shallow little thing to show willing. The same night we were strafed, and you should have seen us digging next day, about four feet deep and all stone!

(You don't think of t'desert as stone.)

Only t'top bit's sand. They get a wind every day called the Carsene, and there's sand and little pebbles in it. If you're caught out in it, it knocks hell out of you, so we had to cover all t'aircraft engines up. They'd special sand filters on them. You couldn't work on them till it had blown over. It 'ould last one-and-a-half to two hours a day. The surface changed all the time. A forty-gallon oil drum would become a sand dune.

I met George Formby twice, once in India, and once in t'Middle East at ENSA concerts. In t'Middle East he'd got Gippo Guts, and he was on and off the stage, and they had to fill in for him. He had his wife with him in India. He'd met her at Cas as he was always popular at Cas Theatre. He called her over and said, "Guess where this lad's from." They'd got engaged in Cas.

Then I came across Mountbatten. He came to give us a pep talk, but he tried to come down to us, and he was swearing. It didn't do him much good at all. To hear a man like him effing and blinding wasn't on. It brought him down to our level.

It was just outside Bombay where Ghandi gave his lectures. Ghandi wallahs used to wear a little white forage cap, and when they were on the prowl we were confined to camp. It was always a blood bath when they got going. We'd one or two tricky situations. I've been chased home a time or two, dropping on Ghandi wallahs. There's that many of 'em. They hate to see you clench your fist. They fight you with the flat hand and the knife. We'd one or two knifed in the Middle East guarding the compounds, so they'd double the guard up.

After I came back from abroad I was in North Wales for VE Day, and then I got back to Fenton as son John was three-and-a-half years old, and it was handy. I'd a Class B offered. They wanted miners, but I wasn't going down t'pit again, so I refused it. Next thing I was posted to Cornwall - from nearest to home to the farthest.

After Cornwall I was sent up to Rolls Royce at Nottingham, and I can remember a lad coming in saying he'd seen an aeroplane without propellers. We all laughed but it was the Gloucester Meteor doing its trials at Hucknall. I got demobbed from Hucknall. They were flying VIP's around and we looked after mainly Spitfires, Ansons and Rapides. There were about fifteen to twenty English, and the rest were Poles, so we were on Polish food - sauerkraut and beetroot that hadn't been boiled and without vinegar, but we had to have it. I ate mostly at t'NAAFI there.

(How did you get to Sherburn aerodrome?)

In 1934 I got summoned by one of your relatives at Fairburn for rabbiting on Fairburn Ings, and had to appear at Sherburn court. David Atkinson from Stream farm was on the Bench, and when I paid my fine, he said I could look after his pigeons and rabbits, and that got me coming to Sherburn on the bus, and into the Swan waiting for it to go home.

I was married to Doreen, Jack Henry's daughter from Milford Junction, when I was nineteen, and we were ten years before we had our own house.

(You wouldn't have much trouble with Old Jack, your father-in-law.)

He just was t'boss that's all, but he'd a good table.

(He was boss on the railway too wasn't he?)

He'd a hell of a reputation, and was t'queen bee at Milford Club. He was very keen at work. I lived with him for a while, and the phone'd ring at all hours in all weathers, and never once did he grumble. "Right I'll be there," and he always was.

But of course when that plane crashed, I was looking after that side of it, and he was the railway man. For t'first time I met him on equal terms, I'd always had to bend and give way. He'd looked after Doreen and John all the war. Mind you, she did earn her keep. Jack's wife wasn't very well and she was mother to 'em all. They brought our John up for t'first three years, and had been so good to them, so I had to give way. He said, "I want this thing shifted and t'railway running," but I said, "No-one shifts owt till t'examiner's been, so I'm afraid tha'll have to wait." It was an Expediter, it looked like a Lockheed Hudson. It belonged to David Brown. The reason it happened, he left his engine idling over 'cause we hadn't a starter trolley for it. He stopped longer in the clubhouse than he intended, and he should have revved up and cleared the oil, but he didn't, and his engines cut on take off. He took all the railway signal wires and all he had was a hole in his ear. We were there straight away witht'yellow peril. I expected to find him all smashed up, but he'd jumped t'dyke, and was walking back.

I filled in at Rostron's paper place in 1947 whilst on demob leave, and then I got a job at the flying club until they moved to Yeadon in about 1953. I worked on airframes, covering wings and fuselages. I used to love that. When they went to Yeadon, I went back to t'pit.

Eddy back at Sherburn Aero Club with ex RAF man Les Welbourn

Arnold G. Wilson and Braime owned it and all the aircraft, but it was an outpost for their sort of business. I was there when they weight tested Sherburn for the Brabazon. The runway is just a mile long. They used to do a lot of charter flights on race days at York, and eight or ten people used to use us for various reasons, mostly business. Bidgood was Conservative MP for East Leeds, Catton had an engineering firm, Wheatley's cars, and a knacker's yard man, Wiles. He used to fly to Ireland buying horses like mad. Then of course there was Kingy. The problem was they started charging landing fees, and they got astronomical - £7 I think at Sherburn in 1950.

(So how did you meet Lord King?)

My mate Harry Hartley was his groom at Hillam full-time, and he was Master of the Badsworth, and I was t'terrier man, I spent a lot of time there helping. He used to drive the horsebox with his spare horse, and of course I knew him through work. I always got on well with him. He was approachable - I won't say he is now. He always had time for you, but brisk, always number one. He always tried to out-do Massarella, but never could. It wasn't the horses. He was a power pack, and kept himself fit, but he was too big for them. He didn't treat you like muck, like some, and when you walked back from an aircraft, he didn't sidle away. He'd walk with you and chatted. I'd a lot of time for him, a lot of time, but I bet he could be nasty when he wanted.

They said he went through his factory, Pollard Bearings, in his hunting gear. He had his own cigarettes made with a red stripe, and above it it said 'Made for the express pleasure of Mr. J. L. King'. They were in flat fifties, and when he left his aircraft, I tried to be first in for any he'd left. One day I was smoking one as I talked to him. He said, "Do you like that Eddy?" I said I'd found it on the floor, but he knew, and said nothing more.

(How about that button story?)

Yes, he gave me a fiver tip as we walked back, a week's wage. He said he'd had a good day, and had bought a button factory. I said, "What the hell do you want a button factory for Sir?" He said, "I'll give you ten minutes to fetch someone without one, and I'll make it into ten pounds. As he walked away he said, "And Eddy, don't bring someone without clothes, 'cause they'll have a belly button."

He was generous. He'd lend me his little car when he was going away, as long as I had it back when he said. I often had it for the weekend. He drove a Bugatti, with twin belts across the bonnet. At night we'd move it from the office into the hangar, but I'd always go straight down the runway and round the outside with it, which was over seven miles. Somebody must have told him, because he said, "Eddy, when you put my car away tonight, go from there to there, not round the bloody 'drome." I could never understand why he was always referred to as 'John King' or 'Kingy' when all the others were Mister this or that. Of course to his face it was always 'Sir' or 'Mister'.

He's really got ahead now. He's bought an estate in Scotland for a bit of fishing. I think he'll be seventy-two - same as me. (1993)

(How did he manage to crash at Monk Fryston?)

I think it was devilment. He was always a bit wild, and he fancied landing in a field near his house, but he hit a ridge, and the nose tipped up. We got a low-loader from Arnold Wilson's. It was fairly straightforward, as the wings folded back on a Proctor when you took a pin out. One from Yeadon crashed on a weight test just outside Leeds, when the wing folded. A lad from Milford got killed, Colin Ransome. Also the Spanish pilot, one of the Director's sons and t'sweeper up who was there to make the weight up. The modification for that was a piece of wood and two screws.

(Eddy at seventy-two don't confuse me too much, but tell me about your cameras.)

I used to have a cine camera, but when I got finished I got five hundred pounds, and I thought, "What am I going to do now?" Videos were a thousand pounds then and taking over from cines, but I couldn't afford one, so I went for a still, but didn't know owt about it. Clarry Addy's son was a manager at Dixons. He explained it all and fixed me up. I got a Chinon CE3, then the CE5 and it snowballed and I've just got a Minolta 700. It's got cross-eye lenses and is in focus all the time. It's got a 2400 shutter speed for sport, a built in flash and four computers in it. You put chip cards in for different things. It has 70-210 and 24-70 lenses. It has eye start, nothing works till you look through it.

(Gosh, Eddy, you've come a long way since that two-bedroom house in Cas and the summons at Sherburn in 1934.)

Eddy and friends ready to pounce

DOLLY BATTERSBY'S WONDERFUL SHERBURN

(Recorded 17th March 1986)

It is over thirteen years since I chatted to Mrs Battersby in her little cottage up Milford High street, which by my reckoning made her around eighty-three then. Her body had been creaking for some time but her mind and memories were in order. Her sense of fun and action came through as I listened to her again.

Older readers will relish this, and some like me will be surprised to know she was Sherburn born and bred and should have written a book.

(We'll put the microphone there because we want to hear you not me.

What I would like from you is to start at the beginning - school, all the friends you knew, where you

went to school, all the farms in Sherburn, all the shops, all the entertainments, dances, drama that you were expert at, a bit of Steeton Hall, a bit about the roundabout, the war and Monk Fryston Hall. Can you get all that in an hour and a half? We'll start with your parents. Do you remember your grandparents?)

I never saw my grandparents because I was born when my father and mother were turned forty so my grandparents were dead. The Tomlinsons weren't from Sherburn. My father originated from Ribston near Harrogate. They were yeoman farmers and had the Bay Horse Inn there. My Grandma, father's mother, ran away from home with the farm foreman and they never recognised her again.

Dolly Tomlinson

That's how she came to Sherburn you see. They lived in the old house that Jacksons had, where David's shop is now. You'll remember that old house. Well that's where they lived and they were straw dealers. My Grandma was as strong as a man. She could cut hay like a man and she could milk a cow. She was the champion milker of Yorkshire.

My mother belonged to the Thornton family and her father was a shoemaker in Sherburn. His shop was where Miss Pullan's sweet shop used to be, where George Jackson had a butcher's shop up Kirkgate. He used to go round the farms measuring all the men up for shoes and boots - all round Fenton, Barkston, all over - then make them. They were a real Sherburn family, a very old family were the Thorntons. My mother went to school at what they called a Dame School in the house where Jack Johnson lived, opposite the old girl's school. Betty lives there now. Well that was a Dames School, and that's the school my mother went to and the school opposite was built when she was just past school age. I went to that school, and in the infants I very often sat next to your father. He used to draw pictures for us. He was very good at drawing when he was a little boy in the infants. I can remember him and Denny Cope. I used to sit with them a lot. Then I went to Leeds to a private school and finished my education there. I got the medal at Sherburn School for being the most popular girl and I think your father got one as well. The Cawthorns gave them. Every Christmas they used to give us three new pennies and an apple and an orange and all these prizes for best work and that sort of thing.

When my father left the house where he lived, Jackson's house, he took the Oddfellow's Arms and that's where I was born. We stayed there - well we moved across to where Qualter's girl lives. It was a farm then. Then we moved back again to the Oddfellow's Arms. I can just remember, but I was only young.

Tipling Tomlinson (Dolly's Father) outside the Oddfellows in Low Street

Kirkate, Sherburn-in-Elmet 1908 - Glebe Farm at end near church

Then we moved up to Glebe Farm, which was opposite the doctor's up Kirkgate when I was about six. I can remember when I was three years old going over the Beck Stees and falling in the water and I was all in white and there were some big girls, the Fletcher's girls - Arthur Fletcher was our man. He came to work for my father when he was fourteen and stayed until my father gave up. They took me down there and I fell into the water and I can remember my father coming - someone had told him and he came down and carried me home. I was wet through and I was only three then but I can remember it very vividly.

Tipling Tomlinson

Before I went to the school up Kirgate I went to a little private school run by Mrs William Thompson. You won't remember her. Well Mr Thompson was the headmaster at the boys' school and she used to have a little private school down Moor Lane and I went there for a while before I went to the village school. We stayed at Glebe Farm and I was married from there. I was christened at Sherburn Church. I was confirmed at Sherburn Church. I was married at Sherburn Church. My son was christened at Sherburn Church. I was twenty-seven when I was married - not exactly young.

(Was your brother married?)

Oh yes, Bob married Hilda Lamont and they went straight to Steeton Hall to live. I'm not sure where she came from but they did live with Mr and Mrs Dick Hayes, the vet. I think they came from down south somewhere. At one time, when she was a child they had lived at Barkston Towers. He played tennis with her you see. She was much younger than him.

(You were talking about tennis courts before. How many were there and were they all private ones?)

Starting from the top of Sherburn there were two at the vicarage, one at Doctor Pickersgill's, one at Mr George Hill's. I don't know whether there were two or three at Cawthorn's. There was one at the boys' school up on the top of the garden. That was Kirkgate. Then starting in Finkle Hill there was one at England's, one at Mr Charley Dickinson's, one at Mr Dick Hayes. There was one at Thompson's in Rose Terrace and one at Mr Joe Potts'. They were private ones but quite a lot of people used to go and a lot of the young ones, when I was about sixteen, we made one in Mr Billy Slater's field. My brother helped us to make one and we had a nice little club of our own then up near the church. You know Kenniwell's farm, well old Billy Slater lived there and my brother took the roller and rolled it out for us and we made money by having dances and things. We made all the money ourselves, about a dozen of us. In those days the Church Hall was very busy. We had wonderful dances, three a week, Wednesdays, Fridays and Saturdays every week and they were really lovely dances. We used to have an orchestra come from Pocklington to play for us. They used to go on 'til three in the morning and my brother always M.C.'d them He always used to bring the orchestra into our house at three o'clock in the morning before they went home. They had some kind of a car. There were three of them. I can't remember their name but they came for years. There were a lot of private dances in Sherburn at that time, very good ones.

The operatic society, the Gilbert and Sullivan society, started when I was about fifteen. Maurice Holgate started it. You won't remember him. He lived next-door to your old farm, practically, where the bank is or somewhere there. He was a very noisy man. He used to say, 'Spit it out!' when he wanted you to get on with it. He was a very peculiar man really. He was married to Wilfred Rhodes' cousin. She was a Lawn and she was an artist. She's dead now; she died in South Africa. She was Mrs George Harrison's sister and they separated. She was very ill and then they separated and he died. They had one son and he went over with her to Africa and she married again over there. She came back several times but she has died.

Then J P Fletcher took it over. We started with 'HMS Pinafore' and I was the understudy when I was sixteen for one of the principal parts. I took principal parts in nearly all of them and we used to have an orchestra come from Knottingley. Mr Gregg was one of them; glass works people I think they were. We did very, very well for years and then Teddy Pearson produced and Mr Fletcher used to conduct – I'm not sure he knew a lot about conducting – but we had a very happy time. It was a very good thing for Sherburn. Madame Susan trained my singing voice first. You'll have heard of the Covers family? They were trained in Paris and Vienna, the Covers girls. They all were wonderful musicians. They lived at the end house of that terrace opposite the park. You know, the largest house that looks over on to that field where they're building all those houses.

Janet Cover's Concert Party
Including O. Lewis (L. with cigar), Mrs Battersby (3rd lady from L.), Mr Cope (ext. R.), and Joe Bradley (next to him)

They had some very good entertainment, excellent, and I was in their shows as well. A long time after the Covers had finished I had done singing mostly and dancing. They used to have a famous man from Leeds come out and give us dancing lessons. They had a room behind the house there and we were taught tap and toe dancing, and I did singing and dancing as a girl. Then when I got older I went to Leeds College of Music for drama and got my certificates so I could teach drama. When I got sort of past singing I started teaching drama for the West Riding and I taught all over. I taught in Sherburn, South Milford, Fryston, Fairburn, Swillington, Whitley Bridge.

We had cups and my girls and boys won them. Stuart won the cup once, strange to say, Pauline Butterfield won it twice and Ruth Kirkman won it once and we did very well. Dorothy Hill was in it too. All the local girls did very well.

Mrs Battersby and trophy winners
Including David Grace, Malcolm Leach, David England, Brenda Poole(Leach), Marlene Wood(Ruckledge)

Mr Alf Wainwright parades his horse at Sherburn Show - 1930s

I have a lot of lovely memories of Sherburn and it really was a lovely village. It was a holiday village you know. They used to come from all over for Sherburn Show, it was lovely. When I first remember it was in the field where they are now building houses, called the Show Field. That's what we've always called it. Yes, it used to be really lovely. My father was always in the ring judging. They used to wear big leather badges and the year after I always used to have the old badge when I was a little girl. He let me pin it on. I can't remember when they moved into The Park. I was quite grown up. I should be in my teens when they moved into The Park but it never was quite the same.

Sherburn Show - Tom Makin from famous horse-jumping family of 1930's

The feast that came with it, when we lived at the Oddfellows Arms, used to be in our orchard. I used to love to be amongst the feast people. Then it moved. It used to be where the Catholic Church is now, but it was a really great thing. I can remember wagonettes coming from Leeds full of people to the show. My mother never got to a show, she was making food and washing up all the daylong. We used to have big hams put on stands. Mother was a professional cook and she used to have them all iced with fancy work, tongues done out like they should be, big things full of strawberries - it was strawberry time was show time - trifles, it used to be lovely. Poor mother used to be all the day feeding people, father's customers from Leeds because he provided straw for Cobras, Melbourne Brewery, Furnaces, the furniture removers, Leightons the sweet people. He used to provide them all with straw and they used to come out and bring crowds out and we used to feed them all day long. We used to start getting ready at six in the morning.

(What was there to see in the show field?

There was a big tent where they had the booze and all that. I can remember my father taking me in there and getting me lemonade. There was a very big covered in stand where you could sit.

(I have a picture of that and all the ladies have fancy hats on. I think there's somebody in the middle we reckon is George Schofield with a homburg hat on. Everybody is well turned out. You would think it was Ascot.)

Yes it was , we used to have lovely clothes. There were rings all round and they used to have people selling balloons and lots of things. I can't remember everything because I was very young when it was there but it was a great day. Then there was sports and all the lads used to be running. There was dancing on the grass to the band, Milford brass band, they had a band then, and that was lovely!

(With drummer Hodgson?)

Baker I should imagine. Mr Baker used to have the big trumpet, Bob Baker who used to live at Mile Hill. Mrs Baker belonged to the Pantons that used to live in Sherburn, but he wasn't a Baker of Milford. He may have been related to them but he wasn't the brother to them. I can't remember really.

When I left school at half-past three when I was a child I used to get a piece of jam and bread, eat that, then run all the way to Mile Hill to play with the Baker's children and the Barker's boys. They were little lads then. They had lovely dilly houses there made of sleeper logs and I used to play there 'til about six then run home – we had a meal at six. I used to swallow that down then run back again to play and come back at eight o'clock. Every day in the summer we did that. I wish I could do it now Don. That lane had a lovely path and it had a what they call 'Jakeman's Hut'. It had a little pool where you could catch boneys, but it's all gone now, they've ploughed the path up and everything. I go down regularly for a ride to have a look.

(Talking of Tom Baker then, did you know R. C. Scriven who wrote in the Yorkshire Post, his poems?)

I remember him vaguely, yes. He used to come to the Ratcliffe's. I remember seeing him in Leeds because Miss Scriven, his auntie, belonged to the Church Institute and so did I. She sometimes used to come in with him and he was blind then.

(He wrote a nice book of his childhood called 'Edge of Darkness'. It was about his schooldays and going deaf and blind, staying at Milford and going up and playing in the Willows. Also about Tom Baker and coming down on the train. We went to see the play about it at the Playhouse with them all in it.)

Of course in Sherburn in the old days Sherburn Church had a vicar and a curate. The first vicar I remember was Mr Glennie and he had a curate called Mr Rowntree and of course we saw a lot of them because, farming glebe land, they used to come every week to our house, especially on baking day. They knew they could get some teacakes you see.

(Did you all chase the curates then?)

Well I was too young but I'll tell you who did chase them. Probably I shouldn't say, but when I was at Sunday school there used to be Miss Lewis and Miss Christabel Squires that taught us and Miss Squires was very friendly with Mr Rowntree. I always remember my father teasing her and she said, 'Mr Tomlinson, if your head never aches until I marry Mr Rowntree it never will ache.' She only wanted fun you see because curates were very poor. That's the only curate I remember and I was only a little girl. Then I remember Daley Atkinson who was a very popular vicar. I remember his children. They were about my age and we had a field behind the vicarage, a grass field, and I used to take my pony right across the front of the house down to the field there. I didn't ride the pony, I just used to drive it in a little cart, and I can remember going there and I played with the children. We had a very good following in church in those days. We had a wonderful Sunday school.

Sherburn Church Choir 1912

Back Row - including Mr Thornton, B Osborne, Ben Wrigglesworth, Harold Hill, Joe Cromack, Curate Shaw, Rev. Reg Glennie, Mr Welburn, Sid Jakeman, Geo Hill

Front Row - including Ch. Weldrake, A Borman, H Borman, Ch. Mason, Bert Robinson, Ch. Walker, Arthur Slater

(Was there a big choir?)

Oh yes, we had a beautiful choir. We used to have the Sunday School feast - I don't know whether they're there now - on the walk down to the vicarage there were some lovely big trees and we used to have all the tables set out under those trees. It used to be really beautiful. There was a Parish room in the old days where the garage or something was. Thorntons lived there, they were the church caretakers, and we used to have our Band of Hope in there.

(Where was that, on the car park where the pub was. There was a pub there, the Rising Sun.)

Originally but that was before my time. Then Thorntons lived in it. They were undertakers, similar to the others, and they were the caretakers of the church. There was a Parish room built on at the end of the house where we had our Sunday school and Band of Hope and Girls' Friendly Society. Really we had a very good following at that church then. At Whitsuntide we used to go round the village, a Whit walk they called it. Sometimes we would walk and sometimes we had wagons as well, decorated up.

Dick Whittington - Eversley Park 1932/3

1. Dorothy Waites
2. Annette Baldwin
3. Fenella Baldwin
4. Beatrice Bott
5. Renee Wainwright
6. Elaine Wheldrick
7. Flora Bagnell
8. Minnie Turner
9. Elsie Dunwell
10. Margery Pouncy
11. Joyce Schofield

12. Kath Carr
13. Joe Wainwright
14. Eric Wainwright
15. Grace Bott
16. Maurice Sissons
17. Freda Henry
18. Jean Gill
19. Kathy Wainwright
20. Nancy Wainwright
21. Mary Thompson
22. ?

23. Margaret Thompson
24. Michael Langrick
25. ?
26. Dorothy Foster
27. Ivy Hewitt
28. Claude Fay
29. Annie Marklew(cat)

(I can just remember that, going on the wagons.)

Can you? As a treat from the church they used to take us to Fryston Park to the zoo. You won't remember that. There was a zoo at Fryston Park and a maze and we were taken on wagons. Fred Hill, he was killed in the First World War, he always used to drive one of the wagons. He was George Hill's eldest son, there was Fred and Harold and Evelyn.

(Wasn't Evelyn friendly with the curate?)

Well Evelyn was friendly with them all and she married Mr Green, you know Walter Green from Kippax, and she died. She wasn't old when she died and left one daughter. I don't know where she's gone. They were on the next farm to us. Oh, I'd forgotten, their tennis court was missed out when we were counting tennis courts.

(We never added them up did we? There must have been at least ten.)

There were a tremendous lot of tennis courts then. They all played tennis. Everybody played tennis.

Sherburn Tennis Club celebrating their fiftieth anniversary in 1986

(There was nothing else much was there?)

No but young people now say there's nothing much in Sherburn, well I never had a spare minute when I was a girl, never.

(There's plenty now if they want but they don't want it.)

No, they won't go will they?

(Was the cricket team going then?)

Yes they would be because my father was great on cricket. He was a member of Yorkshire. My mother always said my father was a stone-waller, and my brother was great on cricket.

(He used to like to go and watch with Reg Thompson. Who was the rest of their gang?)

Arthur Riscoe of course. He was Bob's best friend. I don't know whether you knew or not but Arthur Riscoe committed suicide.

(No, I didn't know that.)

Well I found out in a strange way. My youngest granddaughter, who manages the shop now - I don't know whether you know her. She's a very fair girl, very bonny - she got all her 'O' levels and her 'A' levels and she wouldn't go into the bank though she could have. So she went down to London and worked at the Strand Palace and she got to be the head girl doing the cocktails and she got to know a lot of people there. Her mother went down to stay with her and got to know a very old gentleman who was a retired colonel. They were talking to him one day and he said, 'Where did you say you came from Julia?' He said, 'I knew someone who came from there. They called him Arthur Riscoe.' She said, 'Oh my Grandma knew him. We often hear about him.' He said, 'Oh dear, well I don't know whether your grandma knew or not but he committed suicide.' Well we knew he had died because Bob couldn't go to the funeral. Someone went in Bob's place for him, a friend, and he'd been living with an actress - I can't remember her name - and she'd turned him out or fallen out with him and he'd committed suicide. We never knew, or at least if Bob knew he never told us. Anne came up and said, 'Grandma, I can tell you a bit of news,' and she told me.

(What was he like then? Was he like Claude Hulbert? Was he comedy?)

Yes, he was comedy.

(Did he sing and dance?)

Yes a little bit. The first thing I saw him in was 'No, No Nanette' when I was about sixteen. He did very well but he was a bit wild with his money. Well, as a matter of fact he wouldn't have got anywhere but Bob lent him so much but he paid it all back. He was a very honest man.

(Did his father build our house in 1910?)

Yes but they lived in Rose Terrace first. His sister Lily was living up to ten years ago. She lived at Copmanthorpe or somewhere near there. She worked in York because one of the Clark girls came into the shop one day and said to me, 'We were talking about you to someone the other day.' I said, 'Oh were you?' She said, 'Yes. We were in York and we sat with a lady when we were having a cup of tea. It was Miss Borman and she lived in Copmanthorpe. She asked who was still living and she asked about you.' I said, 'Oh tell me where she lives.' We never got to know where she lived but about two years after Nancy Pickersgill came to see me and she said, 'Do you know Dolly whether Lily Borman is still living?' I said, 'Well when she was living last she was in Copmanthorpe.' She was a very nice person. I'll tell you who she was engaged to when she was a girl, and I saw them saying goodbye. I was only a very young girl but it stuck in my memory and I went home. You knew Mrs Philip Dennison, Doris?

(Just.)

Well her husband was engaged to Lily Borman, and I was walking home from Milford,— only as a bit of a kid I was, very young - and I saw Philip talking to her, and he was really talking to her in earnest on Milford road, and he was very upset I could see that. I went home and told them so Bob said, 'Sh! You mustn't talk about that. They've fallen out.' Bob was friends with them you see. They'd fallen out and that was the end of their engagement and Philip was terribly upset but she didn't want him you see. She was a lovely person, she was really. Now Harold, he was in the navy. He was very good-looking and very smart. I didn't know him that well, he didn't spend a lot of time at home. Mrs Borman was a lovely old lady.

(The father, he travelled didn't he?)

He worked for that big firm, Greenwood and Batleys, the ammunition people and when the First World War was on people said he was a German and they got it about he was a spy. He was found dead on a bench on the front at Blackpool.

(The father, Mr Borman?)

Yes, and they always said that he'd taken something, My father was very friendly with him and he said, 'Borman never did take anything,' but they said he did. My father said, 'No, Borman would never do that!' They said he did.

(Was that why his son changed his name?)

Arthur, when he was a lad they used to say he was daft. He used to walk about with his head like that (obviously demonstrating). My brother went to Leeds Modern School with him and they were always great friends and Bob always stuck up for him. People used to laugh at him so he went abroad. He came over with the Australian Army during the First World War that's how he got back into England. That's how he got on the stage. He got into a concert party in France.

(They all used to play hockey together. There was a hockey pitch at the back of the vicarage wasn't there? I have a picture of the team under the posts.)

Sherburn hockey team 1912?
Back Row - G Thornton, Crossley, T Thorogood, H Marsden, F Thornton
Centre - H Hey, S Jakeman, T Wilson, C Blackburn
Front - J T S Potts, Sydney Potts, Willie Thompson(brother of Reg), P Dennison, Billy Ward

Yes, that's it. They did.

(Yes, Sid Potts and Joe Potts and..... It's a good picture.)

I remember Mr Potts' brothers very well, Sid and Jack.

(I don't think Jack's on it.)

No, he didn't spend much time here. He went abroad. I think he spent most of his time in Africa, but Sid was a right happy lad. He was my sister's husband's friend, Will Clayton; he was a Milford lad. They were pals together.

(You would be friendly with Mr Potts' sister.)

Barbara. Oh yes we were good friends. We seemed to get wrong after Fred died. She dropped me for some reason. Fred and I were great friends as well. I don't think she really dropped me but she got away from me. Not long ago she sent her love to me. You might tell your mother that.

(Was that the mother of Richard?)

Richard and David. They always remember me. I think Susan's bought a place in the Cotswolds, a very large house. I think Barbara, her mother, is going to live with her and have a granny flat there. Miss Shepherd, she's moved from Pontefract now to Kirk Smeaton into a little cottage there, she told me. When I left from down Low Street you see, I'd played with Denny Cope all my life, as a kiddie. I had a picture at one time, but it's gone, of us sitting on the kerb making mud pies. When I went up there Bob had always been friendly with Mr Potts. He'd played bridge and that with him and he introduced me to Barbara. We were bosom friends ever after. I remember old father Cope very well.

(What about him then?)

Oh, he was a terror. 'Now me daughter,' he used to say to my mother. Mother used to say, 'Now what do you want?' and he used to come ringing his bell, 'Oyez, oyez, oyez' and give notices out. When he got to our house he used to come in and we had an old dresser in the kitchen and he used to sit on a stool at that end and my mother was often baking. 'Well, daughter, I could just do with one of your teacakes daughter.' She used to say, 'Well, if you behave yourself I'll give you one when they come out of the oven.' She used to wrap him one up. I always remember one day he had gone and we had a knife box that we put all our spoons and that in. She said, 'Dolly have you moved those spoons?' I said, 'No.' She says, 'The old monkey, he's pinched them.' So she went to the passage and waited 'til he came back and said, 'Come here Cope!' 'Now my daughter I was only teasing.' Three lovely silver teaspoons he'd pinched but he gave her them back again. He was a rum old chap, he really was!

My father was very good to him though and my mother said his wife was a lovely lady. Mother lived opposite at the pub, and when she was very poorly, mother used to take her soup across. He had some lovely daughters that nobody ever knew in Sherburn. They never stayed. There was Lizzie, Evelyn was the youngest and there was another one, I've forgotten her name but she came over. Before the First World War she was a nurse with a German family and before the war started she came over.

When she came she always came to see my mother and she said they were real ladies. She said, 'Mrs Tomlinson, soon there's going to be a war. Germany are getting ready for war.' My father said, 'Well why are you going back?' She said, 'I love the people I'm with.' But, you know, they got her back over to England safely and not long after the war started. I always remember my father telling me that, and Evelyn, the youngest was very bonny.

Father Cope - Friendly Scallywag and Bill Poster 1920's

(That was Denny's father, father Cope?)
His Grandfather was old Cope, Denny's father was Arthur Cope. He was brother to these girls. He stayed in Sherburn and did very well as you know.

(Was that a farm when he got it, the garage?)
That garage was his. He was a very clever man was Cope.

(Denny was as well.)
Oh he was, yes, and Denny was a lovely lad. He was the same age as me. We were children together.

(He had a brother at Aberford.)
That was Sidney. He used to be in the Mercantile Marines for a while. Then he had that other brother, Leslie.

(Was that another brother or was that an uncle from Filey who used to come and help?)
That was his brother, Harold. He died in Filey because I had a flat in Filey at the time when he died. He had an Uncle Sidney that used to come and help him from down Hull way. He used to come and help him, and he had a sister. She's still living I think. I can't remember her name. Oh yes, Olive Cope. I know her husband died and Leslie died. He was living with Olive.

(Who was his wife then? Where did she come from? Denny's wife I mean.)
Denny's wife used to be the maid at Miss Cover's. She was an Aberford girl, his first wife, a bonny girl.

(They had no family?)
No family, no. Denny's father was a good comedian. Yes, he used to be Miss Cover's comedian, and I'll tell you who was another good comedian, Harry Osborne's father. He used to have a concert party and I used to sing for him. We used to go to the Beeches at Tadcaster and give them a show every year when I was young.

(Was it an old people's home then?)
Yes, it's still the same.

(Was it built as an old folk's home?)

Yes, the old type. We used to go every year. There were several in from Sherburn and they used to be waiting because they knew. We took them tobacco. My father used to know them. There was old Harry Marsden and...

(What was Harry Marsden's nickname? Was it the old soldier?)

Yes, that's it. He used to be waiting for his tobacco. He used to walk with a crutch. We had some grand old people in Sherburn in those days, characters. The Battles were characters. Old Mick Battle, bent double. He went to work bent double, to the quarries. He must have been six-foot if he had straightened up. There were all the Jenkinsons, you know. They were all characters, and little Jimmy Battle...this is going back a long way. He was a bit soft and he used to play the accordion and the mouth organ. When you were passing him he'd turn his back to you and play like that. He was a bit silly but he could play anything, anything! He never worked because he wasn't capable of working. That was going back to when I was about eight years old. They lived in that off licence. Well no it's a pub now, up Kirkgate, the Foresters. There was a yard next to it and some cottages at the front, and they lived down there. Jimmy used to stand there playing. It was a wonderful village was Sherburn, it really was. We used to have an old man come round called Yeasty Baines. Has anyone told you about him?

(No.)

Oh well he used to come round with one of those covered carts selling yeast. I think he came from Tadcaster, and it's a funny thing I would go up in the ambulance to the hospital.... I'm going to-morrow, I have to have my blood taken every so often...and I was in one day with a Micklefield man and he said, 'Does anybody remember Yeasty Baines?' and I said 'Yes, I do.' He used to go round Micklefield as well. This was last year and I'd forgotten until he mentioned him. We used to have another old man coming round with a trap selling herrings. I can't remember his name, but you used to go out with your basin or your plate and get herrings from him. We had a lot of people coming round Sherburn.

(Kiddy Hayes, he was in my time.)

Oh yes, Kiddy Hayes, I remember him. I think he came from Micklefield but I'm not sure. First of all he had that fish shop in Kirkgate. That was his shop and a good one it was too.

(Was that the first fish shop then?)

That was the first one I remember. Starrs had it after him.

(Then there was old Parkinson up at the top wasn't there?)

Yes, Tommy had one up there. Before Tommy had it, Jacksons had it. You'll remember Percy Jackson; he used to be up here.

(He had a wagon that went round selling greengroceries.)

Well his parents had that fish shop and Tommy Parkinson took it over from them. They used to have a parrot and when you went in it used to say, 'A ha'porth of chips please, a ha'porth of chips.' Oh yes it was a wonderful village, it really was, marvellous. I was confirmed in Sherburn church with all the Sherburn boys and girls like Teddy Howcroft and Harold Thornton .

(Was my father confirmed then? I don't know whether he was or he wasn't.)

Not when I was. There was Guy Hawley and the two Walker boys. They went away from Sherburn. One ended up in Scarborough as a chemist and did very well. There was Isobel Smart from the Swan, me, Louie Barraclough; she's in Canada now... a whole lot of us. It must have been during the First World War or at the end of it because they didn't give us a tea. They usually put on a tea but they couldn't afford it. We all went for a walk down Aberford Lane and the boys wrote a piece of poetry about us. I can only remember one bit..'And Dolly Thornton with a face like the rising sun.' I often wonder what happened to that piece of poetry. The boys and girls all mixed so well at that time and we were such good friends. Your father was a very shy boy when he grew up. He wasn't as a little boy but as he grew he got very shy and he wouldn't join in with us. He was very shy, especially with girls, terribly shy. As a little boy he wasn't though because I can remember playing in the schoolyard with him, as plain as day. I can see the desk where we used to sit in the school. It really was a wonderful village.

Pupils outside Sherburn Girls' School - Jim Bramley with hands in pockets

No, I haven't got that one. Do you know, I've lost a lot of my things. I think it's with moving about so much.

(Did you ever see that picture taken outside the girl's school, and he's stood there with his hands in his pockets?)

I can remember the old saddler's shop very well. If ever my father was missing mother used to say, 'I know where he'll be, in the gossip shop, the Saddler's shop.' Dad was very fond of old Tom.

(Was he the father of the one that's just died?)

Yes. My father was very fond of him. They were very great friends and he used to sit all day with him sometimes when he was doing his sewing.

(And then into the Swan?)

Yes, then across into the Swan, that's right. Of course when I was a girl the Swan had a little farm and old Mrs Simpson had it, and I spent a lot of my youth there because Isabel and I were bosom friends. She married a title and became a titled lady, she was Lady Litford. She went away from Sherburn and told us she didn't want anything more to do with us. She got right up in the air you know. I should think she'll be dead now, but she was very beautiful. Her mother used to paint pictures. I had two beautiful pictures she painted and I took them to be framed at Wetherby and I forgot to go to collect them for a long time. When I went the shop was closed, the man had died and I'd lost them. I was very disappointed. Someone told me that the school in Wetherby had bought a lot of pictures but I didn't follow it up. We had a lot of quite clever people in Sherburn then We had artists and singers and pianists, violinists. Margaret Dennison was a wonderful violinist, with all the big orchestras.

(What do you remember of the Carrs?)

Tommy England who lives at Boston Spa married one of the Carr girls and they came to the chapel service the other night. Now what did they call the young boy? Tommy England told me about him. He said he's done very well and I think he's done some broadcasting as well. They were a very nice family but terrible socialists. Old Carr was a terrible socialist but they were very nice people. She was a lovely lady was Mrs Carr. They had the little shop at one time before Rapers had it. That shop, Donald, when I was a girl, was a beautiful bonnet shop and they bought stuff from Paris, and that's true, because the last time Cynthia Harrison was here to see me she said, 'Do you know there was stuff from Paris left after my mother had died'. They used to have beautiful things. It was a beautiful shop and I had my first suit made there. After they'd left Miss Denham was there and I had my first little costume made there I remember. It was a really classy little shop. You'd be surprised how many shops there were in Sherburn. They keep saying, 'Oh there's plenty of shops, we don't want any more.' There were just as many years ago. We had some very peculiar old men. There was an old man called Halton. He used to teach the violin, and he lived in that yard where the garden shop is. He taught my brother the violin. He was a big Methodist, and he used to talk all through the service saying, 'Thank the Lord. Yes Lord, I hope you've heard us Lord. Amen, Amen.' I used to go as a child, and this fascinated me. I used to listen to this old man saying the Lord's Prayer and answering. I think he was a bit queer. Sherburn chapel has always been well attended, always. My sister was a Methodist. She wasn't church like me, because my Grandma was a Methodist and brought her up, and she was in the choir. She was a very nice singer, and they always had a lovely choir. I used to sing for them sometimes when I was a young girl.

(The Methodists? They had ladies in the choir then?)

Ladies and gentlemen.

(Not at the church though?)

No, not in those days. They had a wonderful choir. There was Mr Joe Gill, Mr Harry Gill, Mr Dennison, Mr Thornton, Harry Osborne, Walkers, all the boys, and it was lovely to see them walk down. There isn't a lot of pleasure going to church now really. When I was a girl, we had railings at the front of the house, and my father used to like to stand with his hands round the railings, and my mother used to say, 'Tippling, will you come in. The ladies will be coming from church.' 'Well I shan't hurt them.' He used to do it to tease them. Oh he was a tease, my father. Mrs Dick Hayes, Mrs Pickersgill who lived opposite, the doctor, Gertie Lewis, Miss Squires and Mrs Henry Welburn all used to come walking down and my dad used to say, 'Now ladies, have you enjoyed church this morning?' Mother used to be blushing for him, she used to be so angry. If he hadn't got out, they used to stand gossiping at our end, and he used to say, 'I'll soon move 'em.' Mother used to say, 'Oh, you are rude.' He used to walk up and say, 'Good morning ladies, have you enjoyed church?' and they used to scatter. It was a great joke in our house. Mother used to say, 'Your father does embarrass me.' They always went to church. You could guarantee some people always went. I don't think that now they have the following of the same type of people as they had in those days. They haven't that backing they had from the farmers. In those days there was Millie and Hetty Bramley. They'd come up, and there were Welburns. They'd all come up, every Sunday.

(It was the in thing wasn't it, the event of the week?)

Absolutely. We all lived in terror of Mr Welburn. He used to read the lessons. He was a horrible old man, he was.

(And Mr Potts ruled the church too didn't he?)

Yes and Captain Thompson offended me several times. He moved me out of his pew twice. They spoilt it you know. If I go now I always sit in mother's pew. It's where Tolemans sit, you know Miss Toleman, and she'll say, 'Hello,' so nicely, not like the old days. I can remember mother and I sat there, in front of us was Mrs Wilson and Mrs Stevenson, in front of them Mr and Mrs George Hill, in front of them was Miss Denham, and then Mr and Mrs Cawthorne. I can see them now. Across here was Wilfred Rhodes's mother, Potts' here, Welburns and Bramleys across there. I can see them now, every one of them. Wilfred used to be coughing and choking, blowing his nose and making funny noises, and when I was a little girl I used to laugh. The children used to sit down that side. They were never allowed down the middle aisle when we went on our own. The choirboys used to use that other place near the porch.

(It's called the Huddlestone chapel now. They've put a floor in and they have meetings in it. I used to be in the choir before I went away to school. When I went away Rev. McLane sent me my wages on, 3/6d. I thought it would be grand if I was going to get 3/6d every month but it never came again.)

50

I can remember all the lads that used to come. We used to go and watch them, you know how you are when you're young. We all used to start giggling. Oh, and the font, when it was harvest festival Mrs Cawthorne used to make a big frame. It used to be beautiful did that font. Cawthornes were very good to the church. They lived where Veterinary Hayes used to be at Elmet House. They had two or three tennis courts. I learned to play tennis there.

(What did they do?)

They were wine and spirit merchants in Leeds. She was Italian. They were real gentry. They're all dead now. Gerald got killed in a motor accident. I read it in the paper, years ago at Wetherby or somewhere that way. Of course the eldest one was same age as my brother. He died a long time ago in Scarborough. He courted Evelyn Hill for a bit. I think she courted them all did Evelyn.

(Have you told us everything about Father Cope and his tales. He got in the chicken coop didn't he?)

Oh, yes, and Marshall's lads, they used to tell some rare tales about him, but I can't remember them.

(He didn't pester the ladies then?)

Oh no, he was never rude.

(It's just the way people laugh when I put his picture up.)

No, I never knew him to be rude. He'd been a coachman for someone and his wife had been in very good service. She was a real lady, his wife. I've heard mother say she was such a gentle person. The children were brought up nicely; they were really nice children. The Marshalls said he got in through the bob-hole didn't he? He was a devil for pinching though. Oh, I must tell you one thing he did. He went into Dickinson and Ward's and my cousin, Harry Hodgson. Well Harry Grice and him, they were the lads in that shop, and he eventually owned it of course, did Harry. Well they were both in this day and Harry Cope went in for something. Harry Grice said to Harry Hodgson, 'Hey, go Bump up against Old Cope.' Harry said, 'What for?' and he said, 'Just go bump up against him.' So he did and Old Cope had pinched some eggs and he said, 'Tha' shouldn't 'ave done that.' They ran right down his trousers. He was just a bit light fingered, but he had no real badness in him. It was just that he was poor, and he wanted something, so he used to get it that way. Mother was always good to him. She always saw that he had something. I can remember Ted Elliff, he was rather a character.

(I've never heard of him.)

He was a painter and decorator. He worked for Thompson's and he used to be barman for my dad. You would know Jossy Elliff.

(No.)

Didn't You? He hasn't been dead many years. He was the same age as me, and Mrs Elliff worked for me when I was down Moor Lane. Well Ted was a bit of a character. My father always looked after him. While he was living he used to send him a bottle of rum now and then because he'd been a good workman for father. He was a beautiful dancer.

(You didn't learn to dance at Monk Fryston then? You didn't go with Walter Wainwright? He used to walk and pick people up on the way.)

I've gone to Monk Fryston dancing.

(They had dancing lessons on a Wednesday I think.)

Well he was older than me you see. I learnt to dance at Miss Cover's, mostly. My brother took me and taught me. There's a granary behind that house where Covers used to live, looking on to the show field. Well it was a lovely little place and we used to dance in there.

(Was it built as a granary?)

I don't know. I think there was a coach house underneath it.

(Somebody used to live there. I used to go there. A lad at school used to live there and I used to go and play with him.)

Oh, did you? When I was a child Fells used to live there. Do you remember Norman Fell who married Wyn Dickinson. They had mushrooms. Their father lived there, and when I was a little girl we lived at the Oddfellows, and mother used to take me across the road to meet the Fell boys, to take me down Moor Lane to Private School. When they came back to England, they looked me and Wyn Dickinson up, and they married the two Dickinson girls. Bobby is still living. He comes to see me once a year. He's married again and in Scarborough now. His wife died about five years ago, the Dickinson girl. He rang me up and told me. I think this wife is very poorly. I don't think he's had much happiness. Mrs Spear that used to have the shop lived in one of those houses, and Mrs Hick and Gertie Lewis. It was a right select terrace was that you know when I was a girl.

(What about the houses at the other side, this side of Denny Cope's garage?)

Do you mean old Mrs Lewis's house.

(Teddy Howcroft lived next to the garage, then there were some houses between there and the park gates.)

Oh yes. Mrs Tindale used to live there, but I can't remember who the others were. He was the gardener at the big house in the park. What did they call him?

(Was it Walter?)

Yes that's it. He was a lovely dancer. When I was a right little girl he used to say, 'Come on I'll dance with you.' He was a beautiful dancer, but his wife never used to come out. Then he moved from there and went to live at the Pigeon Cote, we used to call it. Near the school. Their eldest daughter only died last year. She was my age, a beautiful girl.

51

(Did they have a son who was friendly with Eric Wainwright? Did they have a market garden down at Fenton?)

Yes. One of them died down there. Was it John? He was married and his wife was Josie. Well funnily enough I went to the doctors the other day and I said, 'Hello Josie.' She said, 'I'm sorry you're wrong. It isn't Josie.' It must have been her double. I thought it was Josie. I sometimes look back and think eeh I've had a lovely life. I don't think today they have it as nice. They think they do. I think things rush past them too quickly. I remember the first VC coming home from the war to Sherburn. They called him Sutcliffe. I remember my father leading a torchlight procession from Milford station up to Sherburn for him. I was a little girl and I was in bed upstairs watching through the window. They called him Sutcliffe and he married a London girl. There was a family of Sutcliffes lived at the top end, some of their relations still live in Sherburn. I can remember that very vividly. I can remember the Zeppelin coming over. My father was very ill. He was two years in bed during the First World War and Doctor Pickersgill lived opposite and he shouted, 'Don't get up Tip, don't get up.' My sister lived in Rose Terrace then when she first got married, and she'd walked across the fields to be with us and we were all sat round Daddy's bed, and he shouts, 'Stop where thy is Tip. I'm going down into t'fields to light a flash down there to see if he's going to drop owt.' My Dad said, 'Tell him not to go.' I can remember that as if it were yesterday. My mother said, 'Tip says you haven't to go, you haven't to go.' Folks said, 'We aren't going to let him go.' People said they held him back. He was going to go down the lane, Doctor Pickersgill. I can remember that even though I was very young.

(You were frightened of the Zeppelins then?)

Yes. You could hear it. I was frightened and crying. We were all sat round Dad's bed, because none of us would leave him. First of all he had a carbuncle, then he had heart trouble, then he had what farmers get on their chest from cutting hay, hay dust. He had that.

(How many were there that didn't come back? Had you any friends?)

I was only young but there was Freddie Hill, Joe Hawley, Laurie Wilstrop. I can only remember those three I think. I remember Fred Hill distinctly because as a little girl I had gone to play a lot at Hill's, the next farm, and Fred was the butcher. I used to help him to scrub his block. He used to say, 'Come on you can do this for me,' and I used to reckon to help him. I was upset when he didn't come back. He was a bonnie lad. Joe Hawley, well I can just remember him, and the reason I remember Laurie Wilstrop was because he was the sweetheart of my cousin Annie that we brought up. She lived with us and he was her boyfriend. I don't remember much else really. I remember my brother was a farmer and he didn't' go, and he kept getting the white feather. I remember people sending white feathers.

(I was reading in the Yorkshire Post that they'd been selling some posters at Sotheby's. The ones 'You're Country Needs You.' Not from the first war but from the Boer War. It said that they'd had difficulty getting people to go. Sometimes it took two years to get conscripts. There was that poster 'What did your Daddy do in the war?')

Doctor Murphy, when he first came to live at Sherburn, used call my father Kitchener. He was very like him. He had a moustache just like him. He used to say, 'Good morning Kitchener.' My Dad did used to get mad.

(Doctor Murphy was in the war wasn't he?)

Yes, he was very badly wounded, very badly. He once told my mother, that he wouldn't have done to a dog what they did to him in hospital.

'New' Old Church Hall

War Memorial

CLAUDE KENDREW AND HIS SHERBURN MEMORIES

(Recorded 17/02/1997)

On 17th February 1997 I interviewed Claude Kendrew, a well-known Sherburn resident who was over eighty at this time. I asked him to talk about his father, grandfather, great grandfather - anybody or anything he wished to tell me, or not as the case may be.

I do not know a great deal because my grandparents on my mother's side died when she was only eight. John Thomas Hodgson was a local cabinetmaker and joiner. I understand he did all the work in Sherburn chapel when it was built - the pulpit etcetera. I am never very clear where his joiner's shop was but I think it was where the milk bar is now. There were originally three cottages there with a building behind. I think Laxton had it latterly - Joe Laxton who lived in Dilkoosha, but the other joiner's shop was where Grice was, where Jack Natriss is now. The building is still there, the one with the nice little windows with overlapping glass.

John Thomas Hodgson was my mother's father. They had a son called Joe who died when he was seventeen. I know he French polished. You remember in the shop in the old days there was a staircase up the middle and a very highly polished banister on each side?

(No, I can't remember it at all but I can remember going into Dickinson and Wards on the other side of the road with the order and all those dummy biscuit things. I had never seen biscuits like that. I used to take the order in during the war and I used to look at those biscuits and look forward to them, but I never got them.)

I don't know where it went. Mrs Cawood would destroy it I suppose. Well, there was a stairway opposite the door and they were highly polished. They said that Uncle Joe did this when he was seventeen. He probably did the woodwork for the shop as well. I never heard it said but it was converted from the Traveller's Inn about 1900-1901. In those days there were three steps up to the pub from the footpath. You went up three steps so the floor level was the same as the back room is now. You walked straight through on one level. When they made it into a shop they dropped the floor level and made the three steps up into the back room instead of into the shop. I believe that Edna Knaggs, Mrs Copley, has a picture of the shop as it was originally. She has been going to show it to me but I have never seen it, though I would like to. I am not sure whether it is a photograph or a drawing.

View from High Street looking towards cross (Kendrew's Shop Right) - 1910

(Did your father buy it or what?)

No, that little Dickinson was first I think, then J.J. Foster. My father worked for J.J.Foster and we didn't take it until probably '26 or '27.

(Has it been the same sort of shop right through?)

Yes, a draper's shop and milliners. There was a milliner's department upstairs. They made ladies' hats. In fact, my mother was a milliner up there. Several girls worked there.

(Was she a milliner before she married your father or did she take it up?)

She must have taken it up. They were left orphans at eight years old. There were three lads to be brought up and she more or less had to look after them.

(Tell me about J.J. Foster then. Did he retire?)

No, he had a shop at Otley after that. He had two daughters, Lois and Muriel. As far as I know Muriel is still living. She will be ninety now. She used to have a private school somewhere on the south coast. Lois used to live up Otley way and a few years ago had a boy at Ackworth Quaker School. Cliff Dunn met her one day at the filling station at South. Milford. The last time I saw J.J. Foster was in about '76 and he had driven up from London that day.

(Had he a special car?)

No, I think not. It was a Standard Ten I think. In the old days he used to drive a Jowett that would go anywhere, but at its own speed. Of course he had a Model T. Ford as well. I heard my father say he rode to Coventry and back on a bicycle on a pocket full of nuts and raisins.

(Did your father start working for Fosters straight from school?)

I think he started with Dickinson's first of all and I think they sold to Foster.

(Did they go across the road then? Was that the same Dickinson?)

I don't know about that. The only Dickinsons that were connected as far as I can tell were William Dickinson who had the shoe shop which is now Selles, and Charlie Dickinson who had the grocer's shop. Charlie Dickinson had two daughters, Winnie and Rene. They lived in the house with the tennis court looking on to the show field.

(Cec. Grimley used to live there and Brian Lockey now.)

Yes, the tennis court was a piece of land taken out of the show field. Charlie and Willie Dickinson were brothers.

(Who was Ward?)

I don't know. He came in as partner with Dickinson. Then they took in Wilcox from Whitby - he had grocer's shops in Whitby. Then there was Barnard and Wilcox and Dickinson and Ward finished altogether except as a trading name. Barnard and Wilcox owned it and Harry Hodgson was manager. Barnard and Wilcox got old and decided to sell out so Harry Hodgson took it over on his own.

Dickinson and Ward's Shop in Finkle Hill - Harry Hodgson left, Mr Ward and Ernest Thompson with van

(Was that during the war?)

No, I think it was a bit before the war in the late '30s and he continued until he died and that was the end of the shop.

(Let's go back to your shop then.)

The Draper's Shop in Finkle Hill

Alfred Kendrew (extreme right) eventually became the owner.

Well, my father took it over in about '26. He started there straight from school. He was there from about 1901. I think he was about thirteen when he went and he was there until he was seventy-eight. He retired a few years before that. At one time we used to sell motorbikes but that fell through. We sold TV sets, radios etcetera.

(It was a draper's wasn't it? Is that just clothes or shoes as well?)

Drapery is textiles but we did sell a few boots and shoes in the early days. We used to sell dresses and material for people to make their own. We used to measure ladies for coats and costumes and men for suits. There were various places where we had them made. We used to deal with a firm in Leeds, one in Nantwich and another in Norwich. We used to take measurements and send them off with suit patterns and so forth. We had dozens and dozens of suits and coats made.

(Did you make hats to order then?)

Ladies' hats, but that was before my time. I think it finished with the war.

(Where did you live then? Did you live above the shop?)

Oh no. Tomlinsons had Glebe Farm. You know where I mean? - Opposite the old doctor's entrance - Beals lived in it - the double fronted house opposite the doctors. There's my dad's new house on the corner, then Glebe Farm and Glebe Cottage next to that, where Dolly and Bob lived. I lived there from being born in 1916 to 1927 when we moved down to live in the house attached to Dickinson and Wards. That would be when Harry Hodgson took over. The house would be empty and we moved in in '27. Then in '37 we built the house at the top of the lane here. We were there from '37 onwards.

View looking towards church - Kendrew's house through trees on right, Dolly Tomlinson's Glebe Farm with railings

(What do you mean 'the house at the top of the lane'?)

The vicarage. My father had it built. R.M. Thompson built it.

(Did you take over the shop from your father? Did he retire or did you both continue like we do in farming?)

He didn't live long after I took over. He died in '66 and I think he had only made it over to me in that year.

He'd had angina for some time then he had a stroke. He hung on for a while. We all lived together in Ellerton Garth as we called it then. This field was called Ellerton Garth and we gave the name to the house. Of course they've dropped that name now and called it the vicarage.

(Yes it's sad isn't it? What have you called this house then?)

Athelstan.

(You could have called it Ellerton.)

We could have done but you see Athelstan is across the road. We resurrected the name and since then there is a house at Saxton called Athelstan and they've used it for Athelstan Court, Athelstan School and so forth. We found out on a survey map that this was Sir John's Lane so we used it as our postal address, then the council came along and put a name on it officially.

Sir John's Lane was mentioned in the Yorkshire Evening Post feature 'Down Your Way' by Jim Greenfield and reads as follows - 'Sir John's Lane, Sherburn-in-Elmet keeps alive a memory which otherwise would have died with the man six hundred years ago, for the name of this thoroughfare commemorates Sir John Langton of Farnley, Leeds who in 1385 leased his famous Huddlestone Quarry near Sherburn-in-Elmet to the Chapter of York so that they would have a supply of good quality stone for repairs to York Minster.

Picture taken from Old Garth near Sherburn Church looking down Kirkgate and showing Ellerton Garth (front left) before the Kendrew House was built

The stone was carried to Cawood, probably via the Bishop Dyke and then by river to York. Sherburn is said to have been the Capital of the Ancient Kingdom of Elmet and at one time it possessed a palace built by King Athelstan. It still has its handsome Norman Church - one degree below a cathedral according to an old opinion. During the last war its tower was a watch point for the Home Guard. In 1461 it is believed that Edward, Duke of York, went up the tower on the eve of the Battle of Towton to examine the dispositions of the Yorkist and Lancastrian forces

(I have a picture from the top of the church and there is nothing in this paddock. The windmill is still there so it must be pre 1920.)

Well I watched the windmill burn down. I wouldn't be very old at the time. I lived in the cottage and there was a window with a wooden frame and frosted glass at the bottom. I could stand in the window bottom and just look over it. I remember well standing there and watching the windmill burn with the sails going round, all burning. Quite a sight!

(It was windy. The wind was blowing up the park. If it hadn't been it would have burnt our stack yard. I have

Charlie Gardner talking about it. He said it was a wonderful sight. Were you taken to see it afterwards?)

Not that I remember. I remember going with a load of corn before it burnt down. Afterwards... no.

(When you went up to the picture house, where was the mill then?)

The mill was at the end of the building. It was just round the corner from where you went into the pictures. I remember we used to take salted pigs down there into the cellars underneath the picture house.

(We used to take an odd pig down there during the war to keep it out of sight. I used to be scared stiff in case

somebody caught us at it.)

I've taken a few pigs down there to get salted. In the old days, when I was little, my dad used to keep pigs behind the shop. There used to be a pigsty right at the top, before that wooden hut was put up in about 1921. We used to sell second-hand furniture in there. J.J. Foster used to have auction sales. We never had any. When it was new, we had half of it and Dick Yeaman had the other half for his garage.

Yeaman's Garage 1960's with Laurie Winship and Big Jim Grace

It still stands. It was an ex-army hut from the first world war, but where it came from I don't know, but it's been up there for 75 years.

(It's a bit perilous now isn't it, on top of that wall?)

It strikes me that that wall is going to have to be rebuilt. I can't see it is going to stand. The buildings that have been built up to it have been acting as buttresses. Take them away and I can't see that it will stand.

(I think they have plans to buttress it, but it would be better if it was cleared and sorted out.)

Yes it looks very dodgy.

(Have you been into the school?)

Not inside - no.

(I bet it will cost the doctors twice as much as they expected.)

It's a terrible price, and then it's to equip when it's done,

(And they don't get on very quickly. That wall they're doing, they must have been doing it two or three weeks. They have got it opened up a bit now. I keep going and taking photographs. I did it when they started and I go every two or three weeks.)

Doctors and Staff at Grand Opening of Hungate Hospital

Did you go up the back passage to our shop when they were trenching up there? They exposed the whole of the school wall; right up to the top of the passage where the window is and they tell me they found either a stone trough or a stone coffin or something. Did you see it?

(No. Is that recently?)

About a month ago. I haven't seen it, so whether they left it where it was I don't know. The worst mistake was when they took the doors off on Finkle Hill side, opposite the chemists. Old studded doors they were. I've asked and asked about them but I can't find out. Presumably whoever took them off took them away, but they deny all knowledge of them. No one ever found the honours board did they? My name's on it but I don't know what happened to it.

(Back to the shop then.)

I took over in '66 and retired in '83. It was my property and business and I sold it to Martin Hurrell. I think he worked for the gas board and she took the business for her entertainment. She didn't keep it long.

(It's been various things since then.)

Yes, but the property still belongs to them. It's been pulled about and various things tacked on. They've taken all the character away from it now.

(England's grocery shop was next-door wasn't it?)

Next-door to us they had a boot and shoe shop, then the post office was included in there. The post box used to be a slot in the window, then they took it out and put one in the wall. Well, they're all dead now, the Englands. Mary England became sub-postmistress and built the shop next to the Co-op *(the post-office was actually at the end with the Bacon Factory shop next to the Co-op)* and they lived there until they retired. Of course the shop next to us has had all sorts of uses - hairdressers, furniture shops and all sorts of things

(It was a good set-up in its day wasn't it? I have Lloyd Carr's brother talking about it because he married the daughter.)

Yes, he would know better than I.

(He says that John England, the old man, was up at six o'clock every morning and had his staff doing everything. They said that any girl who was taken on there and survived was a good catch to get married to because she knew how to do rabbits and pluck chickens.)

The only female I remember working there was Mrs Harry Fay, Emma Heels she was. They kept the off licence in Garden lane.

(There weren't any more then?)

There may have been but that's the one I recollect. There was Jimmy Gallagher who lived in what is now the Wheelhouse.

(Where Pawson's were?)

Yes. There were two men - Jimmy Gallagher and Charlie. Then there was Lily. She married Harold Hickman from Micklefield. They lived in one of the cottages to the right that have now been pulled down. The first one was Bradley, a bell-ringer I believe, then there was Fred Wainwright who was father to Mrs Alf Wainwright from the farm. One of the Gallaghers worked at England's and Charlie worked at Newthorpe Quarry I think. There was an old lady as well — their mother I think.

(Fred Wainwright - there was a Wainwright when we used to come to school. He had a hankie. Was that Fred?)

No, that was Wilf and he had Parkinson's disease. He and his mother used to live in a cottage down Moor Lane, somewhere where the clinic is now. Latterly they lived in the cottage where Ronnie Knaggs lives now.

(What about the shops then? Have you got a list and dates?)

No dates but I just wrote down all the shops I could think of. In Moor Lane there was Stoker's butcher's shop, built into the White Swan. Then there was the Saddlers, Jackson, across the road. They tell me that that was a blacksmiths at one time. You can see two arches and they were open at one time and if you look there were rings in the wall where they tethered the horses.

(What about Bestwick's, where was his shop?)

Ken came from Doncaster in about 1928 to drive and sell meat from a Bacon Factory van. Two other drivers were called Haddock and Fish. He started on his own and had an extension built on to his house for the shop just below Thornton's garage. Cliff Dunn left us to work for him in 1951.

Ken Bestwick (leaning on van) and Oliver Yeaman

Then there was Edgar Simpson. They had a little sweet shop and he was a plumber and pan maker. Across the road Thorntons had a sweet shop. There were two or three cottages where the petrol pumps are now. Then below Simpson's there was Shipley's, the blacksmiths.

(Yes, I used to take horses there. What about Thornton's - the garage, the wheelwrights and the undertakers?

How long have they been there?)

The wheelwright, undertaking and joinery have been there as long as I can remember, maybe before. The garage, just before the war I think. In Low Street - Billy Osborne's on the corner, gents' outfitters and shoe shop.

(They lived at the bottom of New Lane.)

No, that was Harry Osborne, his son. Billy Osborne lived at the top end, right opposite the church entrance, where Smith, who married Pat Culkin, lived until recently — the house immediately after the telephone box. I would think it was an old farmhouse at one time. Then there was Miss Denham, which was next to your farmstead, more or less.

(Which was then Raper's?)

Yes, that has been various things, from millinery to confectionery.

(Lloyd Carr's mother turned it into a confectionery tearoom didn't she? They used to serve tea upstairs.)

Yes, there was a spiral staircase and they used to carry everything up there. The only other shops in Low Street as far as I remember were Walter Wainwright's butchers and Cope's garage.

(And Mrs Mills sweet shop.)

No, that's more recent. It was the New Inn.

(Was it the New Inn or the Sun?)

The New Inn, the Sun was near the church. The other business in Low Street was Beck, the blacksmith. Do you remember Beck?

(I've heard of Beck and Hawley.)

Oh yes. Beck was where the Westminster bank is.

The One That Claude Forgot - Alfie Lewis, Mrs Lewis and granddaughter Rachel on their retirement from their Low Street shop after thirty-five years, March 31st 1973. Outside of shop (Inset)

(Near the Swan. It was a bit busy around the Swan wasn't it but of course in the old days you would get the Stagecoaches coming in.)

Yes. I've now resurrected this (producing a photograph), there's the old Swan. I think that is Sykes' Model T.

(The interesting thing with that is that it was a left-hand drive).

They all were. That one of ours was and that one of Dickinson and Ward's was. I drove to Scarborough in that.

(This is almost the same signpost as it is now.)

Yes, except that then it was square. The actual width of the road then was to opposite the Halifax window. So the road then was about half as wide again as it is now. The new Swan was built in the angle of the old Swan in 1929 before they knocked the old one down. The old Swan was L-shaped; it followed the corner round so they were able to build the new one behind.

(Was it for horses at the back? Were there stables like at the Red Bear?)

Yes, there was a weigh and a stack yard. There was a farm with it and the main way in was down Moor Lane. That was Stoker's butcher's shop there (obviously pointing to the photo) I think. It just used to have a wooden shutter to open. He just used to push it up. There was no glass in.

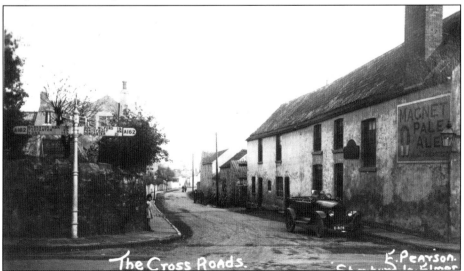

Photograph showing Old White Swan and Stoker's butchers shop
(Coming up the hill from the lights. Whose was this farm? Was it Bielby's?)
No, Tomlinson's. The entrance is where the Co-op car park is now. The next one was Harry Hey's.

New Co-op store with Bet & Stan Levick and friend in foreground (left), which replaced Chapel Yard (right)

(When I was at school sometimes the rumour went round that the bull was loose and we were all scared. Would it be Bielby's bull? Had he a bull somewhere in Sherburn? Harry finished up down over the level crossing.)

Oh, that's right, at Ash Row farm

(Who was Joe Bielby then?)

He lived in the house that is now Child's, the accountants, opposite the Forester's. You know the house I mean above the girls' school. (Obviously looking at the photograph again) That is the Butcher's Arms opposite our shop and the White Hart.

(Where was that then?)

Where the paper shop and the wool shop is now. If you stand at the school side and look across at the doorway you can see the keystone where they drove through. The shop doorways are actually built into what was the old archway.

(So it was just one archway? I've photographed that recently from the school.)

It's the same at the Red Bear. You will have seen the keystone at the arch there. The White Hart was built but I understand it was never licensed. It never was a pub but it was built as one.

(The Butcher's Arms - was that a pub?)

Yes, well I suppose it would be a beer house but not in my time. There was a butcher's shop next to it, a stable door type. I remember there was a ring in the floor and a slaughterhouse at the back. I also remember that in my time it has been a fish and chip shop. Latterly it was a cobbler's shop. Howie had it. First of all he had the shop, which is now the entrance to the Dentist's. The Registrar for Births and Deaths used to be there, between the Red Bear and Osborne's shop. Then they took part of it into the Red Bear and part of it into the Dentist's.

(Didn't Tim Bortoft have a place somewhere down Low Street opposite our farm? Was Bullocky Kendrew any relation to you?)

Claude Kendrew's grandfather 'Bullocky' Kendrew at Home Farm Low Street 1930's

Yes, he was my granddad. He lived in the cottage opposite next to Stanley House Farm. Of course John Backhouse was his cousin. His name was John but they always called him Jack. He was my dad's cousin. I always thought John Backhouse was very much like my granddad. Of course he was an old man all the time I knew him.

(I have one or two good pictures of him.)

I've seen them on the screen.

(Tim Bortoft, did he have a shop in the cottage at the top of Orchard Cottages that is now the Bon Viveur? And there was another chap, was he a cobbler? We got a lot of paper out of there. Was it a printing works?)

That was Bywater's property. They were painters and decorators. Charlie Bywater. They have a place at Selby somewhere. I always called that Panton's Yard. A man named Panton lived there.

(Where did your grandfather live?)

In the double fronted cottage next to the fold yard. It's no longer there. It was more or less where the bus shelter is now. You could stand in their room window and you could look straight up Jack Habesh's yard straight up to the church and tell the time with the church clock.

(Was that the picture house yard?)

Yes, so you can more or less picture where it was. So that would be looking up the side of your farm.

(What about Denny Cope? Was he a bit older than you?)

Yes.

(They were a clever family weren't they?)

Oh yes.

(Further down Low Street you would get to the electricians, Levitt's and Howcroft's. Was there a little shop before that? - Opposite Walter Wainwright's.)

Yes. Horsefield had that for a time. It was a strange building, single storey.

(Back to the shops.)

Kirkgate - the blacksmith's was the first one. That was Hawley's. Then I believe there was a tailor's shop. He used to sit cross-legged on the table.

(Did all tailors do that?)

Yes, it was a recognised position. I don't know why. That was behind Cromack's, where the fire was. I understand there was a tailor's shop there. Then there was Arthur Jackson's sweet shop on the left. Across the road from there was Miss Alice Pullan. She had a sweet shop there at the yard end. Then there was Pullan's butchers shop - a little lean-to place in the yard there. It was a good butcher's shop. When you think about regulations today I don't know how they would cope. Then Miss Thorpe, she had a shop where Nattriss' garden is. The first house was Johnny Henry's, then there was Grice's, then there was her little sweet shop, then Natriss's, then Thorpe's.

Father Grice's Joiners shop - still there behind Jack Natriss's house

(What was there before the school was built?)

I have heard there was a barn so there must have been another farm there.

(Where Henry's garage is, what was there?)

There were three cottages there. Winfields lived in the first one after Betty Johnson's, Mountains in the next then Fosters.

(Which Foster?)

Billy Foster. Do you know Lizzie Foster, Mrs Hardy? She's eighty some years old. Her brother, he died. He used to live in the house that was Miss Thorpe's shop. I think they called him Billy. Those cottages, Harry Mountain used to live there and his sister, Margaret, Mrs Jeffreys who lives at Highfields.

(What about the Forester's?)

Well Wrigglesworths had it first as far as I remember, then Joe Firn. He had a son Roland who married Nancy Tindall, Walter Tindall's daughter. Walter lived in Dove Cottage, down at the end of Garden Lane and was a gardener in the park. Roland Firn was an auctioneer and valuer eventually. I think he went to Scotland. He would be a bit older than me. He had it quite a few years, before they started pulling it about. It was a grocer's shop and off licence. You went in at the front and there was a counter to the left where they sold groceries. Then at the end of the counter there were a couple of pumps. Then you could go through there into a snug with long settles in and on the left there was another quaint little room with a table in the middle and a long settle. That will all have gone now.

(Did they serve food in pubs then?)

No not much whereas now of course it is their mainstay.

(What was next then? Was it Parkinson's fish shop?)

Well that was Percy Jackson's greengrocer's shop. Eventually he worked at the Bacon Factory as a grader. He had a greengrocer's shop there. Before you got to Percy Jackson's there were a couple of yards. One was called Leaden Hall Square but I don't know why. Then there was another one called Broomhead's Yard. Leaden Hall Square had little cottages built all round the square. Of course they were a feature of Sherburn at one time. There was also a square, behind what was Griffin's shop, with cottages on all sides and Chapel Yard up the hill and Lemon Square. Have you heard of that?

(No.)

There used to be a common lodging house on there and most of the Irish lived there, I would say it was where that big evergreen tree is that grows on the hill, where you turn left onto Beech Grove? The tree they light up.

(It's a bit like a square behind where Graham Beal lived.)

Oh, that's Happy Valley. There are four or five houses there, but you can scarcely see it now with the building around.

(There's one down Low Street at the back of the hairdresser's where Molly Henry used to live.)

Yes, East View.

(Then there is Dilkoosha up here. Where does that name come from?)

I can't find out why it is called Dilkoosha. To me it is an Indian sounding name. There has been a terrace of cottages there. Now there is only one left.

(Have they a date on them?)

I haven't seen one. There is a date over the door of Glebe Farm that was Tomlinson's, but it's in Roman numerals so it isn't easy to decipher. I was going to copy it down and sort out what the year is.

(Parkinson's fish shop. He was a bit of a character.)

I think he may have played football in his younger days.

(What was his job? The fish shop would be just part-time.)

Oh, he would be a miner. Then going up Kirkgate there was the doctors then Henry Foster's. He had a little farm. Then there was Rowley's farm, where Henry's house is now. Next to there is Church Hill house, as they call it now. That was somebody called Barraclough and there was somebody called Gaythorne Hardy but I can't put a face to him. He was about when I was a kiddie, he lived in that house. Then there is what is called Gilgreen, where the scout hut is. It was just a grass paddock at the top there.

(Do you remember the Church Hall being built? Was that about 1920.)

I can remember it when it wasn't finished. I just have a recollection of seeing scaffolding and builders' things. In the same way I can remember Highfields being built. They brought all the water for mixing the concrete from Milford Beck using horses with big barrels on the carts. Of course that was originally called Hunger Hills, probably because it was poor soil up there.

(After the Church Hall there is a shop isn't there?)

Yes at Top Cross as we used to call it. It was a grocer's shop until a few years ago. The only other shop was the Off Sales down the Poddle as we call it. Whether or not that is a corruption of Pod Hill I don't know.

(Then there was Billy Dennison's. Billy Duck we used to call him.)

Yes, Billy Duck, like Lloyd George with his hair long down over his collar.

[....Discussion re Tom Fletcher, son of J.P.Fletcher who Don met in Harrogate, Lloyd Carr's fancy for Christine Fletcher and location of one or two tennis courts in Sherburn — Fletcher's in the park, Dennison's, Kendrew's, Captain Thompson's, etc. Tape apparently ran out whilst they were talking about doctors - George Metcalfe and Dr Thirkill.]

...

(Did you go to Sherburn School?)

Yes.

(Did you go into Mr Potts' class?)

I went into Mr Thompson's first. He was the Headmaster then.

> *(Lloyd Carr didn't rate him very highly. He said he used to sit by the stove and read the paper. They used to practise a few hymns for church and that would be a morning's work.)*

Standards three and four used to be in the bottom room. I suppose I must have been in there.

> *(I was with Jackson when I was there. Fred Jackson who used to lodge at Ashfield Terrace I think.)*

Ah yes. A Lancashire man, fresh faced.

> *(I think he used to wind the clock, the one near Sissons', on the wall.)*

I believe there was a clock there. It was for the buses wasn't it? I had forgotten about that. That would be H, B and R - Hartley brothers and Rhodes who came from Kippax. Do you remember it saying number two garage at the end of Sissons'?

> *(No.)*

The old barn, at the end of the house with a door facing Milford, and across the lintel it said number two garage. They must have kept a bus or two there at one time. They ran buses to Leeds. Then Smith, Buckle and Winn followed that. The first people to run any kind of transport were Winships. They had a Model T Ford truck with a bench down each side and a canvas tilt, and they used to take the colliers to the pit. That was the first bus of any kind. Then H, B & R, then Smith, Buckle and Winn, then Walton's from Fairburn ran buses from Fairburn to Tadcaster, because I went to school on one of their buses. Then B & S came along. Cockerham's from Tadcaster bought out Walton's and they ran this route in competition with B & S.

> *(Then there was the West Riding. We used to take our time from the buses. When I left school, none of us had watches. At first we didn't have drinkings then one man started bringing a flask and we all started having drinkings.)*

I never knew anything about elevens's until I went into the army. We never used to stop at the shop.

> *(We had two express trains, which crossed at 10 o'clock, on the Selby line, and two did the same again at about three. Then at five to five a train came up from Selby. You spent half your time watching for them.)*

Didn't you ever hear the whistle at the wagon works? They used to blow a whistle down there.

> *(So you went into Mr Potts' eventually did you?)*

Yes, then I went to Tad Grammar.

> *(You would go on the bus?)*

Yes. Les Gilbertson and Dick Wilson went at the same time, though they were a bit older than me.

> *(How did you rate Mr Potts then?)*

Well, he was a disciplinarian and I think they could do with more like him today.

> *(Did he ever give you the stick?)*

No I don't think so. I remember George Lund put his fists up to him one day. Mr Potts chased him all round the school with a stick.

Mr Potts in gentle retirement

(Where did you get to during the war?)

I was six years in the Royal Signals. I spent two or three years at Catterick on admin., officers' training unit.

(Did you get abroad at all?)

Yes, I was in India. I was also in Northern Ireland, Chester, Aldershot.

(What was happening in India? Was that after the war?)

No, I was in India on VE Day. I was there for about a year. We went to the North West frontier, near the Khyber Pass. We had Indian scouts. The camp was like a little village with a wall all round and barbed wire. You couldn't go out. We also had outposts, outside the camp. The Indians used to go out there and they acted as early warning posts because it was tribal territory and they used to attack us. I have a photograph of some of the scouts. There was this chap, George, one of the scouts, and he got the British Empire medal. They always said it was because he murdered his mother and father. There was a programme on television about two years ago showing the area where I had been and they introduced this fellow, George. He looked a bit different from what he did then, but obviously he is still there.

(What did you do on VE night? I was at school and it was a free day.)

I think we went to the outdoor cinema to see a Charlie Chaplin film. I remember we were more interested in watching the fireflies flitting about than we were in the film.

(Do you remember the first talking picture you ever saw?)

Yes, it would be Al Jolson.

(I found one of my dad's diaries. He used to chunter at me for going out but at the time he was going out

with mother and it says 'Went to Fairburn and to the pictures with Win.' about three times in one week.)

I remember going to the Rialto at Leeds. For part of the picture there was writing at the bottom of the screen, but in some parts they were talking. I think it might have been The Singing Fool but I can't remember. It would be about 1928. That was the first talking picture.

(You didn't go to Sherburn pictures much then?)

Oh yes, at times — the twopenny rush.

(It was sevenpence, a shilling and one and nine in my time.)

They used to have concert parties down there as well. They used to get you up on the stage doing things. I remember once there was a wooden roller suspended from the top and you had to try to climb onto it. Of course you couldn't because it used to spin round and round all the time. You provided the entertainment.

(What about this picture then. It is a marvellous one of a car with white wall tyres.)

Daimler in Ropergate, Pontefract, with chauffeur Harry Pargeter

Yes, it's a Daimler with an outside gear change. The photo is taken in Ropergate in Pontefract. Harry Pargeter came from Church Fenton and at one time was Chauffeur for Dr Pickersgill and his wife was nanny to the children. They lived in the first house in Dilkoosha Terrace at this end. I presume the car belongs to Major Archer.

SHERBURN WINDMILL

Last Saturday, September 6th 1997, was the opening by Lady Clegg of the Old Hungate Hospital, to be used by the Sherburn doctor's group practice. It brings back to life and use of the village's oldest and most treasured buildings, the former Hungate Endowed Boys' School.

Sherburn Windmill before the fire

The windmill down Low Street was one of the last working windmills in the area until its spectacular demise. The people that can remember the tragic fire that destroyed Sherburn's mill in 1921 are becoming few and far between but luckily I have a few memories of the occasion safely on tape.

Saddler Jackson would have been thirty then but was too busy in those days to remember. John Thornton was into crystal sets and he was never short of a job. One of them was to help Jack Habesh, the owner of the cinema and windmill, to grease up. He had a grandstand view from one of my grandfather's corn stacks next door. Charlie Gardener, who later worked for us and had been visiting relatives at Ulleskelf, tried to help with a bucket chain but it was no use. Worse still he lost his mother's best bucket! I quote Charlie, "I shouldn't say this, but the best bit was when the sails broke loose and started going round in the strong wind with burning bits flying off towards the church." The wind direction was exactly right otherwise our farm next door, the chapel and half of Sherburn could have gone too.

In the dim but happy recollections of Sherburn Cinema I always thought the mill had been at the top of the yard behind the pay box and gents. According to this map of 1938 Low Street it seems to have been at the top of Mill's sweet shop yard.

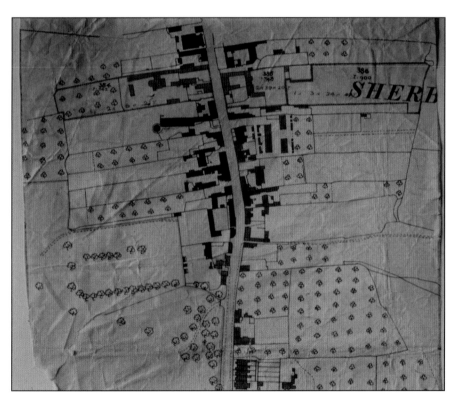

Map showing Sherburn windmill

Here also is a report and editorial from the Skyrack Courier, 4th November 1921.

BIG FIRE - The Selby Fire Brigade were called out about two o'clock on Saturday afternoon to a big fire at the windmill at Sherburn-in-Elmet. The brigade, under the command of Captain G. Clayton, proceeded to the scene with the motor engine. They found a five-storey windmill belonging to Mr J. Habesh enveloped in flames. It appeared that the wood bearings in the mill had become over heated while the machinery was at work, this giving rise to the outbreak. Mr Habesh combines with the occupation of miller that of cinema proprietor, and the brigade took steps to protect the picture-house situated close to the mill. Soon after their arrival the top of the mill fell in, causing the flames to mount up, and the sails, which had been turning, fell heavily to the ground. The brigade could only draw a limited supply of water from the new main, which carries the Leeds supply through Sherburn and on to Church Fenton. The supply had been turned on but a couple of days, and only sufficient water was obtained to keep the engine pumping slowly. The windmill was destroyed, but through the efforts of the brigade in protecting the adjoining property, the picture-house was saved, being only damaged by water, and the buildings used as granaries were only slightly damaged through proximity to the fire. The damage, which amounts to nearly £3,000, is covered by insurance.

The windmill after the fire

An editorial column from the same edition:-

It is a matter for regret that one of the best-known landmarks in Barkston Ash, the famous windmill at Sherburn-in-Elmet, was gutted by fire on Saturday afternoon, when the huge sails crashed to earth and smashed into fragments. Though the loss to the owner was covered by insurance to the extent of £1,000, there can be no adequate compensation from the point of view of sentimental value of a structure which has been a feature of the landscape for sixty years, and which has now been reduced to the semblance of a venerable ruin. Experts enquiring into the cause of the outbreak attributed it to grit under the stones, causing friction. It is doubtful whether the mill can or will be repaired, and though the stonework still remains intact, the great wooden sails, now lying in fragments on the ground, appear to wait the ignominious destiny of being converted into firewood, rather than restoration to their former activity. A somewhat similar structure is the well-preserved windmill at Barwick-in-Elmet, which is a prominent landmark for miles around, while at the Austhorpe end of Barrowby Lane there are ruinous remains of another windmill, familiar to residents in Crossgates and Whitkirk.   J.D.B.

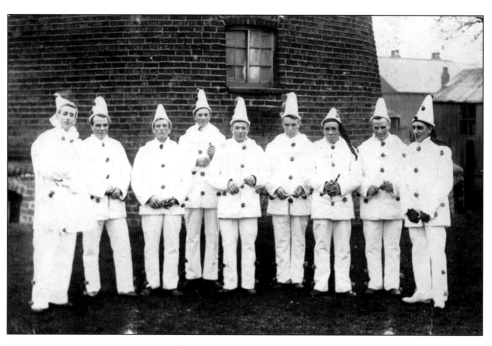

Sherburn Pierrots outside mill

THE CINEMA

There are still a few of us left who remember the CINEMA Sherburn-in-Elmet, better known as Sherburn Pictures. In those good value days of no adverts 7d, 1/- or 1/9d would get you in to see one or two cartoons, a black and white cowboy, PATHE news and the main feature. If the big one was a good cowboy, most of the young lads would dash down the yard slapping their backsides, and off up the street.

This all readily came back to me as we visited a similar, but slightly superior set up at Wetherby, with posher accents around, and amazingly well over half full. The well reviewed, French, feel-good film Amelie had been at York for a month but had escaped us so Wetherby was a last resort and a pleasant experience. The smart foyer and pay kiosk are similar in memory to Sherburn's, but no Mr Mills. Inside are a wide screen, newish blue seats, smart decorations but no-one flashing a torch, telling certain people to behave, and better still no breakdowns! Our Gents was badly lit (if at all), and the remains of the famous windmill were just around the corner. The Mills family ran it for as long as most of us remember but David Booth tried valiantly to compete with television at the end.

This is chat I had about those times with Joe Mills on 12th January 1995. J.D.B.

The end is nigh for cinema and catholic church

JOE MILLS

I was born in February 1923 at Blands Cottages, Micklefield. My brother George was a year and three months older. Father worked in the pit as did his brothers Arthur, Len, George and Billy. Two of them were deputies. Grandfather Mills was a Derbyshire man and very strict. They were characters and all did well with little education.

We came to Sherburn and lived at number five, Highfield Villas to start with, and Sherburn and eventually Joe Potts was my first school. Joe and my dad were on opposite sides of the fence, which didn't help, but he had a lot of time for me and said I'd make out. When I came home on leave later I used to go and put money in his bank. He'd say, 'Can you come in school time?' - real proud that I was one of his pupils.

In 1941 Blackburns were making Swordfishes down on Cawood road. I was apprentice of the year twice and was deferred twice. I enjoyed it, doing wing structures and sternposts, swagging and riveting. They were wheeled through and Topham tested them. He was an Errol Flynn type. He did a few circuits and they were away next day. They had Pegasus engines, no speed but a quick climb away!

But we're getting ahead. We started a little fish and chip shop somewhere near Walter Wainwright's butchers shop. There was an L-shaped row of old cottages there at one time. Old Mrs Beck lived in one. We got fish sent daily from Hull, and fetched it on a trolley from Milford station. Mother had peggy tubs out, and had them washing potatoes and cutting fish up. She'd served her time in Youngman's in Leeds, and was trained properly there. They'd come for miles; it was a gold mine.

Jack Habesh was from a Harrogate money family - jewellers and orientals, and he wanted to start up on his own. He bought the Mill and granary, which was ninety-five feet long. It had steel stanchions and forty-foot 14x10 inch pitch pine beams. The Mill caught fire one windy lunchtime and was destroyed. People said he'd done it, but Jack would just laugh, and got paid out. He also got paid when George Hill slandered him, when he called him a Russian Jew. He took him to court and won.

Jack came to lodge with us and was friendly with my mother's sister, Aunt Jess (Joe Wrigglesworth's sister too). He was a clever engineer and started with silent films and dances. Pictures were maybe twice a week to start with, then three or four times, and eventually two houses on a Saturday.

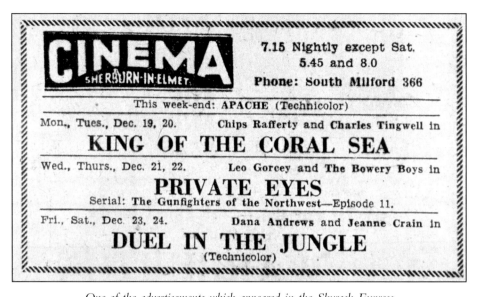

CINEMA
SHERBURN-IN-ELMET

7.15 Nightly except Sat.
5.45 and 8.0
Phone: South Milford 366

This week-end: APACHE (Technicolor)

Mon., Tues., Dec. 19, 20.   Chips Rafferty and Charles Tingwell in
KING OF THE CORAL SEA

Wed., Thurs., Dec. 21, 22.   Leo Gorcey and The Bowery Boys in
PRIVATE EYES
Serial: The Gunfighters of the Northwest—Episode 11.

Fri., Sat., Dec. 23, 24.   Dana Andrews and Jeanne Crain in
DUEL IN THE JUNGLE
(Technicolor)

One of the advertisements which appeared in the Skyrack Express

I was really interested in engineering and read lots of books. To start with I got pocket money doing odd jobs and sweeping up. At fourteen I was a full-blown operator and loved it. Cyril Stockdale was in charge and helped 'til I could take it on. We got on well together.

They were hand feed arc lamps and I used to be winding up downstairs. You could tell by the change of noise if there was a break, and I could run up those steps without hands. It was all on the floor otherwise. I'd stop it, stick it together, rethread it and back on again. You could hear them stamping, Bill Knowles and all those. I'd stick it together with amilacetate - scrape one side off and overlap one sprocket.

I was never ill. I could eat three dinners a day and never stopped working. We were happy. Father ran the pay box, cashed up, and then went to the Red Bear for a drink. Mother had the ice-cream sideline from her shop, and Tom Flowers came to help his wife with her torch. We had taken over when Jack and Aunt Jess went back to Harrogate. He had bought two or three pubs. They had no family - I think we were it.

The Mills Family outing -

(L. to R.) Pat Mills(sister), June Gilbertson, Nora Mills(Joe's wife), Joe Mills and Mrs Mills(mother)

David Booth got it from us against father's advice, as he thought picture days were about done. His father Charlie ran Pollard Bearings at Knottingley for J.L.King who owned it. They were producing atomic plates for power stations and David was apprenticed there. J.L. knew everyone who worked there. I started as a charge hand and then became a manager.

But back to David - I stayed and helped all I could but couldn't fill the house for him. Sometimes we only had two-dozen people in. It was inevitable. He came to terms with it and sold to the Catholic Church.

Wartime auction in cinema - Bid up for War Effort
Olive Cope, Harold Mills, Fred Harling (Bacon factory boss) Miss Harling and Pam Denby

Senior citizens outside cinema in '50s
Front - Cyril Stockdale, Harry Osborne & Geof Marklew with many well-known faces behind them

HAROLD MILLS

I think I would have been eleven or twelve when I was first allowed to go to Sherburn pictures. In the pay box was a man with glasses who insisted on tossing for double or quits. I never paid even if I lost and I had discovered my father's mate Harold Mills, but always Mr. Mills to me.

He never talked of his time in Micklefield pit or World War I and I regret I never asked him. I don't know how long he had the cinema but his supportive wife Belle, who ran the sweet shop, gave him space (as they say) for his council work and other activities. He didn't drive a car but most Sundays he arrived at our house about eleven, primed for debate with other characters, and all against him bar my mother who was trying to get dinner ready. It was all 'thee' and 'tha' stuff and all talking at once, and no-one won.

Mr. Toleman was a Welsh banker from Rose Terrace. Harry Butterfield was a fish and game man from South Milford, as was the up and coming farmer Councillor Cawood. Our foreman Jim Bellwood rolled up to report and my father puffed his pipe and kept the pot stirred. 'Tha's no idea what a million is Harold. They'll never allow anyone to build on that Bacon Factory field.'

One morning Arthur Cawood arrived early with his tape recorder to set it up in the quiet of the room and with some loaded questions for Mr. Mills. Eventually, one by one, the debaters arrived and it became a rabble, not helped by my father banging the poker on the hearth and next to the microphone. The victim was most upset with Arthur over it, and with my mother for condoning it, which was quite unfair as she was getting his dinner ready in the peace of the kitchen. Towards twelve o'clock he always began to hint that it was time for them to go, as it was getting on for dinnertime. Afterwards I sometimes got him to play the piano. He could play anything I could whistle and had some nice Arthur Askey style ditties - 'I do like a nice mince pie' etc. He liked to go for a walk with the gun but I can't remember him letting fly at anything. Once I took a photo of him in a Huddersfield jersey after a kick around with a rugby ball.

He had a wicked sense of humour, which never left him even later in most trying circumstances. In respect for his early days he would always call a foxhound a dog, and I've seen him deliberately pick his nose while being filmed on ancient cine. One Sunday afternoon he came walking with father to see how we were getting on combining near the Willows. The field was full of dog men waiting for rabbits, but as they went back over the hill Mr. Mills got his handkerchief out and started putting things in it. It looked as if he was picking mushrooms, but really he was only pretending, and I watched with pleasure as various men sidled off to investigate - brilliant! Jokes and slow timing seemed to be the order of the day then, and Harold could both give and take - he had to!

One of the best was when I was his pea-growing partner on the patch behind the cinema. It was a good crop and we were justly proud of it. One morning when they were ready for pulling he phoned up very annoyed, there were pea swads (pods) all over his cinema steps. "If they'd come and ask me they could have some, but to sit there and leave that mess is beyond contempt," he fumed. It was an Uncle Wally prank with half a bucket of mother's swads stealthily done before going off home to Pontefract.

Testing peas behind cinema - Guy Br., Walter Wainwright, Harold Mills, JDB, David Heath & Jim Bramley

Another was when I thought father was going to pass out when he read in the old Skyrack that 'even as far afield as Spain Sherburn's new street lights had been praised.' It was father's printed pigeon English letter addressed to the Mayor of Sherburn and posted by Harry Butterfield on holiday. The joke rebounded somewhat as we hadn't the heart to tell him the truth! In the war he held auctions in the cinema in aid of the Red Cross and to send money to local boys abroad, so with that experience he fancied himself as a wide boy at country house sales. Once at Methley Hall, father left him to bid for nearly a hundred-and-fifty London Illustrated News. He thought he had a bargain with one huge book for just over five pounds. He took some convincing that he had bought three carloads of them. On another occasion at a farm sale with an uncle he started scoffing rationed sweets he had lifted from his wife's shop. Uncle Wally was soon wanting some, but was told the canteen lady had plenty under the counter, but to be discreet. They enjoyed watching his antics and the discomfort of the lady in the ensuing pantomime. Another trick he pulled was to buy some cheap rubbish and get someone to drop it off at home, so mother would be raging mad when father got back!

He was great fun at Christmas parties, which hardly varied - plenty of food, dominoes for the men 'til midnight, then silly games and a singsong 'til two or three in the morning. Once he had an ancient bottle of wine, saved for a special occasion and given to him years ago by his friend Mr. Willie Thorpe. He poured it for the domino school and proposed a toast. We said it was great and he went off to serve the ladies. The wine was terrible. We all looked at one another. Someone said, 'What's tha think?' and with one accord we all tipped it into the flower vase.

For many years he served on the Parish Council and the District too. In 1964 he was awarded the OBE for services to the community. It was a proud day to be presented with it by the Queen at Buckingham Palace, especially for a mining lad from Micky.

Latterly he spent a lot of time in hospital, having both legs amputated. His bungalow was always overflowing with visitors, all still 'thee' and 'thaing'. His missing legs used to twitch and he was desperate to scratch his toes, he said. Whether it was true or another of his jokes I'll never know. His bravery was unquestioned, and everyone went home the better for his company. He was keen to have artificial legs but it wasn't to be. At Pinderfields, and a great joker to the end, he'd line three or four wheelchair mates up and give the order, 'Wagons roll,' and away they went.

This piece may give anyone passing the Harold Mills Centre some idea of the man whose name it bears.

THE RED RED ROBIN

Saturday morning when I first left school in 1950 was the busiest part of the week in winter, with normal work going on till about eleven, then having to feed up to a hundred bullocks, and chop and bag enough turnips for Sunday too. So it was a rush and not exactly relaxing to catch the ten to one train to Selby, bus to Camblesforth, and taxi to Drax to play for the School Old Boys' side. No one had cars and every game was an away game. Getting back to town was easier as a hitch on the opposition bus was usually the answer.

Selby on Saturday night especially, when I embarrassingly admit that at seventeen I had hardly ever been in a pub, was dead. It wasn't until 1954 when we amalgamated with Selby, and I began to feel a man of the world with the Londesborough our headquarters. But at that time, for Pete Mumby and me, upstairs at the Four Seasons Café for sausage, beans, egg and chips, the Hippodrome or Ritz, and home on the 9.32 train was standard procedure.

According to my diary of 1950, and before our black and white tele of '53, I saw twenty-seven films. Amongst them was Jolson Sings Again, and I remember coming out of the Hippodrome on something like Cloud Nine. I already knew some of his songs but until then I'd never heard of Al Jolson or his Story which had come out in 1945. Eventually I saw one five times and the other four! Fifty years later his songs are still as good as ever and I'm trying to sing them Barber Shop style.

Progress over the years has brought the video, and a sister's perfect present to an ageing fan has me working repeat and fast forward with enthusiasm. Mama's horseradish sauce is as hot as ever, but I never knew men kept their hats on in the synagogue, and interior house designs are nothing new!! Larry Parks, miming to Jolson's voice, really earns his money doing both films and many energetic numbers. Most people will remember him as Jolson, and I understand that the original was not the best of characters. It seems appropriate that I learned of his death coming out of Belle Vue, after watching Wakefield Trinity, but with this video – I'm just a kid again, doing what I did again, singing his songs!!

Selby and Sherburn Films of 1950

The Kissing Bandit

Bedtime Story

Hamlet

Fiddlers Three

Four Just Men

Phantom Light

Task Force

Morning Departure

North West Passage

Last of the Mohicans

Unconquered

Passport to Pimlico

Under Capricorn

Contact Man

Yellow Sky

Bride of Vengeance

Whisper Smith

Yank in King Arthur's Court

Jolson Sings Again

Stop Press Girl

Big City

Inspector General

Johnny Belinda

Wooden Soldier

Sorrowful Jones

Flags West

Road to Morocco

Happy Days!   J.D.B.

CHAPTER 5

SOUTH MILFORD

ALEC JACKSON

(Interviewed by Don Bramley 16th January 1995)

I must admit that I always feel quite proud when I see my photo of Mr Tom Jackson hanging on the wall, a foot or two from his favourite spot, at the end of the bar of the 'Swan' Hotel at South Milford. I had taken it outside his Saddler's shop in Sherburn when he retired. A few years later I spent a pleasant evening recording the tough life of this gentleman and the intricacies of wax ends, making horse collars, and much more!

His younger son Frank had been an Alec Bedser style stalwart of the cricket club before moving to Selby and retiring too early. Brother Alec also played, but before my time. Living these last years on his own in Hill's Terrace, near the doctor's, he was a mine of information and kindly company. Sadly Alec died at the end of November 1999 and a full church paid their respects to this genial gentle giant.

Alec Jackson waiting for opening time with John Hodgson

(So here we are at number 4 Hill's Terrace. What's the history of it?)

They were originally built by Batty's, going back a long way. Hughie's uncle built them. I'll tell you where they lived. You know t'back lane where Elsworths had their allotments. There were two houses. A Mr Barker lived in one and a John Batty lived there in t'other.

(Did he have the grocer's shop?)

No, a relation. I remember t'little man who had that. He wore a bowler hat and had a beard. That must have been in the early 1920's. That's where Harris's are now, opposite the doctor's surgery. Moons had it after them, then there was t'chapel and t'Co-op!

Stan Batty used to have these. He married Elsie Barker who taught me at school. He worked for his Uncle David Atkinson at Stream Farm, Sherburn, and went on his bike every day with a pipe in his mouth and a knapsack on his back. - I can see him now.... They lived up back lane where John had lived and every Saturday morning he'd come through our stackyard. "Hello Alec," he'd say, "What do you reckon to 'em - Yorkshire? I don't know!" - and even in them days they were on, that they weren't as good as they was - if you understand me.

(Who else lived in this row?)

You'd know Jim Lacey at Sherburn? He knocked about with Tom Flowers and his dog. He's still going! There were some Newby's, Harper's, Pawson's, big Dick Atkinson at the end, Hull's, you know Roy?

Actually I used to take bets in this row when I was about sixteen years old. John Kitching, that were another one - he'd have a bet. They'd have sixpences on, tanners, that sort of thing. I'd take 'em for Harry Smith. He worked at t'Maltings, and he'd take 'em to Tad Acaster at Sherburn.

Where the doctor's car park is now was just a made-up yard. It'd paddle in when it was wet. We used to have sandbags keeping water out when the beck came over. It was a funny thing that. Mr Butterfield, you'd know him, he was on t'council. They used to come down did him and all t'councillors, but nowt was ever done. But once it came extra heavy and went through Mr Butterfield's house. It wasn't long before they made a proper job of it and we'd no more trouble!

In 1936 the culvert blocked at Wain gap where you turn left to Lumby, and it ran like a river down the street. Guy Wilson told me there was a mark on the old bar in the Swan where it came up to. Me dad's cellar was full, and just past in the quarry George Riley and Rex Sutton paddled around in a tub!

(Can you remember your Grandma Carr?)

No, she was dead and he died in 1929, but I was fortunate because he retired from farming in 1919 and he still had his pony and trap. He kept that, and Batty's rented the farm. We used to get all over in it, in a radius of five or six miles – Ledsham, Lennerton and Church Fenton - so I knew all the lanes around.

He always called my mother Bett. "I'll take 'em out of your way for a bit, Bett." We had an auntie at Ledsham, and he'd have a couple of gills at the Chequers. For us kids it was great.

(How did you break your leg?)

I did it footballing at Halifax. It was just an accident, but I was in bed eight weeks down there. Rowland Harrison had broken his about a year before. I was at the match at Ledston Luck and you could hear it crack. Doctor Radcliffe set it, and I remember Rowland telling me of the gyp he gave him adjusting it. Luckily mine was potted up at Halifax and he couldn't get at it.

We used to have a right do at our house. How my mother put up with it I'll never know. All t'lads 'ud come. There'd be t'piano going, our kid had t'jam jars. Teddy Elsworth -do you remember Teddy? - He'd play t'piano, Ernie Atkinson t'violin. What a racket! Mind you t'house was by itself so we didn't upset anyone. People amused themselves then.

(Can you remember your Grandfather Jackson?)

Oh yes, he lived opposite the Chapel at Sherburn, next to Walter Wainwright's shop. He'd come from Lincolnshire to out here. Uncle George and Uncle Percy had a slaughterhouse at the back where Chris is now, and 'Slowcum' Bradley killed for them and I'd get him a sheep out. It was a cruel job if they didn't hit cattle right.

We used to fatten about thirty pigs for t'Bacon Factory and they supplied the grub. I finished up looking after them but they didn't pay then either! But around the back we'd a couple of those saddlebacks for ourselves, and fed them on their stuff. Later in the war I was down the pit, a Bevin boy, but earlier I had Uncle George's van and collected stuff from the Factory to take to Castleford. It was all rationed, coupons, a bit of this and that, and in them days if farmers hadn't paid I went round collecting and I'd come home with quite a bit of bacon. So we were all right in war time and I loved home-fed bacon. I can see me Dad cooking it now.

(Did you work in the shop?)

Yes, I did the binder canvases - father didn't like doing them' - and the dust got me.

(I first came across your father when I took the canvases to be mended - up those wooden stairs. That had its own smell of leather and beeswax I think, and had racing calendars on the wall. He talked very polite for Sherburn. I'd never been in a pub before, and sometimes I'd to look for him over the road. It was a bit scary.

You said Lloyd Carr was at Milford school in your time.)

He didn't teach me, but he coached us. I played right half and my brother Frank left half. John Goldthorpe played but we left and went to Leeds Central - twenty to eight train on a morning and back on the twenty to six at night. They were long days but in summer the cricket fields were up at Lawnswood, past Headingley and nearly where the tram sheds were. We'd walk back into Leeds and catch the quarter to eleven - the last train. Once we woke up at Selby and I'm saying to our kid, "It's Cross Gates," but father fixed a taxi back; and we were at school t'next day!

We used to watch Lloyd play for Milford. He'd always a bit of a swagger, and I remember them winning the cup. He writes about it in his Steeple Sinderby book. We weren't very old but father took us. You all supported your local teams in those days. Granville Hepp played in that team and Freddie Boston and Frank Poole. Bill Anderson was the goalkeeper that swore a lot, not Dennis Sutton.

(Do you remember Freddie Boston taking his bat home and going to play cricket for Hillam? What's your version of that?)

Well I don't know. He was a bit to blame ower that was Les Boston, he was captain of that team. We called us t'Bodyliners. Fred had gone in for some tackle or something. He used to play for Mr Lyons at Hillam Hall midweek, and they seemed to think he should have got permission. Fred didn't think so after all his boss George Harrison had done for the club - and he'd probably bought the tackle. Harry Batty seemed to take over, but then Phil went to Hillam.

I remember playing them down t'common there, and they only got about thirty-some, and we thought, you know, we've won this. But it was one of them shooting pitches and nowt got up. Any road Freddie was laiking for them, and he walked through us and we got next to nowt! You know what I mean.

(Well what's your earliest memory of the Swan? You'll have known some landlords.)

Alf Johnson had it when my Granddad was there so I knew the place. I can smell it now. Them pubs they smelt of beer and 'bacca - and also I tell you what I remember, those steam brewery wagons filling up from the beck with water. They just stopped at the side and a pipe went into t'beck.

(So back to the landlords, who else was there?)

There was a Linaker, Bob Holt's father and mother had it, and just before the war Laurie Oliver had it. He was from Hull and he went off on t'merchant ships. Then Harry Spencer came from Leeds, and when he died they wouldn't let his missus keep it on.

Then Joe Hill took it. He was Lester's brother and had been a Captain or a Major or some'at in t'war. He went to Hambleton and Lester took it over. Then Lewis, who married Alcock's daughter from the top end pub. Then of course Brian (Stocks) took it on after him.

It's a different world now. It was all separate little rooms, and I don't know whether it's better or not, in a sense. It's all this canned music now. All we had was the old piano and homemade stuff.

(Did you pick any bets up from t'Swan then?)

Milford Swan and Gibson Bortoft's Poplar Farm and his car

Oh Lester, he thought more about taking bets than he did about running t'pub. I think officially they'd get a shilling in the pound commission. I used to take t'locals up to Harry Smith, but I used to help Teddy Spencer too, at the Club. It used to be full, and he'd get on the phone to Sammy Balderson at Kippax, and get the winner through.

(Were you allowed to do it?)

Oh no, you could have got done. I was fortunate and never was. They'd catch Tad Acaster with a slip or two on him and march him up to t'police station. But in Cas they had illegal betting shops with teles in. When it all became legal they had to take them all out. In the south they thought it was great 'cause they could have teles in - funny that.

(Who're your best Milford cricketers you can think of?)

Well I should say that Freddie Boston was one of what I'd call good all-rounders. He'd hands like buckets. I don't really remember him dropping a catch, and he put his heart into all he did, even practising. And our kid wanted a bit of beating. I just kept wicket mainly. Folks don't believe me when I tell Graham Hill and these. You used to shout, "Lost ball," and you could run up to six. We used to think it was marvellous. When Freddie played for us he used to come with t'grass reaper and cut the outfield, and it looked great. T'way it is now, it's no wonder they get these big scores. You had to hit it in the air to get a four! You got them behind because the wicket was the other way on then.

Jack Hill was a good batter. He was younger than us and we really brought him on. When he got married he went and played at Fairburn, but finished up here.

It's all altered now - wickets today - in them days you got shooters. You can't compare it really. We only had about two yards of t'pitch cut. That was yer lot. That great heavy roller we pushed, that needed six at least on it. We'd nothing else to do, practise and roll. They don't do either much nowadays.

T'dinners they had were above the Swan where they live now. Soup, rabbit pie, and always apple pie, for half-a-crown! Homely it was, and just villagers there! Actually I never went to another after it finished at t'Swan.

(Those are the thoughts and memories of Alec five years ago, slightly poshed up and minus quite a few "you know what I mean like," and unfortunately without his infectious chuckles.

By the time you read this, a photo of Alec in appropriate pose, sitting on the wall waiting for opening time, will also be in a place of honour near to his father. Although the slow timing and banter has ended their presence will still be around.

--- You know what I mean!)

J.D.B.

VIC WILLIAMS

(Interviewed by Don Bramley 13th February 1996)

I spent an enjoyable evening taping Vic on February 13th 1996 in his well-kept cottage filled with railway pictures and model engines. He even has a working train set across the flower filled yard in a shed.

It's through his flowers that I got to know him. As chairman of the cricket club at that time I was informed that returning rowdies from our barbecue in the Batty's corn store had either desecrated or stolen his hanging baskets. I had to go and make peace and what a pleasant job it turned out to be. J.D.B.

Vic Williams at his door

I've a book I lent to Alan Sunderland. I had it bought for Christmas. It's all railways including Ripon, Harrogate, round to York, Selby and Hambleton, and it's surprising how things have altered. Beautiful village stations and their car parks now all pulled down and rubbish - Oh dear, things have altered.

You can't understand it because, let's be fair, you can't stop progress and railways had had their time, but things have gone to the extreme - because as you know pea pulling time - when I was on the railway coal trains would come in, and the guard used to ring controls at York and tell them what had come in, how many wagons, etc. They'd say, 'Go to Milford and fetch peas in. Go to Hambleton, go to Burton Salmon.' In them days peas had to be in cattle wagons and only one bag deep or they sweated, and they'd come to Gascoigne Wood and on to Selby from all round the district. The pea train would have about fifty wagons on and a big K3462 engine used to come from Doncaster to take them to be sorted out there to go to t'Midlands, London, etc. I remember George Harrison got his brother Ernest to take them to Sheffield and Leeds etc. in his lorry. They were four or five bags deep. I bet they were right peas when they got there - but that was the beginning of the end of peas by rail.

(So what was your job then?)

Carriage and wagon examiner - wheel tapper.

(Go on then, explain that.)

How can I explain it? You went round tapping wheels, that was the novelty of the job - but when you were going round examining wagons, you knew what you were looking for. You knew how a wagon was constructed, and looked at all the weak parts to see if they were all right. Draw gear, if the draw gear was loose on a specification wagon, they pulled from the hook on the buffer spring and the rod went to a cradle in the middle. That cradle was about two feet long and there was a volute spring in, but they were tightened up, real tight so when the wagon was pulled it pulled on the spring. If the draw gear was loose it was pulling on t'buffer spring and all t'pulling was on t'head stock. And a simple thing; a wagon could be loaded with coal and t'safety loop missing. Well a safety loop, yer brake blocks on the wheel and the push rods, and if anything failed in the hanger it dropped in the safety loop. You'd think it silly stopping a wagon for that, but if it fell on the track and dislodged the points that would be it! You'd be looking at simple things - draw gear doors and everything, axle guard bolts and load bearing springs. Then there would be hot boxes, you couldn't miss them.

(How about being overloaded? Was that your job?)

No, you didn't bother about that.

(So did you tap the wheel? Did you get a sound out of it?)

Yes. Well you see I was twenty years on the railway and examining about twenty year and I've only found one cracked, and funny enough it was a brake van that came from York. The tyre was split straight across as though you'd cut it with a sharp knife.

Well you see they got them in with loose tyres. A tyre is set from the wheel. Your wheel is on the axle and you've got two on one axle. When you are re-tyreing them your tyre is in a well with gas heaters round, and it was smaller than the diameter of the wheel so it expanded and the crane dropped the wheel in. Then you put a retaining ring in, and they used to wear loose and you had to watch for loose tyres.

The wagons would vary. If you took a brake up that was slack when the wagon was loaded, when it was empty it used to rise and lock the wheels, and then they'd skid and wear a flat part and bump, bump, bump, and then it'd split and crack. - Things like that.

You always had to be at the nearest point to the arrival of the train, and when the wagons passed you'd have a casual look to see if door cotters were all intact, and end doors, etc. You did all that as the train was passing.

(Were you popular with everyone then if you pulled a wagon out and caused an upset?)

Oh no, because if you went round a train maybe averaging sixty to eighty coal wagons, well you see it came on to a reception where you put a 'NOT TO GO' card on in front of the traffic label. So when the pilot drew them off the low road, that's up to Sherburn gates, and push them over the hump, the red card went into what was called a cripple siding, so all the 'not to goes' were in there, and then they'd shunt the yard at morning.

(So how many would you pull out?)

It varied. Sometimes none, sometimes three or four,

(And how many others were there at Gascoigne Wood?)

I'll tell you. Now then, we're going back now - Dave Terry, Frank Reynolds, Harry Hanby - that's going back a bit - John Willie Towriss, Doug's father, Alan Baker - he used to do a bit of reffing - and that's it.

(Were there night shifts?)

6 to 2, 2 to 10, and 10 to 6 on the up side, 7 to 3 and 3 to 11 on the down side, and we had an 8 to 4 shift to do outside examinations of wagons. We'd go as far as Castleford, Sherburn Junction, wagons that were damaged at the pit, see what it was and go next day and mend them. When you stopped a wagon you made a report out which went to York and they had them all there. What they did with them I don't know.

(And it was all before computers?)

Computers, in the days of my railway life, they wouldn't have competed with it. They'd have been buffer locked. I mean, there's not the traffic by any means now.

You see, in 1922 t'railways were in dire circumstances then because of the 14 -18 war had knocked the stuffing out of t'railways - lack of maintenance and everything. They were absolutely kn-------! Eric Gedess, who later became Sir - he was same as Beeching but he didn't slash railways because it was all busy - but his prophecy was 'you'll only make them pay running them from A to B'. But he was before his time 'cause there was more traffic across country from C to D and D to C. You take this area, Selby, Leeds and Gascoigne Wood. There was a railway to York and one to Monk Fryston, then the main line from Sheffield to York. All the traffic that went that way to York, Harrogate, Starbeck through Fenton, and the other way to Sheffield and Castleford. All the traffic going left and right from Gascoigne Wood had to coincide with that from York to Normanton and Sheffield. You don't know how they coped with them.

I mean, in my days take Gascoigne Wood junction box going to Sherburn, there was Sherburn South and Sherburn Station. Going to Leeds there was only South Milford, but going to Normanton there was Milford East, Milford Junction platform, South Cabin, Monk Fryston, and two at Burton Salmon - 'cause Burton Salmon was a big depot in its hey day. Of course it all went till there's only Milford South now - oh, and Hagg Lane of course. Aye, there was some traffic. We used to have trains departing at half-past five in the morning to Doncaster area and to all the collieries round Castleford and Pontefract etc. They'd come back with forty-five's, fifty's, seventy's and eighty's on because Sharleston and Bowers used to bring some coal in. The 2.10 to Bowers took empties to Fryston, Wheldale, Allerton Bywater.

(Bowers, where's that.)

On t'Kippax road between Kippax and Castleford.

(Never heard of it.)

Haven't you ever heard of Bowers Row? - I'm not kidding!!

Well another aspect is this. The mainstay of British economy before the war or just after was coal - make no mistake.

(And steel?)

No because you can't make steel without coal. But if you worked at a pit you were t'scum of t'earth - you was; true - and if you saw some of the hovels the miners lived in, it was beyond you - especially Bowers Row. Oh dear! But those things have altered. As I say, the coal that came in, you'd know where it came from - no mechanisation then you know. You'd wonder how they got it out of t'pit, the lumps - massive lumps, they were that!

We went to Gascoigne Wood in 1916 and I was five the following March - from York and we lived in the vee between the Sherburn and Leeds line.

(Where were the houses exactly?)

There was t'line and t'culvert to t'farm (Norden Barn) and two houses faced there where Deagle Sutton and Panton lived looking towards Milford. Then there was one big house where George Pickup was born, then there were four built when Gascoigne was first built in 1834 - and you went over t'Leeds line and our two were there, eight and nine, and they built the offices in 1907.

You see that engine SI (showing photo) 2008, it was stationed at Scarborough and it ran from Scarborough to Gascoigne Wood and back for years. - I can still see t'driver now with a white beard on. Aye, and you can see how the mineral trade deteriorated because - well take Malton and Scarborough. The coal for Malton Gas Works and for Scarborough Gas Works and Electric station and all that; they ran a special train to Malton taking all household coal, domestic coal and for industries that required it. They hadn't any electric at Malton. Well, as time went by they went on the grid and over a period of years you lost that coal and it all diminished. Then in t'twenties and thirties they were going themselves to t'pit with lorries, and that did domestic coal at the stations. Ernest Harrison used to get his from South Milford station.

(Was the coal the Station Master's perk?)

Yes, but I'll tell you this, farmers have ruined more Station Masters in t'north-east than soft Mick.

(Go on, explain that then.)

You know Bert Rayworth, he lived on Fenton Common, they ruined him. I'm going to be fair with you. In these rural areas farming in them days was a struggle, and farmers thought they were the elite but they hadn't two halfpennies for a penny. They hadn't you know, but when they were ordering stuff they had to pay for it and it hung on and hung on 'til their debts ran up, and of course the station master had to suffer.

Well, owd Raines at Monk Fryston - I've heard Walt Hill say t'same many a time - 'cause there were some cheapjack farmers round there, no doubt about it. There's an owd saying, 'It i'n't what we were, it's what we are now.' - Bear that in mind! At harvest time one of t'farmers went to t'station. 'Has our band come, has our band come for t'binders?' 'Yes but leave it there.' He never got t'band. Owd Raines saw to that, He kept t'band 'til he sorted hisself out. The farming community broke many a station master.

(So you'd walk to Milford School when you first went to Gascoigne?)

I started when I was five in March and Easter was late. My mother took me t'first day - eight inches of snow and we didn't get there. She took me t'second day but never again. I went with t'rest of t'kids and took our grub. Allison lived at Norden Barn then, before Farrars came. He didn't keep milk beasts. We used to walk to the back of Maltkins for the milk - where Cromacks lived. Farrars came in nineteen twenty or twenty-one and they had cows. I remember owd Farrar. He was ready for t'uppers 'til t'war came.

(George's dad that, was it?)

Yeah. Well Henry and Jack went on t'railway but George stuck with his dad and he kept milk beasts. - I can see it now. - He had a separator, and my dad was handy - he was a shoeing smith by trade, and served his time at Malton - and there wasn't a week passed when he didn't bring this separator down, soldering this and soldering that. There was more solder than original. We'd no bother getting milk then.

(So there'd be a right gang of you going to school.)

I'll give you an idea. There were Farrars - George, Jack, Henry, Linda and Lucy - Arthur Wisely, then two of Pickup's (George wasn't born then - George's uncle had two daughters) - three of Barkers, Tom, Kath and Ken and them, and then me. So that's how many. We'd walk there and back and think nowt about it. When we were eleven or twelve we got push bikes.

(Who was headteacher at Milford then?)

Wise, and then Captain Leggat.

(How did you get on with them?)

All right, but I hadn't as many brains that would have blown your hat off. But when I look back at some of those clever kids, I could lose them hands down now. I've learnt as I've got older. I left school in 1926 and I should have gone to Micky as apprentice fitter but the strike started so I went off and worked in Blackpool. (another episode) When I came back home I worked at Burnett's Wagon Works 'til I was sixteen and started on the railway on June 3rd 1928 and I finished in '59.

Gascoigne Wood was built for coal. It came in block loads for t'shipping. You won't know 'cause you're too young, but I've gone to Hull and you couldn't see the skyline for trawlers, hundreds of 'em and all of them wanted bunkering. All export coal down to the south and east coast, and export to the continent and all that caper. But war made a certain amount of progress. They started using oil around the First World War and coal diminished. You can't stop progress. The line from Church Fenton to Tadcaster and Wetherby in the thirty-nine to forty-five war was wick. You'd wonder where all the iron and steel had come from. I was in the war in the RAF for nearly five years so didn't see a lot of it, but I know of it because when I was demobbed I sorted a lot of jobs out.

There was always a lot of Irish in Sherburn. They came to build the railways. They opened the Leeds to Selby in 1834 and when they got to Newthorpe going through the cutting, they found out that farm labourers were getting more money and they did a runner. A lot of them settled in Sherburn - Culkins, Narreys etc.

BOWERS ROW – WHERE'S THAT?

Bowers Row

Regrettably my tape recording sessions seem to have taken a back seat lately. There are still plenty of interesting people to talk to. First hand experiences of the second world war are getting hard to come by and I would like to think that youngsters might read this and set about getting their grandparents, and parents even, down on tape. They have the tackle and they won't regret it! It is a privilege to be let into people's lives, and it is surprising what can come out of it, many years later.

I got to know Victor Williams when attenders at the Cricket Barn Dance had desecrated his hanging baskets on their way home down Well Lane.

In February '96 I didn't have to ask many questions as he could talk forever on his beloved railways, his time as a wheel-tapper and sorting the world out. An added bonus was being in the RAF, and salvaging crashed aeroplanes. But, embarrassingly, I lost some respect when I revealed ignorance of Bowers Row. The conversation went like this:

Vic. The two-ten to Bowers Row took empties to Fryston Wheldale and Allerton Bywater.

Me Bowers, where's that?

Vic. On t'Kippax road to Castleford.

Me Never heard of it.

Vic. Haven't you ever heard of Bowers Row? – I'm not kidding!!

Me No – Sorry!

It was nearly as bad as years before when I told Harry Butterfield I'd not heard of Nat Gonella!!

In 2001 I helped start a Local History Society at Fairburn and was asked to speak at their first Annual Dinner at the Chequers. I gave some examples of the pleasures and fun of taping and I mentioned the Bowers Row episode.

At their February meeting at Tucker and Enid Makin's Beckfield Farm to study old maps, I was delighted to be lent a book called 'Bowers Row' by the late Jim Bullock O.B.E. I am now an expert on the Bowers Row era, which has thankfully just about gone, although I intend going to check on the village. It was built in the 19th century to house miners and disappeared when the pit closed in the 1950's.

Jim Bullock O.B.E.

The community produced many fine sportsmen, unionists and characters but Jim Bullock must have been the outstanding one. His story tells exactly of the same hardships and comradeships that Eddy Edmonds told me about on tape in January '93.

Jim Bullock had also written a more humorous book about the men and the bosses aptly named 'Them and Us'.

I really wouldn't be boring people with all this, except that at the South Milford Cricket Club's Chinese Banquet night I had been telling my neighbour about Bowers Row, and she was telling me more about Jim Bullock - being most knowledgeable about Castleford hierarchy. Eventually she said, 'Mrs Peter Beckett opposite will tell you a lot more - she's his daughter.'

- and that made my night!!

J.D.B.

"That Was My Dad"

When I was a child, oh he was so wild
Yet gentle, and loving, and kind.
He'd go to the mine, ne'er a moan or a whine
Of the dust, of the sweat, of the grind.
His back was so strong, his lips full of song
And on his broad shoulders I'd ride
And he'd breathe in God's air, and perchance say a prayer
But I doubt if ever he cried,
That was my Dad

When I was a boy, his time I'd employ,
On telling me tales of the pit.
And his strong embrace, was my favourite place
Where he'd thrill to bits, with his wit.
And scars tinted blue, gave me the first clue
Of the hazards he faced, at his trade,
Yet of them not a word, at least I never heard
Seems that's just how miners are made.
That was my Dad

When I was a youth, I first saw the truth
How the pit was taking it's toll
His temples did page, the white frost of age
And his breathing he couldn't control.
His back slightly bent, his jaunty walk spent,
But still doing the job he knew best.
A good-bye kiss from Mam, a snap tin full cram,
And befitting a collier was dressed.
That was my Dad

And when I was a man, I honoured his plan
And donned on my pit boots and lamp,
And he taught me to fill, be of iron will
And a nod, was his approval of stamp.
And the proud N.U.M., was a brotherhood gem
And how he'd always be part
And the day he retired, happy but tired
But I knew he was sad to depart.
That was my Dad

And when I sat by his bed, and cradled his head
As he coughed up the dust from the past,
With a hand scarred and weak, my own it did seek
And the words "stick together', were his last.
And in death as he slept, his promise I kept
Of that N. U. M. gem be a part
And his epitaph reads, U.D.M., a Sir breeds
I thank God, that I ne'er had a part.
That was my Dad

Benny Wilkinson.
The South Yorkshire Poet Laureate

80

MR ALFRED BURNLEY

November 26th saw South Milford Church full but not bursting, as it should have been, for the dedication service to Alfred Burnley, former headmaster of the village school. During this service two Sanctuary Chairs were dedicated to his memory, along with a Bishop's Chair in memory of the Reverend Dr. Aylmer Kelly.

Aylmer was a newly ordained non-stipendiary priest based at South Milford and Monk Fryston, whose untimely death shocked the many friends he made in both parishes and beyond. Aylmer's wife, the Reverend Val Clarke participated in the service.

Roger Chapman, Rector of South Milford between 1968 and 1975, now retired, but wearing well, preached about his hobby of reading biographies and of other notable lives, which remain, as yet, unprinted.

Mr Burnley succeeded Harold Parker into the old school house, and was probably the last village headmaster brave enough to live amongst his pupils (and parents). He told me that fact probably got him the job! He will be remembered as Chairman of the Parish Council and Church Warden. The village saw his commitment to many other organisations, the children's sports, the show, pantomime, cricket, football and badminton clubs. He was also a keen bridge player, and latterly as a keep-fit lone walker around the lanes.

It was a real role reversal for me to be questioning a headmaster at his bungalow in March 1999. His beloved wife Muriel left us to it, but kept us fortified with good coffee!

Mr Burnley was born at Garforth, but the family had originated from Batley. In keeping with the area they were miners and rugby people, and his mother sang in the chapel choir. He could just remember the hard times of the 1926 strike, and the Garforth pit flooding and subsequently closing as a result. He went to Garforth Parochial School and then to Castleford Grammar, where he was Captain of Football. He had to leave to help out at home. Money was scarce and his father was out of work. He caddied at the Golf Club for the sum of ten shillings a week. He passed exams to join the railway but when war was declared on a Sunday, he was in the queue to volunteer on the Monday, joining the RAF, where his life changed for the better.

Mr Burnley couldn't understand where his sporting talents came from. He played good cricket with Garforth Parish Church, and for various football teams at all ages. The highlight of his career was playing for North versus South in an England trial. Then the Arsenal scout John Plows earmarked him for a five-day trial, subsequently playing for their 'seconds' against Norwich City. He met many of their famous players, all internationals, who at the time were on £8 to draw and £10 to win. Names that came readily to his mind were Eddy Hapgood, Les and Dennis Compton, Alec James, Wilf Coppin, and Cliff Bastin, who had been at Leeds. His never to be forgotten advice as he went out to play, and in the broadest Yorkshire accent, to the young Alf was, "Doan't ferget lad – get stuck in!" Sadly manager Tom Whitaker's words were not as encouraging, but he did use his Sunday name. – "Alfred, we like your football, but you're a little bit too old for us." He was twenty-one at the time.

Two spells in Leeds Infirmary, one for a serious appendicitis operation hadn't helped his football, and failing a colour vision test for aircrew was another setback, especially as he had passed similar ones for the railway. Undeterred, he re-mustered as a PT Instructor, and was posted to Uxbridge. He also acted as a parachute-training instructor at Ringway Manchester, all the time applying for an aircrew position. Luckily a bridge playing doctor friend sorted out his vision problem, and he joined pilot training courses to Cardington, Butlins at Skegness, and finally to De Havilands, to fly Tiger Moths. All the time he was playing football and cricket for his station. At one place he was the only non-pro in the side, which included the Huddersfield and Ireland winger Peter Docherty.

Mr Burnley's next adventure was a cheap but hair-raising six-week cruise to South Africa, to join the Commonwealth Air Training Scheme. It was none too pleasant, with some five thousand passengers packed on board ship. Midnight one night saw him on deck to witness passing the Rock of Gibraltar. The ship was then subject to many attacks during its seven days passage through the Mediterranean. Seventeen WAF's and Wrens were killed, and Mr Burnley didn't care to talk of the part he had to play in their funerals. The journey then took them via Suez and the Red Sea, finally to dock in Durban. It was then on by train to Jo'berg.

Going solo in a Tiger Moth was no problem, and Mr Burnley progressed to Oxfords and Wimpeys. They were destined for Japan! When the atom bomb was dropped, he felt rather cheated, but admitted that it might have saved his life, together with thousands of others.

Whilst this was all happening, he was enjoying some good cricket, and playing on one occasion on the famous 'Wanderers' ground against R.W.V. Robins of Middlesex and England fame, who got him out with a 'googly'. He also met again Dennis Brookes from Ledston Luck, who played for Northants for many years, and later for Sherburn Eversley.

So after six and a half years of training, travel, and excitement, Mr Burnley was back home, and still without a job. He enrolled at the City of Coventry Training College to become an emergency trained teacher. Needless to say, he represented them at football, cricket, and table tennis!

Following his training he was back to his roots for seven happy years at Garforth Secondary Modern, teaching Maths, Geography and PE. Marrying the daughter of Micklefield headmaster, Mr Harry Pawson, was a shrewd move, and together they beat more than one hundred and twenty other applicants to start a new and long life in South Milford. In his interview Mr Hugh Batty was the one who asked if he was prepared to live 'over the shop'. Harry Butterfield must have voted for him too, and they became lifelong friends and workers on many village events.

I hope these few lines help to throw a bit more light on the life and times of a very modest man. Three times during our chat he said, "Are you sure I'm not boring you?" Hundreds of local children were very fortunate to be taught by Mr and Mrs Burnley at South Milford school, which still maintains its good reputation.

Councillor Harold Mills, Micklefield born Sherburn Picture House owner, was proud to have been taught by Mr Burnley's father-in-law. He told the story of being left in charge of the class for a while, with instructions to bring out any misbehavers. On returning, the head found nine or ten waiting at the front. " Them's 'em, Sir, that talked," said young Harold proudly. Unfortunately he ended up having to write a hundred times, 'Those are they, not them's 'em'. This anecdote amused Alfred Burnley.

Two sanctuary chairs and Bishops' chair dedicated at the service

Next time you contemplate the 'Mouseman' Sanctuary Chairs near the Altar in St Mary's Church, I hope you will know a little more about the man they commemorate, Mr Alfred Burnley.

J.D.B.

BOB COCKERHAM

Bob Cockerham was a great man and a super character, but most of the time I was pleased to see the back of him in his working days. His arrival, usually late at night with his threshing set, meant two or three hectic days of hard work but pleasant companionship and team spirit. Men were borrowed from neighbours to make up the team, and drinking times, as well as being a much needed rest, were a real chin-wag and an exchange of news and views. Bob never said a lot, but when he did he was listened to, and dry would sum up his sense of humour. George Riley was an early assistant and later Bill Marshall when, in steam times, both would come in for a 6.30 breakfast. Son Dennis joined them when he came back from National Service in Malaya in the early fifties, but combines were here and gangs pulling beet and peas, picking potatoes and having threshing days were soon to be no more.

Bob had his own tried and trusted way of doing things and even at the end of a long day, when he was getting everything hitched up to move on with his bike, his only transport, on the back, he wouldn't be helped and we left him to it. It was a wonderful sound when, much later, he could be heard pulling out on to the road and chugging off to set up elsewhere for an early start next day.

J.D.B.

BOB

I was born in 1900 at South Milford Maltings, and have been interested in steam engines all my life. As a little boy there, just nicely walking, I would make for the engine house where the driver would sit me in a window out of the way. One morning he lifted me down, sent me home and went off somewhere else. I'd not been gone long when the cylinder head blew out and shattered the window where I'd been sitting. So my mother thought it was time to go off to school.

I walked to Milford school with my sandwiches and had a midday drink at the school pump, but had a good meal when I got home, That went on until I was fourteen and got hired to Mr Parkin at the bottom of Monk Fryston Common. I stayed with him for two years - all for five pounds ten shillings a year! Then in the First World War I went to feed the threshing machine for my brother-in-law William Bradley until I was eighteen.

Thinking I could do better for myself I went to a firm of steam ploughing contractors in Lincolnshire - Kitchen and Sons of Crowle. I stayed there until I was twenty-seven. They were long days. We worked from daylight to nine at night in the summer. The wages were two guineas a week, sixpence for every acre ploughed and sixpence extra after we put in fifty-four hours. We made do with two guineas and left the rest in the firm till the end of the season, drew it in a lump sum and took care of it for later. A hundred pounds went a long way then, and most of those that worked with me could start their own little businesses.

John Fowlers of Leeds made the engines, one positioned at either end of the field. The plough was pulled across between them with a wire rope. There were six hundred yards of it on each engine. On a good day we'd do up to twenty-five acres depending on soil type and field size. The plough weighed four tons, and it took two men to manage it. At the side of the Trent and Ouse we could go eighteen inches deep to get to rich soil. There was a man looking after each engine. At the ends they pulled the plough out, moved on whilst the ploughmen balanced it, then back again. The fifth man looked after the van and got the meals ready, took them to the field and stood in, in turn, as the others ate. We never stopped. The farmer supplied a man and two horses to fetch water and coal. We charged a pound an acre for ploughing and a pound for cultivating twice over. The second time over we could go with eleven or thirteen tines, but the first time nine were enough for it to pull. If it was too wet we didn't venture in to get stuck, and quite often we had to pull gate-posts up to get into the fields.

We lived in a caravan very cheaply but at twenty-seven I came home with 'flu and never went back. I married and started with a gentleman by the name of Mr Fred Burland, driving a set of threshing tackle for him. My area was Sherburn, Barkston, Biggin, Lennerton, South Milford and the Common and Burton Salmon. Herbert Myers did Ledsham, Ledston, Newthorpe, Peckfield and Micklefield with the other set. We all had our own areas. Greenwood went beyond Barkston and the Castles were at Saxton.

The farms in Sherburn were Milkly Mason's next to Levitts, Marshall's, Greby's, Wainwright's, then at the other side of the road was Fletcher's and yours farther up with Eshelby's opposite (Ozy Lewis later). Mrs Simpson had some land with the White Swan. Up Finkle hill was Hey's and up Kirkgate were Wainwright's, Pullan's, George Hill's, Foster's, Rowley's two, Mr Dennison's and Summers' at the bottom of Bottery Bank opposite the lane to Huddleston Grange where Captain Thompson was before Hawkings and after your father's Uncle Jim. Mr Hodgson was at Huddleston Grange but didn't last long.

It took about eleven men to thresh. Carrying chaff was the worst job but men used to follow the machine from farm to farm. Tom Hey, Jim (Music) Fletcher and Tommy Narey later on were all characters who did.

Mr Burland sold to Mr Clarke in 1933 and I bought some tackle of my own, and eventually we went from steam engines to tractors and then to pick-up balers and combine harvesters.

Threshing Gang

They were mostly Milford men that followed me - Jim Bullock, Dick Atkinson, Dennis Sutton, Albert Saunders and George Dacre. Most farmers needed at least five and borrowed from each other as well. Ten ton a day was about the average yield, but I remember doing eighteen tons once at George Harrison's.

During the war I only had one set, and in slack months in summer, I used to go to S. H. Baker's at Kellington to help repair their equipment and other people's. I have a photo taken there showing nine Fowler engines (three of them mine), six Clayton and Shuttleworth machines, six Hornsby straw tiers and four straw choppers - quite a yard full. Sadly that yard is now full of bungalows and is called Baker's Field. We'd put new beater plates in the machine and new concaves and bearings. We'd re-tube the boilers. Every two years we drew out the tubes and cleaned them. They had either thirty-eight, forty or forty-two and they'd get furred up. The engine was examined twice a year and hydraulically tested periodically. We never had problems with steam pressure when they were properly looked after.

Fire was a different thing. Once, at Flaxley Lodge on Selby Common, I left the engine at night near a pond to fill with water but mysteriously the stack yard caught fire in the night and I lost my machine. Another time at Webster's at Burton Salmon the stack caught on with a spark just after they'd got going. Luckily a man called Bailey was passing with a tractor and pulled the machine into the street with Bill Marshall brushing off burning straw as they went. George Riley followed with the engine. We lost nothing but the stack yard went up. In 1935 a new machine and straw tier cost £428, and prior to 1914 a new traction engine was £500 and the machine then about £130

Bill Marshall and machine at Home Farm 1949

I remember Harry Hudson getting his first tractor. He was an excitable sort of fellow and hadn't time to talk much. He was giving someone orders and walking away at the same time. He was going to take the tractor to the bottom of the field. When he got on it wasn't running. "Oh dear," he said, "I'll have to fetch John to start it." "No need to fetch John," I said, "I'll start it for you." So I got it going and he said, "I didn't know you knew anything about tractors." So I said, "I just knew sufficient to get it going for you."

Ozy Lewis managed for Mr Fletcher in the park and he went to him one day when he was cutting corn with horses. He said, "Don't you think you're driving a bit fast Oswald?" and he said, "Well we haven't much band left and we want to get finished before it runs out!"

At another place we stopped for drinkings around ten and three - usually home cured fat bacon or cheese sandwiches. Poor old Mr Barker used to go into the house for his drinkings but it was up to me to get mine as quickly as I could, to get greased and going again. But he came out and said, "If you aren't going to give t'men time to have 'em, there's no point in bringing 'em." The point was they'd had half of them whilst he was walking about!

Low Farm, threshing. March 1957

Photo taken by J.D.B. and shows Charlie Farrar from next door taking over band cutting from Bob Cockerham, Jim Bellwood checking corn bags, Tom Narey casting his chaff sheet and Jim Bramley coming round corner with drinkings.

GEORGE WATKINSON

(Interviewed by Don Bramley November 1991)

George Watkinson (centre) in charge

THE SCHOOL

(So when did you come to school? Were you with my dad or Mrs Battersby?)

No. They were before me. Your dad was a bit older than me Don, I can't remember him being at Sherburn school. T'lad that I went wi' to Sherburn school was Hardy, down here, Reg Hardy and Teddy Lewis, Alfie Lewis and all them. Them were t'lads I went to school wi'. I think I started at Sherburn when I was seven years old.

(And you walked from Milford?)

No I used to bike it.

(Why did you come to Sherburn then?)

Cos we got thrown out of Milford. Well it was a matter of two lads fighting up in t'yard, and I were never a fighting man, but I went down to try to stop 'em. Well two lads taller and bigger lads than me like, they were on to this lad and I tried to stop 'em and o'course Schoolmaster Jimmy White came down to see what were 'appening and he picked on me, straight up you know, like that and I spat in his face. That were it. I'd out to go. So I had to come to Sherburn. Well, when I came to Sherburn I went down to Miss Pickersgill's, down here. Can you remember her?

(No)

She'd a private school. I went there for about two or three months an' I got thrown out of there. I were t'only lad among all t'lasses.

(Not for spitting again?)

No. She locked me in t'coal-house, and I broke t'door down and run home and that were it.

(So you didn't like school then?)

Oh, aye. I had some of t'happiest days of me life at school. Then I came to this one here and finished me time here...

(Was Joe Potts back at Sherburn then?)

Oh Joe hadn't come out o' t'army then, but we knew when he did come. We got him and he used to drill us like soldiers, in that schoolyard up there. He did. Me and him could niver agree. When I finished up like, and I wanted a reference, he gave me one o' t'best references anybody could have...

(Tell us a bit more about school)

Well I finished up down there at Sherburn like, you know. George Holdsworth, you remember George who used to work down at Burnett's?

(No)

He was t'foreman afore he finished. His dad used to be t'foreman. Me an' him used to sit together at school down in t'bottom room. Of course old Joe always 'ad it in for me. I could do everything bar sums. I'm better now than ever I've been at sums. Anyway, one day he got me out on to t'front. This long division was written across t'board and I just stood looking at it. He put his hand behind me head and pushed it straight into t'board. He says, "You'll do it before you leave 'ere." Well I wouldn't do it. T'door, which came out on to t'main street then, is blocked up now. There were two doors, t'big door out onto t'street and two sliding doors inside. He pushed me in and said, "You'll stop there 'til I tell you to come out."

Anyway, I'm feeling about round t'door and of course they'd forgotten t'key were in t'lock. I twisted it and out I went, on t'bike and home. I got it t'next day when I went back. He gave me a good hiding.

(So did he give you it with his stick on your hand when you went back?)

Oh, aye! Oh, he'd a lovely stick! Nay, when I went back t'next morning they said, "Oh, he's got some hoss hair in his pocket." I niver thought about hoss hair in me pocket. They used to say if you put it across your hand and held it at t'back and he hit it , it wouldn't hurt. But I didn't bother w" t'hoss hair. I could take all he gave me. Anyway he said, "I'll see whether he has any horse hair or not. Hold your hand out." Three right across, bang! I didn't flinch. I just laughed at him. I thought, "Yes, but wait 'til you get back on that seat at that desk." He kept saying to me, "Take that grin off your face." I kept laughing at him. Anyway he got sat down on t'stool, and it were a high stool, which he used to wrap his feet round. T'stove were at t'other side of him for t'heating of t'schoolroom. I waited while he got his feet round t'stool, then, bang! I gave him a tupp and over he went, straight over t'stove. I galloped out and as I'm coming out I got t'bell pull and gave it three great pulls, then I'm out and on to t'bike and home. That cured him! I had no more trouble wi' Joe Potts! Oh no, I'd finished wi' him.

(So how old were you when you finished?)

Fourteen.

(And were there any lady teachers?)

Aye, Miss Atkinson. I wasn't with her much though. Thompson was t'best man.

(The Headmaster?)

Aye he was t'best. I could get on wi' him lovely. On t'top of his desk he'd a row of chalk. Any lad he wanted out of that room he used to pick t'chalk up and throw it. Never missed. On a Friday night he used to say to me.."Come here!" I used to go up. "Now then, you go home sooner to-day. I want you to take Muriel's cycle to South Milford station and come back with her. Then it'll be home time." Well t'three o'clock train, t'collier train came from Leeds, down from Micklefield, all t'colliers on. I used to go up with her bike, and take me own as well, like. I used to push hers and ride me own. Three bananas and sixpence I got that every Friday afternoon when I met her. Then I used to go home. Monday morning, chalk, "Come here! I thought I told you to come back on Friday." I used to say, "Well I didn't think there was any point in coming back." He never used to scold me or owt like that. Then he used to say, "Now then, just go across to the Chemist's shop and get me an ounce of acid drops. Sixpence." I used to go across and get him his acid drops and come back. They were in them little three cornered bags at that time. I'd give him 'em and walk back to me seat. Chalk 'ud come. "Come here. How many have you had?" I used to say, "None." "Let me smell your breath." Bang - one across t'side o' t'face, then sent me back to me seat. By, what a time I had there!

(Did he use a stick then?)

Not on me. John Able, he farmed where Bob Cockerham farmed, again' t'garage there, he used to come wi' me on a morning. Eddie Bullock, he used to go to Barkston to t'Catholic school. We used to ride on together. When he got sat down - always in t'far corner were John. Chalk. "Bring all those things you have on that desk up here John." He used to bring about a dozen spanners and keys, and that, and line 'em up on t'desk. He used to fetch 'em out and take 'em there and he used to put 'em on his desk 'til home time. John had to carry 'em home but he used to bring 'em t'next day just t'same. Aye! And poor Digger Potts, he used to throw t'chalk at him and he used to cry like mad when he used to fetch him out.

(What was up with Digger?)

Well he couldn't take it. No, there were one or two that couldn't take it, but I could always get on with Thompson.

(Did you take your dinners with you?)

Oh aye, we used to take 'em with us. We used to sit in t'bottom room where Miss Atkinson was, at t'top end of it where t'stove was and have our dinners there. Dennis Wrigglesworth, that lives at Highfields, and his brother Bob, they used to walk from Newthorpe to school. Well all t'Newthorpe lads came there. Norman Summers - and at dinner time we'd go for our dinners, like, you know, packed up, and Dennis used to wait while Horace fetched his out, then he used to grab. He used to turn round and say, "You sin fiend." He always called him a sin fiend did Horace. Poor old Dennis!

(You had a teacher looking after you, did you, whilst you had your dinners?)

Oh no, there was nobody there at dinnertime.

(Where did they have their dinners then? Where did Edie Atkinson have her dinner?)

She used to walk home to Rose Terrace, and Joe Potts lived up against t'doctor's, up Kirkgate there at that time. You know, where t'Dilkoosha is - t'far end house. He lived in that row at that time. Then he moved from there. He went up Rose Terrace and then he finished up in that house...

(Clarendon)

Two old ladies had it hadn't they? They were elderly when I went to school, and the house was smothered in ivy.

(It was when I was at school. Scarey wasn't it?)

I used to go up once a month with all t'Sherburn church magazines and take 'em all up that way, and where you live today - that was my last call.

(What were Sherburn streets like at that time?)

When I used to come to school on a morning from Milford to Sherburn, there used to be potholes in t'road from John Smith's big wagons, you know, t'old steam wagons they used to be with t'solid tyres. If there was one going back to Tad, I used to click hold o' t'corner and they used to pull me to Sherburn. If they were looking out and they saw you, they used to pull to t'side of t'road to knock you off. Oh, I've got many a pull wi' them.

(I've heard of that before. Did you know Lloyd Carr?)

Oh, aye. He went to school at t'same time as me.

(Did he? Did you know his older brother Raymond?)

Yes, I knew all t'lot.

(Raymond's written his railway journal. It isn't published but it's a marvellous book about being a junior clerk at Milford station, and he used to get rides back like that.)

Oh aye, I knew them lads, t'girls an all like. Well one o' t'girls married...

(George Wright)

Aye, and one o' t'other girls married an England.

(Tom..)

Low Street when George Watkinson cycled to school

THE MILL

Low Mill, South Milford – I went there when I were nine and stopped there 'til 1926 when I was nineteen. Alf Atkinson had t'top mill. He wanted to sell, well it was his wife's really, it wasn't his. Well a chap called Ledger was at Hensall Mill. He'd been at Low Mill before, and he came back. He bought it. I used to play pop wi' me dad. He could have got it for £400, mill and t'lot, and if we'd been down there now Don I would have kept that mill as it's always been.

(Mm. It would have been grand.)

I mean, to me Milford wants rubbing of t'board. Neither t'top mill nor t'bottom mill's there now, it's all gone. He's going to build on t'top one. He's got planning permission to make it into houses, luxury houses. There's a big crack right through it. Where do we go? Oh they make me sick does t'council. There should have been a preservation order on that.

(So what did your father do? Did he manage it?)

Well we milled it right away up to grist mills coming in. When your dad lived at Sherburn here, I don't know whether you can remember it or not, but I can remember it 'cos I came to Sherburn school and he had an old Titan tractor he used to do his grinding wi'. Can you remember it?

(I've heard of it, and seen pictures of it.)

I can see it now up t'yard and there were only three Titan tractors around here at that time. Piggy Farrar had one at Milford. Peter Porter had one at Steeton, and your grandfather, he had one, and they were t'only three Titan tractors that I ever knew.

(And that was what, after the First World War, 1918.)

During t'First World war, aye. When we went to t'low mill we bought a tractor. Me uncle Tom that worked for Dr. Radcliffe, Tom Baker, he'd been down t'low side, Lincolnshire way, and he'd seen this tractor and he came back. He says, "I've a right thing for you for t'mill." Me and me dad had been down to Sykes's, down here below Sherburn station, where , what d'you call him, he went to t'same farm?

(Dick Atkinson.)

No, Bielby. He went on to that farm. He had a portable engine and we wanted to buy it but he wouldn't let us have it.

(What, instead of using water?)

Aye. Well there were two sets of stones in t'mill, one for t'machinery, y'know for t'engine to work it, and t'other were t'water wheel. When you wanted to do any extra work up on t'second floor, there were a big spindle went wi' two clips, and used to join 'em in like that. They like fingered in to drive owt you wanted, because we used to roll oats, but that was only because we could connect up to t'mill wheel. We couldn't do it wi' this tractor because it were too powerful. It shook t'mill when it started off. We took t'big wheels off t'back. They were spud wheels. We took 'em off, and I went to Sunderland's and got a pulley wheel specially made to fit on to t'axle, wi' special wood for to drive it, and it were too powerful then. Aye, it were a big massive thing were that.

(You'd have trouble in a dry time. There's no water in that dyke now you know. It's completely dry.)

Aye, well I mean, t'pond's gone, everything's gone now Don. It goes behind now, behind t'little paddock there. It doesn't come down t'original run.

(Yes. There's nothing down the side of the cricket field.)

No, well there won't be wi' t'dry weather we've had this time.

(I've never known it dry before though.)

Well, when it flooded we used to get t'blame, when Milford flooded, down at t'mill.

(For holding it up?)

Well we didn't. We made another cutout to let t'water off, besides t'one that were there, t'old one. We made another one to let t'water off and still they blamed us. Aye.

(Did you have any rivalry with the other mills.)

We did wi' old Piggy Farrar.

(What about Piggy Farrar then. Was he at a mill?)

No, he were at t'farm here at t'bottom of t'street there, again' t'Swan. He were a bad old bugger were that.

(So what did he do to you?)

Well he had his cattle in t'field, which went down t'side of t'cricket field, you know, right away down below t'mill. All that grassing went down there and he used to blame us because t'water used to run out. When we were holding it up a bit, like, his cattle used to come to drink and they paddled it down. Well, when it got to a certain height, it used to run into his field. But that were his fault, it wasn't ours. Anyway, he fetched all t'chaps down from Wakefield. He says – he used to talk a bit short tongued did old Piggy, "I'll 'top it, I'll 'top it, all this." Anyway, they came down from Wakefield, t'council lot. Me dad had to go up to see what were 'appening. Course Piggy would 'ave it it were us. Me dad says, "I'll throw you into t'dyke." He were going to throw him in.

(So, we're going back to the mill then. Who brought the corn to the mill?)

Well, all t'farmers from round about.

(You would all have your customers like threshing men used to have?)

Mrs Sunderland that was t'postwoman, they used to live up at Peckfield... what do you call it?

(Where Wilkinsons were?)

Aye. Well her and her sister, they used to do t'ploughing – he didn't. They used to do it all. She used to come down once a week wi' t'grinding, you know corn to be ground. And her sister, she were married and lived down t'low side of Selby somewhere on a smallholding. Then there used to be Scatt House.

(Where Woodalls are?)

Aye. Now what did they call them? Anyway he used to come down. He'd been a major in t'army. He lived on his own. Lambert lad 'at lives up top here, he worked for him for a time. Then we used to get it from round about. But at that time Perkins had t'mill at Newthorpe. Well, he used to grind first, did Perkins, then it used to come to Alf Atkinson at t'other mill at t'top end o' Milford. He used to hold it up 'til he got what he wanted done, then he used to let it come down to us. There were many a time when we hadn't any. We were having to wait for him. You see, it were from one mill to another, and we were t'last to get it.

(So in a dry time you would hardly be in business.)

Well in t'summer time, like, you didn't get a lot of grinding. We used to do about a hundred bags a week, a shilling a bag. They used to bring it on two-wheeled carts. What d'you call him down here?.. His wife used to work at England's shop at that time, when I was at school... Dick Askham. He came from t'low side and...

(How did you get it to the top? Did you hoist it or carry it?)

No. They used to back up to t'door, and there were a chain from t'top o' t'mill, down through two trap doors – two sets of trap doors – and when you hung on wi' t'chain on to t'bag – there were one down below and one up on t'top floor, taking off. You used to pull a rope, and there were a round like a mangle roller, and it used to bind on to a pulley there. Then it used to wrap round, did t'chain, to bring t'bags up on to t'top floor ready for grinding. Well we used to stack 'em all up on t'top floor, and then we had a pair of wheels, and we'd wheel 'em to t'hopper and just drop 'em in. It were just a slit in t'top floor, went into a big hopper over t'mill wheel, t'grinding wheel, t'mill stone, and then it used to come down to t'bottom through a chute. I've had me hands under there many a time, when a rat's dropped in! And nails, six-inch nails, used to come out like knives. We used to bag up in the same bags it came in.

(Was it a two-man job then? Was one man tipping and...)

No. One man could manage t'grinding, 'cos when it were nearly ready, he used to keep bobbing up t'steps, having a look to see how t'corn were coming. If it were nearly ready, he used to bob up to t'next flight, and drop another bag in. They were all named, every bag were named.

(So the man who fetched it. Did he bring it in a morning and come back for it at night?)

No, no. He'd leave it two or three days. It just depended on how you could manage it you see. There were many a time when you couldn't grind it just at that time. It were all right in the wintertime, you had plenty of water then.

(So how many people's corn did you have in at one time?)

Oh, we might have had maybe ten.

(They didn't have to make an appointment?)

Oh, no! They used to come down wi' t'hoss and cart, and take 'em out. Then when they came to take it away, all t'corn that had been ground were on t'second floor. All t'meal were on t'second floor. They used to come wi' a pair of wheels in there, and wheel it to t'door. They used to back up to t'door, and t'door were practically level wi' t'cart back, and they used to pick 'em up and drop 'em into t'cart.

(When did they pay then?)

We used to send 'em a bill. Old Piggy Farrar still owes me dad for some grinding. He'll not get it now 'cos he's gone - well both of 'em has. Aye, that's a dead loss!

(So when did you finish at the mill?)

1926

(The big strike?)

Aye, it were on when we left. We left there and we didn't know where we were going. I were about seventeen.

(Who took over the mill when you left?)

Ledger came back. He got t'lot for £400. At that time in t'mill over t'barn we used to keep hay and straw to chop up for fodder, and drop it down into t'bottom. Well, one o' t'mill wheels, t'grinding wheels 'at drove t'stones, had wooden cogs. I used to have to shape 'em and fit 'em in and put four-inch nails in through t'hole in t'woodwork and they used to drive t'stones round. And I were shaping one up...

(What do you mean, shaping them up? Lining them up?)

They were just like teeth. They were shaped like that. You just used to drop 'em into this notch in t'wheel, and then put this nail in. Then you had a full set of cogs. You used to make all your own cogs for that wheel. They were all wood. There were only two types of wood you could make 'em out of - crab apple or thorn. Well, I was shaping this cogwheel down on t'bench, and I heard these feet coming across on t'second floor, galloping. Me dad's coming down wi' his thumb hanging off - he'd sawn his thumb off, nearly. Course I stopped t'mill, went across home to put his hand in a bowl of water. It were all blood. Me mother said, "Nip up to t'doctor's and bring him down." So I went to fetch him, Dr. Radcliffe. He came down. He says, "Now then Alf, what have you been doing?" He says, "I've sawn me thumb off I think - It's only hung on." He says, "Let's have a look." Well, in t'same little house - I dare say it'll be there yet - in t'living room, there was a big beam went through in t'fireplace, straight across. It were very low. So me dad's sat on this stool, t'doctor says, "Let's have a look at it." He dropped some iodine in. Me dad jumped up in t'air and bumped his head on t'beam. He were off six month.

(With his thumb or with his head?)

Both on 'em. By, what a mess he were in.

(He wouldn't go to hospital, the doctor would treat it?)

Doctor Radcliffe did all t'treatment.

(Somebody broke a leg at Sherburn school, and Joe Potts set it in wood. He never went to hospital with it. What other accidents did you have in the mill? Can you think of anything else that happened? It never caught fire or anything like Sherburn?)

Oh no, no!

(Did water mills ever catch fire?)

No. Only thing you had to watch, you hadn't to let your corn run out 'cos if you did and t'stones rubbed together, that's when they used to heat up. There were an old chap used to come every three years, a stone dresser, to dress 'em so you could grind again. He were a wonderful fella were that. All his hands and face were pitted wi' granite.

(No masks or gloves or anything like that?)

No, nothing. It was all chisel work. It were an art of its own, you know, cutting them out. It was that. He were a topping fella. He used to sleep in t'mill. In t'end o' t'mill there were a fireplace and he used to sleep in there. Then when old Ledger took over, after we'd gone, she used to come across, did his daughter, once a week. "You'll have to come, me dad can't get t'engine going." He'd got one of them big paraffin engines, and I used to have to go across and help him start it. One morning I went across. His wife were where t'big wheels were inside, for driving t'stones, wi' a crowbar. She's trying to crowbar t'stones round. He has t'paraffin thing underneath heating t'engine up to start it. Course he were impatient. He couldn't wait while it got heated before he tried to start it. He's laid inside. He had one leg and a hand off, had old Ledger - by t'top his leg were off. He had his good foot pressed again' t'wall, one arm on t'belt trying to pull it, hoping with him pulling it, it would start. Well, when I went in and saw what were 'appening, I shouted at her, "What the hell d'you think you're doing?" I says, "Don't you ever put a crowbar in there again. If this sets off, he's had it and you've had it." Steam were coming out of his cap! I says, "What do you think you're doing?" "Well, t'damn thing wain't start." I says, "Well there's no wonder 'cos you haven't waited 'til it's heated up." I says, "Come out. If that 'ud started you'd 'ave been wrapped round that big wheel." So he came out, and of course after about a quarter of an hour I said, "Now we'll try it." So I got hold of t'big wheel - you know they were about five or six feet across - just pulled, and away it went.

(You would be used to it.)

Aye, I told him, I says, "Don't ever do that again, or you won't be here to do it any more." Well he stopped so long then he left it. Course a chap called Wood took over and turned it inside out. It were an empty shell t'last time I looked in.

(That won't be so long ago then, because I can remember Wood being there.)

Vincent had it for a long time.

(What, before Wood or after?)

No, before him, 'cos Bob Tomlinson, he were in wi' Vincent an' all. He wanted me to go down and live there and run t'mill. But I wouldn't take it on, like........

Milford's Queen of T'Owd Thack before George Watkinson's time - 1890
Left to Right - The maid, landlord Nehemiah Copley and his wife

GUY WILSON

After attending his granddaughter's moving funeral on 29th February '00, I took out the tape of Guy Wilson to listen to happier but harder times. Thelma Tate and his daughter Mavis did the interview in February 1988, assisted by a list of questions I had supplied them with to keep them going. Guy lived in Milford all his life. These names, facts, figures and memories were all instant recall. Not bad for a man whose eighty-fourth birthday was in the July following the interview.

Early Days

My parents came from Beningbrough and I was born at the Maltings in 1904, the second youngest of eight boys. Five had left school before I was born. We went to Milford school and no other. When I was seven years old I had to walk to Milford Grange with four cans for four pints of milk. It was a good half mile away, just over t'railway and round by Lumby Dock. Then I came back and cleaned me shoes; I never went to school with dirty shoes. Then it was a good mile to school and I was never late in my life. I left school at thirteen and a half. On Thursdays me mother used to come and meet me with a meat and tatty pie. There was a set of three trees, two trees, one tree and t'turnings off. We'd meet her anywhere there, me and me brother, and back to school for one o'clock. Every Thursday she'd meet us.

Same at night, if she wanted some separated milk for teacakes I'd go again. Old Daniel had it then a man called Joseph Cromack came to Milford Grange. In those days they grew flax, and we'd go pulling that to make a bob or two. We had nothing, nothing at all!

Milford Feast and Sports day was on July 12th in Swan Croft - funfair, musical rides, the lot. You'd go pulling peas to earn sixpence to spend at the feast - at twopence a peck, four to a bag (4x42 lb). After a while the weigh man let us have a sack. If you were a bit short he'd knock a halfpenny off, but he didn't give you it back if there was over much.

Milford Maltings 1890

Back Row (L. to R.) Tindall (Station Master), Brownridge (Foreman), Newsome (Postman), E. Laws (Station Porter), Roberts, Bacon, Unnamed, J. Cockerham

2nd Row (L. to R.) W. Cockerham, Brown, Kitchen, A. Cockerham, F. Hirst, Richardson (Engine Man), J. Smith, ?.

Front Row (L. to R.) F. Hawley (Joiner), Hodgson, Unnamed, Unnamed, P. Furniss (Pussy), J. White, F. Newby

Milford School

(Were your school days happy?)

Yes, they had to be. I think Mr Wise's son married a schoolmaster's daughter from Hillam. My wife went to Monk Fryston School although she was in Milford Parish. She later went to Priory Street Girls in York. You had to work at your lessons, learn some good manners and not be rude to other people.

Oh yes, in June 1912 when the Titanic went down I was in class four. We all stood to attention and Mr Wise told us it had sailed yesterday, hit an iceberg and sank with so many drowned. That went through the school. It was important that!

Mr James Wise was my schoolmaster and he had a daughter Cecily who taught the infants. Mr Barry was t'parson and his daughter, Miss Barry, took first infants. Then there was Miss Braim who eventually married Ernest Todd. She'd come on the nine train from Garforth. We hadn't a man teacher, only t'head. Miss Garnett was the other - lived in that house that little Mary Harrison used to live in.

Before Mr Barry the Rector was a Mr Young and a Mr Causeway. I don't remember them much - then Mr Stockdale came. In the twenties he went to Wheldrake, then to Sherburn near Scarborough, then in '36 back here again and took over from Mr Hyde. Then there was Mr Harwood, Mr Roodhouse, Mr Taylor and Roger Chapman. Mr Murfleet followed him then David Wilbourne who's now at Helmsley. That's eleven parsons and there were eleven landlords at the Swan since 1929. I can remember them too - Mr Alf Johnson married my half cousin, Mr Reg Linnekar, Micky Colliery manager's son, Mr Holt, another Mr Johnson, Mr Preston from Bridlington who had a milk round. Laurie Oliver had a trawler at Hull and was there for just a year. The wife and I used to go to Barkston Towers for a dance with him. Then Harry Spencer took it. He's buried in Milford churchyard. Joe Hill was next, then Lester Hill, then Lewis had it.

Family

Grandfather, my father's father, died in 1902 before I was born. Grandfather Brownbridge was foreman of the Maltings when they went to live there. He finished in 1894 and flitted to Yeardsley Crescent York on a dray. He was a farm hand at Beningbrough and lived in Grange Cottage. Father went to Shipton by Beningbrough school.

I was born at the Maltings. I'd no sisters but had eight brothers. The oldest, Jim, was a wagon repairer at York. Fred went to Canada in 1929 and came over in 1969. Herbert had the fish shop after Johnson's left it. Mrs Johnson's husband had the Swan and left it in 1928. Louis was a signalman at Milford station. His wrist was blown away in World War 1 but he still worked in a special signal box after. Victor was a farm labourer all his life. He worked for George Harrison at t'Lodge and married Bill Kay's daughter. Harry was a market gardener at Macclesfield Hall. The youngest, Claude, started in the Maltings till he was twenty-eight or nine then drove buses in Leeds after the war. All lived into their eighties except for Frank who died at fifty-six. He was manager at Pleasley Vale Woollen Mill in Macclesfield.

Sports

As time went on I went in bigger races. The dyke race always set off from the cricket pitch. The Mill Dam was nine foot wide and three foot deep, and you had to jump it, go round a flag in the field near the mill and back again. I was the only man to jump it and not get wet. My brother Frank came second to me in 1921. It was a real race, that, once you dropped in there and got your pants wet. Oh, dear!

Then there was dart throwing. They'd stick a ham up, and them that got nearest to t'middle took it. They'd only cost about five bob in those days. That went on till t'British Legion opened and we went up there. Then we came back to George Harrison's at Burley House. We'd a Horticultural Society Show there. That finished in the fifties, about the last of little village shows. Sometimes there were fifty in a race. Seventeen ran from round here. We'd nothing else to do! Saxton was the first meeting, then Sherburn Show, South Milford, Brotherton, Monk Fryston Gala, Hambleton, Byram and Wistow. I had two brothers, Fred and Louis, that ran and I joined them training round the Maltings and Swan Croft. I started getting some cash prizes. My first big prize was that salad bowl. It cost fifty shillings but is valued at a hundred and fifty pounds now. Fattorinis supplied all clocks and prizes. At Selby Bowling Green I got that clock and a case of cutlery at Sherburn Gala in July. I finished in 1925.

I played football at Monk Fryston with Granville Heptonstall and Frank Poole. I went two years to Roundhay Park on Monday and Tuesday. I left here at twelve, 1/9d return then a 2d tram ride from City Square. A balloon always went up on the Monday. One time a gang of us cycled there and when we were coming home down Westfield Lane the same balloon was in the field nearby.

Fryston Football Selby Shield winners

Back - Walt Hill, Jim Lewis, H. Skelton, F. Nutbrown, T. Stainburn, Joe Longbottom, Geo. Longbottom, Percy Baker, Vic Wilson, J. Foster, Tom Foster.

Front - J. T. Whitley, Wally Lee (with ball), R. Baker, Capt. V. Stainburn, F. W. Hooper, Guy Wilson

The first aeroplane I ever saw was in 1913 when a plane landed in a field near Mr Bramley's Low farm. The teacher let us go to look. There were some plate layers on the line and they helped him start up, and take off over the Leeds-Selby line and on to Doncaster.

Farming

I left school at thirteen and went to George Harrison's up at t'Lodge farming, and I worked fifty-one weeks for him. He then came to this farm here with his brother Harold and I'd five pounds, a white five pound note for my fifty-one weeks and me keep! He came from Milford Lodge and ran it. He put Albert on it and when James Hill came out of Burley he went into that and he died there.

(What sort of work did you do there?)

Just ordinary casual work - six cows to milk before eight o'clock, pea pulling. Mrs Harrison was a hard working woman. She was never in t'house, always out. There were five horses, all to feed.

(Did you plough at all?)

Oh yes. If you did an acre a day you walked ten miles with a single furrow plough and to do it you had to start by half past six. In harvest we got Irish men. They'd come and sleep rough in that barn. There'd be one up the street at Inglenook at Bartofts. September was harvest month. It was never ready before, and they stayed to take potatoes up and then go home.

There were fourteen farms in and around Milford at the time I'm talking about. Now there's two. None were more than seventy-five acres. I can name nine or ten, but we'll do that another time.

Shops

Coming to little shops. There wasn't one in Sand Lane till about 1928. Miss Mason started it. Coming down the street Bradleys had a fish and chip shop in Poplar Terrace. That turned into a little grocer's shop and Mrs Gelder had it. Just across Harry Lunn had his cycle agency. He used to cycle to t'pit at Ledston Luck every morning and do cycle repairs later. He bought that farm there off t'railway company, that building and house where Granville died. There was a slaughter house at the end. Then we come to Miss Holgate's - that little shop where Samples live now. You got two warm buttered teacakes there for twopence. Then you got a chap at the cross here. He was a manager for Moons of Keswick before Wards took it. Then the little shop at the side, Mrs Bragg was Mrs Ward's mother. You went there for a pennyworth of all sorts. James Hill's, butchers, was next and across Atkinson had the Midland Bank.

Richard Batty was next-door. He'd open a barrel of cheese and cut it with a wire. Old Nabob they called him. The Co-op next door was quite something. Joe Baker was the last man that delivered. He'd a dray and one horse. Mother always went in for bits on a Saturday and to pay old Bruce, Ernest's father, 'cause you didn't get paid till Friday dinnertime, and he delivered Thursdays and Fridays. Norton Stainburn was an errand boy there.

They were hard times. An Insurance man called Hartley lived next-door. People paid him their Stores cheques and they got their money back in six months. A bit further up old Pettinger was a tailor. He'd measure you for a suit and bring it back from Leeds after he'd made it. Mrs Pettinger sold sweets from a room to children as they went to school. There was the Post Office then Powells, then Pettinger and the fish and chip shop. Alf Johnson's mother lived in it. Percy Paver was another cycle agent and lived in Blacksmith's Yard. There was Jimmy Farrar's butchers near Bond Brook Farm, and at the end of the Nook was a shop old Clayton had. His son Billy looked after it. You could get anything there. At one of those houses opposite the church you could get hot teacakes from Mrs Sutcliffe. Binks Broadley lived there. Mrs Sonny Watkinson's mother had a drapery shop in Springwell Terrace. The well supplied the village from there. It's still there today. Sunderlands pumped it. There were taps at the doctors, Post Office, one near Arthur Cawood's. You got wet though if you weren't careful. In 1935 we got Leeds water but the extra pressure burst a lot of underground pipes.

Doctors

Doctor Jack lived next to the policeman next to the Bull. When he finished there Doctor Harold Ratcliffe came into the Terrace. Doctor Pickersgill at Sherburn died in 1933 then Doctor Murphy came. Him at top of t'hill was Thirkill and Doctor Metcalfe was down Moor Lane. He was a rummish sort of chap and Doctor Thirkill always wore a swallowtail coat covered in dog hairs.

Water Mills and Cars

Water started at Garforth Trench Pit, Micky Pit, it came past Newthorpe Mill, under the railway to the top Mill at Milford, past the Swan and the cricket field to the Low Mill and away to Cawood and the River Ouse. Now there are 3,735,322 acres in Yorkshire, the biggest county in England, 61,000 square miles and I've been in most of them. What I want to know is, is there another place with three water mills as close? Someone might hear this and let me know. We'll have another sherry now Don!

(Tell me about your cars)

The first I had was a Singer Nine. I got a licence in 1926 and didn't have to take a test.

Then I got a Kino, then a Ford, a Hillman and then a little Morris Eight and a Standard Eight and a Fourteen. I had a 1949 Ford Eight I sold for five pounds. I repainted it beige myself. Fred Sunderland mixed me the paint. I stored it at the Gas House for years, SPY 798 it was. Then I had a Lanchester Ten with a Wilson pre-selector gear box, then a Ford Anglia and a Toyota Thousand. I changed that for a Fiesta and now I have a Peugot. Cars were for nothing then. If I hadn't done the repairs myself I couldn't have afforded to run one. There were only two garages, Copes and Battersbys at the round-about. In 1941-45 I did seventy-five percent of the repairs when Tommy Battersby went on to gas fittings. Tommy was a grand chap. I used to take him a crate of Magnet every Friday.

THE BELLES OF ST. MARY'S

When I venture into St. Mary's Hall in summer collecting tables and chairs for the cricket barbecue, no-one present would ever guess the thoughts and memories that are stirred and the friends from long ago that come to mind.

Having just attended the funeral of George Mytum at Sherburn Church, similar feelings come over me. George, a gentle little man was a prisoner of the Japanese for several years and came home weighing six stone and must have had horrendous memories of his internment. In my taping sessions I have talked to a First World War veteran, two shot down Lancaster fliers and prisoners, and a Desert Rat, but George quietly and kindly side-stepped my requests to chat and his nightmare years are laid to rest with him.

From George's war to Milford Badminton Club of the fifties is light years apart but it all happened for a short while of my life too. How and when the club started I don't know but Mr Butterfield and Mrs Battersby could have been involved, and the Girls' Friendly Society might have been its parents. Money was short but Reverend Gerry Roodhouse helped by exchanging hall rent for members' attendance at church I'm told!

For me one night's rugby training a week was sufficient in those days and a night or two at St. Mary's and playing in matches much more civilised. At school table tennis helped pass the time and we all got quite good. I had tried badminton one lunchtime, and although it looked so simple hitting a feathered shuttlecock, I couldn't manage it and spoiled the game of the experts I was amongst. I think it was Phil Batty who talked me into going down mainly for the table tennis which was set up in the schoolroom. Harry Fields was Avery's champion and was always keen for a game. We had some great battles until I started beating him, then it wasn't the same for either of us. It was just exactly so years later when my twelve-year-old son could beat me at snooker!

I eventually succumbed to trying the feathered game again next door and soon got to enjoy the delicate touches and the crash-bang smashes. Our hall was so tiny that we played most matches away. The sidelines were only six inches from the walls and visitors could break racquets. Spectators gathered round stoves at either end to gossip and keep warm.

It was real private enterprise and before expensive night classes, the rule of Fuhrer caretakers and out by 9.30. First to arrive collected the key from Mrs Hey next door - wife of postman Jimmy - and the last out dropped it through the letterbox. A certain few liked to stay on when all the ladies had departed and enjoy men's doubles 'til well gone eleven! It wasn't the best of gentlemanly games, in that you went on in the order that you rolled up, and could be soon on and off if it was a mismatch, and sat out waiting again for better things. There were two unpopular ways of avoiding this and having a better game. One was just to play to the better player, and the other was to play hard on your opponent's serve but keep losing your own, as, unlike tennis, at badminton you only score points when you are serving. It was very frustrating watching when this was going on, and hard to disguise when doing it!

I think I liked being in the team for the suppers, which I can remember better than the games. This was before tea and biscuits only, the pub, or Rosemary Conley. It was all home-made. There was always a cream cake or two, jam tarts, butterfly buns etc., sometimes a trifle, preceded by various assortment of sandwiches and pork pies. We never finished in a pub as it was usually too late. Mode of transport at first was Mr Butterfield's fish van or Harry Fields' motor. If you had a car you were in the team.

As at any sport, it was always a struggle to win at Cawood. In their Old Boys' Schoolroom the ceiling was low at one end, so if in trouble you hit that and played it again. We always had difficulty finding St Saviour's in the middle of York where a stocky chap with thick glasses, Arthur Milling, and his wife were their star turn, but always helpful to beginners. Most village halls still had regular dances then, and slippy floors were a problem. At Allerton Bywater a green marked out sheet was stretched tight over the floor, but that became dangerous over the years as it lost its tautness.

Naburn Hospital was a fraught fixture for some, as the team had to negotiate long, grim, tiled passages and many locked doors to reach the large court in the magnificent theatre. A brilliant mural of 'Entertainment through the Ages' had been painted on the fire curtain by a patient in his better moments but the eyes seemed to watch your every move. Some of our opponents wore long black socks and had starey eyes (they were the staff), and the suppers weren't so hot. It was good to get home to bed and although tired out, sleep was never tranquil after Naburn.

Birkin and Beal were always great suppers with farmer cricketers playing, like Doug Walker and Jack Brears who was also a stalwart of Whitley Bridge Cricket Club. After playing at Osgodby one night and all in Mr Butterfield's fish van, I persuaded him to avoid paying the toll at the bridge by shouting 'local' as the locals did, and zoom on. Unfortunately the van only stuttered on as the suspicious keeper set off after us.

The highlight of the season for men was the team that I used to take to play the masters at Drax. They had an elderly ambling father figure, who must have been at least fifty and had represented Ulster at rugby and badminton. Tom Steen ran us all over and never moved himself. One night we all finished in Selby Hospital around midnight after Ken Powell turned an ankle in the deciding game. Ken had played for Somerset and was in a good Eversley cricket side at that time. A starchy matron was not impressed by his reply of 'Please Miss I think I'm pregnant' to her query about his problem. He always looked it. Mr Butterfield liked me as his partner. Because of his gammy leg he relied on guile and I often finished up with blisters. Latterly Fred Bent from the Limes joined us. He was a dapper salesman of some sort, and had tried and equipped himself at every other sport and finally badminton. He was serving at Drax on another occasion when the clock above us started striking twelve. Like a batsman with a wayward spectator, he walked away until it stopped. We had a fine Christmas party at his home, the Limes, with the bachelor Drax schoolmasters adding spice for our ladies. Music was from my old record player - no discos then, and someone somewhere may still have my long players, Claire de Lune, and Oscar Peterson playing Pretty.

In the summer Fred Bent invited some of us to tennis on his grass court. When sitting out, silver-haired, whiff-smoking Fred could be persuaded to tinkle on a grand piano à la Charlie Kunz, and I came away with Inkspot, Mills Brothers and Hutch records which were piled up in a corner. I'd never heard of them before. Mr Butterfield was always shocked that I'd never heard of Nat Gonella, his favourite trumpeter of the thirties. I can now appreciate his sentiments. It's called the generation gap. In those innocent days it was a shock for me to learn that the Bents hadn't been married, and one day Fred just went off into the blue, and was never heard of again.

Married couples seemed to get on at badminton. I don't know how it is now, but before equality of the sexes, and with the odd exception, the wife sort of scurried about at the net, whilst her husband ran around at the back slamming away. Harry and Mary Fields, Fenton headmaster Ron Thornton and Joan, Mike and Alma Rucklidge, and treasurer Jack and Pat Horton, together with sisters Jean and Rita Harrison and Valerie Hutchinson, the policeman's daughter, were the hard core of the club back then in the fifties before the power of television and wives going out to work. I think I finished up playing at Birkin as well with Phil Batty and Molly Turner. I wonder if the old school rooms will ever again echo to the sound of ping-pong balls and the swish of the feather? Who knows?

Partying time at The Limes
Back Row -Mike Rucklidge, Harry Butterfield, Fred Bent, Mary Fields, Alf Burnley, Joan & Ron Thornton, Betty Stoker.
Front - Pat Horton, Alma Rucklidge, Rita Harrison

J.D.B.

INTERVIEW WITH DENNIS HICK

It is Thursday 17th April 1997 about 6 p.m. and I am inspired by a wonderful evening last night at the History Society when Anne Batchelor came over from Leeds and gave us a wonderful story about finding her ancestor Daniel who played his lute at the court of Queen Elizabeth I at Walsingham. The night before that I was in the company of Dennis Hick and Rod, a former policeman, who keep the football club going. I have been very conscious for a long time that I should interview Dennis, ever since sitting next to him at Milford Hall at a dinner, when he told us the story of how he went there as a lad and the owner, when it was a private house, treated him more like a son. It was unbelievable and now thousands of pounds have been spent on it and shortly it will be opened as a theme pub. Also Dennis is a character who can remember everything about the village and about the football and the school. He has also had time in the army and worked at the Maltings.

Later.

(We are in business. He hasn't got his pipe lit, the dog is quiet and I have got Dennis ready to tell me everything. We will start with family. Go back to your parents)

Dennis Hick and dog

Well I can go back to my granddads. They were both colliers at Micky Pit. Me mother and me father were both first cousins so me grandfathers were brothers. Me mother's dad, he was injured in Micky Pit explosion.

(What year was that?)

I'm not really sure. Maybe early nineteen hundreds.

(Did he work again?)

He couldn't go back down t'pit. They said he wasn't fit so he went as postman and I didn't know a reet lot about him. I only got to know a week since that the woman he married, my grandmother, I thought she was Scotch but I was told she was Irish. I said 'Oh bloody hell' and me other granddad, he worked down t'pit and they seemed to keep theirseves to theirselves. Well I was only young and I was scared of 'em because they were rough, t'old pit type y'know, rough and if they said 'Sit down' you sat down. So I didn't have much to do with 'em. But me granny, what I called Granny Ruth - her name was Annie.

(What about your granny on your mother's side?)

She was a Mitchell before she married and I always said that were Scotch because Mitchell is a Scotch name but I was told about a week ago she was Irish by somebody who was eighty-five so they should know a bit more than me.

(Did they live near each other?)

They lived in t'same row at Micky, The Crescent, which is that first long row of houses on your left-hand side as you go into Micky. It's still there. One lived in forty-seven an' t'other lived in fifty-six, at t'other end. Me mother's mother had a shop but it were t'same as lots of shops then, it was t'kitchen. She used to get up at five o'clock to get everything ready for t'miners going to work at t'pit to call in for their baccer and matches and all that. She selt spice and that for t'kids. That was about it. I remember t'co-op being nextdoor. You see I was born in Micky in '22 and came to Milford in '23 and we lived where t'swings are today. That was called Haystack Farm. T'field that they call t'park was Miles Garth, that was t'proper name for it. We followed Poulter into there. As you walk up you can just see his grave with A. Poulter on it. Me dad came out of t'pit for heart trouble bought this and he set up with fish and chips at one stage then he had a grocery round so we had an old - well it wasn't old then but it was old to me - an old Ford one ton lorry. You undid two bolts at t'back and you took the passenger seats off and put the flat lorry seat on, did the bolts under and took your stuff out, took it off and put t'back back on to take you for a ride. T'handbrake were outside, everything was on t'gear lever. I learnt to drive on that. Most I remember about it was if it were night and you went round a corner t'lights went out, 'cos it was on a dynamo so you went that slow round a corner that dynamo wasn't doing enough to make t'lights work. We had a shop at t'end of t'house, then we got a Bull-nosed Morris. T'house was where t'tennis courts are.

(Was it a farm you were on then?)

Yes, it had been a farm. There was t'council thing at t'end where they used to keep t'sheep.

(The pinfold.)

Aye, t'pinfold and there was t'house, t'hos stable, t'barn, t'cow mistles and t'pigsties. It went in that formation.

(The house looked on to t'road did it.)

Yes, t'house looked on to t'road and the yard at t'front were red ash then we'd a bit of a garden and there were a big wall round and a big gate for t'hosses and that --- we never had any of course --- and a little gate for people coming to t'house. You used to go down past t'shed. We'd a little shop at t'end. It was a building that had been used for something to do wi' t'farm, maybe t'tackroom or some'at like that 'cos that's what it was big enough for. We had a shop there selling potatoes and greens and spice and all that. Me mother used to stop open to eleven o'clock at night wi' t'gas lamp, leave t'top door open --- it was a stable door effort so as you could tell it was something to do wi' t'farm buildings --- leave t'top door open so you could see t'light in and outside, again t'door, we had a big Players Weights tin in a frame that they put up when we started selling Players cigarettes. They put it up for us and there used to be George Edward Farrar and Jimmy Farrar and

98

Billy Costigan and Fred Boston and Raymond, his elder brother, and if they were coming from t'pub or owt – they used to turn out at half ten and they used to be calling and if they thought they wanted some cigs or owt, instead of shouting or owt they used to just bray t'tin wi' their fists and you could hear it all ower Milford. It used to fair rattle! Then if we were having us supper, 'cos it were always a late supper, I were never to bed early, me mother 'ud go to t'door and whoever it were would say, 'It's me Annie, I want some cigs.' 'Well I'm getting me supper. Get what you want, you know where it is, and put your money on t'counter.'

'Aye all right.' And Billy 'ud come and just give t'tin one bang when he were off to let you know he were going. T'tin 'ud bang again and it 'ud be George Edward Farrar or somebody like that. 'Can I have some Gold Flakes Annie?' – They all smoked Gold Flakes. 'Yes, I'm getting me meal. You know where they are. Put t'money on t'counter.' And when she went up after her meal there'd be bundle – it weren't much mind you – all across t'counter.

(It would be mainly pennies wouldn't it?)

Pennies and sixpences, that 'ud be about t'dearest, all across t'counter so as they knew how many pieces of money there was so she knew how many 'ad been. T'folks that went in never touched any of that brass and they had nothing, you know. They just put their money down, got what they wanted and went. Then of course things got bad. Mother was limping, she was lame and they said, 'Oh it's rheumatics Annie, you're alright.' That were Doctor Radcliffe but it wasn't, it were cancer and she died when she was forty-five and I were ten so me Dad just kept doing a bit of t'rounds and trying to look after t'shop with our Alice if she were at home.

(That was your sister.)

That were me eldest sister amd Jessie, me youngest sister had t'three wheeled tricycle 'cos her legs were terrible. She had 'em broke fourteen times 'cos it wasn't bone, it were greenstick. If she just sat down hard she broke her legs. Then me Dad went to bed wi' t'heart trouble and he died when I was sixteen so that left me and my younger sister. Me elder sister had got married and come to live at Sherburn.

(Who did she marry?)

She married a Petch and they went to Canada. He used to work at t' Bacon Factory and – there's a lot of Petches in Sherburn.

(Are there many left in Canada then? Do you hear from them?)

Oh yes. They come over every two year and there's her daughter and a son in Canada and Reg is still alive and he's eighty-six. He comes over. She died out there. She came over for a holiday and I remember we were at t'gate and she said, 'We're off to catch t'train and I won't see you any more our Dennis.' I says, 'Don't talk so silly.' And eighteen months later she were dead. They brought her ashes over and spread them at Bridlington on t'North Sea. They keep saying, 'Will you come over?' but I'm not going over, oh no I don't want to go, not now.

(What was your fist job?)

That were Milford Hall. It was Mr Coates what had Milford Hall and they'd a big factory in Leeds that made furniture, upholstery, French polishing and what not, and I went to work for him straight from school. I left school in '36. Well, when you broke up for t'Christmas holidays, if anybody wanted anybody for work they used to come to t'school. Well John came, I knew after it were John, t'son for Mr Coates, and Mr Salisbury says, 'Well when we break up from school you won't come any more will you, Hick? Because you'll be fourteen in December.' I says, 'Yes, I won't be coming back.' 'Right, come out here. There's a job for you. Now you talk to Mr Coates and he'll tell you when to go...'

Milford Hall where Dennis Hick worked

It wasn't 'Do you want to go or what do you think.'... 'He'll tell you when to go and meet his father and all t'rest of it.' So he took me outside and says, 'Well can you come Friday evening and meet my father?' His father was blind and that's what my job entailed, I were a gentleman's gentleman. I'd never heard the expression before.

(Did he tell you that?)

Yes. He says, 'That's your official title.'

(Did that impress you then?)

Well no because I'd just left school. T'only thing that impressed me were t'size of t'house. That's what impressed me most, and I saw him and he says,'Well you've broken up to-night,' which was Friday before the Christmas holidays, ' Will you start on Monday morning?' Cos he were a gentleman I thought, well I'll go. I says, 'Yes Mr Coates.' I never called him sir nor nothing. I called him Mr Coates but Len Gelder, t'gardener and chauffeur and the other man that were there called him sir when they spoke to him. Len used to say to me, 'You should say Sir when you speak to Mr Coates.' I says,'No, it's Mr Coates, it's not Sir so-and-so Coates.' I says,'I've only just left school but I know that.' So I always called him Mr Coates. So he says, 'Right, don't have your breakfast. You come here for your breakfast. Be here for half past eight. ' I says, 'Right you are.' So I put me best clobber on and went down for half past eight. I went to t'back door of course, t'tradesmen's entrance, and one of t'servants answered t'door. He had three servants and a cook. So I said who I was so she fetched t'cook and cook said, 'Oh we're expecting you. Dennis isn't it?' So I says, 'Yes.' So she says to one of t'maids, 'Will you take him through to the breakfast room.' So I went through to t'breakfast room and there was Mr Coates and t'son and his two sisters. So they shook hands with me and Mr Coates says, 'Right Dennis, come and sit at t'side of me.' He says, 'You're my right-hand man. That's what the job entails. If I go anywhere you'll go with me.'

(How long had he been blind?)

I remember 'em saying in t'village, 'Oh, Coates is a so-and-so. You've got to get off t'causeway for him.' But he'd t'white stick and he was doing this, so that's why you got off t'cawsway for him, to keep out on his way. He didn't tell you to get off.

(Had he had another right hand man before you, another lad?)

No, I was t'first one and 'Come on, get your breakfast.'

(His wife had died?)

Yes. He had two sisters. They were very fussy. I think they wanted a young lad about the house because they used to say, 'Come here.' And I used to say, 'Yes Miss Coates, what do you want?' They'd put their arm round me and say, 'You're a grand lad you know.' They were both t'same. They wanted somebody to fuss over, 'cos he was a bit strict with them..'Don't fuss with me!' I used to have me breakfast, all t'things I'd never had you know. Mine used to be a slice of jam and bread or some'at and I went there and it was a cooked breakfast.

(Kidneys and...)

Aye, and kippers and t'old man used to put hands over me and say to t'sisters, What do you think? Yes, he wants filling up I think.' So they used to bang it into me, you know. About nine o'clock he'd say, 'Right go tell Gel to bring the car round.' So I went round to tell Gelly. You could always find him in t'garden. 'Will you bring t'car round? We're off to Leeds.' We were going to t'factory. He used to go every morning. He didn't do nothing. He sat at his desk but didn't do anything. He just listened to what people were telling him. When I'd been there about a week he says, 'Now then Dennis do you know anything about Leeds?' I says. 'No, I don't know one street from another in Leeds.' 'Well, you'll have to get to know because we might want you to go to a shop in Leeds and give an order in.' He never thought about using t'telephone, somebody always went in to order. They've closed down now but they were in.... I've forgotten what they call it now.

(What order were you taking then?)

For French polish, button shelack, stain, order wood and all sorts and they used to send it round on a lorry. I says, 'Oh very well Mr Coates I'll do that.' 'Well when you go you don't get lost.' So he says, 'I tell you what we'll do Dennis. Gel will take you into Leeds and he'll drop you at t'front of Woolworths and you have a wonder round. Everybody will tell you where Woolworths is so you'll get back. We'll give you an hour and you can stand outside there and Gel will come and pick you up.' Well when he did everybody looked. He'd one of these big Chryslers. Everybody stared because Gel used to open t'door for me and I used to get in. The good thing about it was, he used to say. 'Now you'll be an hour. Now here's half a crown, you can get yourself some sweets or a drink.' Well half a crown then was a lot of money. 'When you come back give me the change, what you've got left give me it back.' I used to just give him the change and he never asked what I'd got or what I'd done. He didn't want to know. He was a really smashing bloke. I looked after him for about a year and he used to have a nap in t'afternoon. He used to come back about two, half-past one to two, then he could have a nap at half past two till five, then he'd start stirring for a late dinner. He used to say, 'Go entertain yourself somewhere Dennis. I'm going to have a nap. Go play with the maid.' She was about my age you see. I used to say, 'Alright.' And used to go out and go down two of t'steps and turn left and that went under t'hall, no under t'garden. There was t'billiard room down there and..

(Underground?)

Yes. Course everything then seemed bigger to me. It wouldn't seem as big when I got older, you know, but that was new to me and it seemed massive but it wasn't that big. If you went down, they used to hang game down there, and at t'bottom end was t'wine 'cos it were cold. I know I went down once and I saw these two pheasants hanging and there were maggots all over 'em and dropping off. I couldn't wait for him to waken up to tell him that t'pheasants were rotten. So when he did get wakened up and I went to his bedroom to fetch him down again 'cos he'd to get hold of me arm you see. That was me job, to steer him about

(Could he dress himself?)

Yes as long as I put t'clothes there for him and told him what order they were in. Then he used to say, 'Right I've got that Dennis. I'll get dressed. You can just go and wait on the landing. When I open the door you can take me downstairs.' So I took him downstairs and took him straight to t'breakfast table you see. I couldn't wait for him getting up. I went to fetch him downstairs and I says, 'Before we go any farther, there's two pheasants down there near t'games' rooms and they're rotten.' I says, 'When I've got you down there I'll go and get a shovel and go into t'garden somewhere and bury 'em.' He says, 'Don't bother Dennis. See Gelly, he'll bury them.' So I took it for granted and I saw Gelly and I says, ' Oh Mr Coates says I've to tell you 'cos there's two pheasants down there and they're rank, maggots all over.' So Gelly just laughed and says, ' Alright Dennis, I'll see to it.' Well it were about four or five days later and we went to have us dinner. We had us dinner about half past seven and they always used to pile your plate up, well they did mine. They thought I was starving. So Mr Coates says to t'maid, 'Make sure Dennis gets enough.' So they gave me a right plateful with plenty of this meat. So I scoffed it all. He says, ' Would you like a bit more Dennis? I can hear you've emptied your plate.' I says, 'Yes please. Can I have some more of that meat?' He says, 'Yes, of course you can.' So he rang t'bell and t'maid came and he talked to her and she came back and brought me some more. Then we had a sweet and he said, 'Well, we'll go up to t'reading room now, the library.' It was a big room and it was just choc-a-bloc from floor to ceiling with books. He says, 'Now then I've something to tell you Dennis. I didn't want to tell you at the meal table...' He'd gotten to know me then because sometimes I used to come out with bloody this, and I used to speak broad. Gelly used to pull me up over it, 'You don't speak broad to Mr Coates.'....So he says, 'You know that meat?' I says, 'Yes.' He says, 'Well, that's that bloody, rotten pheasant tha were going to bury.' Ha, ha, ha.

(Did he talk broad to you then?)

Yes, and he used to enjoy it. He laughed because it was a mistake when I did it. I didn't try to do it, I just wasn't thinking. I was only fourteen. I used to take him up t'steps to t'car. I think there were ten to t'back door. I remember taking him up once and getting him stood at t'bottom watching me. I could see he wasn't going to lift his leg so I says, 'Lift thee foot up, there's another.' He just laughed. 'Alright Dennis.' he says. They got to accept us as one of them. When I saw Gelly he says, 'Don't ever again say to the boss, lift thee foot up.' I says, 'Well I didn't think anything about it. It just come out. I didn't mean to say that but it just come out.' He used to laugh away to himself did t'old man. You could see he was smiling. He used to titter away to hissen as though he enjoyed it that somebody was just natural because everybody that met him they weren't natural you know. They said, 'Yes Mr Coates, sir. Three bags full Mr Coates.' And it seemed as though he wanted to meet somebody that just spoke to him naturally.

And Tom, t'youngest son, he'd a Buick and I know we were coming from Leeds and we'd got past t'roundabout at Wakefield road and Hook Moor.... Well it wasn't a roundabout then, it was just a crossroads... we got past t'crossroads and Tom says to me, 'Have we to see what we can get out of it before we get to t'Boot and Shoe?' I says, 'Yes, go on.' Well he put his foot down and before we got to t'woods at Micky t'old man says, 'Tom, slow down. You're going miles too fast.' He says, 'What speed was he doing then Dennis?' I says, 'Fifty.' He was just doing ninety-eight. T'old man says to me, 'He was doing eighty and another ten on top. I could feel by the ride of the car.' He had a sixth sense with being blind. He used to go into t'library and he'd take it upon himself to teach me English more or less. He used to say, 'Read to me out of this book Dennis.' He'd sit down with a cigar and a glass of brandy. He used to say, 'You can have a glass of lemonade.' He used to sit there and say, 'Now read that book,' Well they were all big books same as that book up there. Well it didn't make sense to me. There were words I'd never seen before, never mind tried to say 'em. So I'd be reading away and it didn't make sense 'cos it was all very highbrow stuff, and when I got to a big word and I didn't know what it was I used to say, 'And some'at else.' And then carry on reading, Then he'd stop me and say, ' Go back to that some'at else. Now what does it say?' I'd say, 'I don't know, I can't say it.' He used to say, 'Well tell me what it looks like.' So I used to say it and he'd tell me what it was and he used to tell me what it meant. Then he'd let me read on a bit farther, then he'd stop me and say, 'What was that word? What does it mean?' All t'big words I couldn't say he used to tell me all about it, then let me read on, stop me and bring me back to that word. 'What was it? How do you say it? What does it mean?'

(Testing you.)

Yes. He used to do that till I got fed up. It was as bad as being at school. Then he'd put the book away and say, 'Well, our dinner's digested now Dennis. We'll just do a few exercises. Get a walking stick.' There were about four or five walking sticks at side of t'door. He always had one and it used to be, 'Now do this with me.' He used to stand with his back to t'mirror with t'walking stick, bending sideways and being a kid I used to think, well he can't see me so he used to do it and I used to go 'sh, sh, sh,' Then he used to stop all of a sudden and say, 'Do you know Dennis you haven't lifted that stick off the damn floor.' I hadn't and he says, 'That puffing, your doing it with me.' When he breathed out I did it with him. He says, 'You're trying to con me. You haven't done a damn thing. Well if you're not going to do it we might as well pack it in.' He used to put it down and we'd talk. He used to talk about anything and that was interesting to me 'cos he used to talk about things that I'd never been interested in because I'd never any money to go to that sort of thing. But he used to tell me all about it and he used to have business men there 'cos he had a big business and they used to come and have a meal. It was always a working lunch and then they used to go in and talk about what they were and what they weren't. If his solicitor came...once when his solicitor was there talking about some'at he says, 'Well I think we ought to be in private Mr Coates.' He says, 'Well Dennis is going nowhere. He won't tell anybody so if I'm here, he's here so you might as well say it.' I used to see all sorts but it used to just go over my head. I didn't know what they were talking about. All I knew was if I got above five shillings I was well off so if they were talking about thousands I used to think oh. I really got on well. I liked it till it started to get a bit much. T'sisters wanted to dress me in a coat wi' t'mandarin collar, like a little Chinese lad. A lovely coat, black with these designs on. I hadn't to wear a hat but I used to hate it. T'old man used to insist that I went to t'top of tstairs where they branched to t'landing, and hit the gong when it were lunchtime for him to get up instead of going in to tell him but I wouldn't...I never did. He used to say to me, 'You don't like the idea of ringing that gong, do you Dennis?' I used to say, 'No Mr Coates, I don't like it.' 'Well there's nobody in the house but us, nobody knows, nobody's going to laugh at you. Do it on a morning for us to get up.' But I still used to open t'door and get hold of his shoulder and say, 'Tea's ready.' Then give him his cup of tea and he used to say, 'You haven't rung that blasted gong Dennis.' I never did ring it. I thought things seemed to be getting a little bit strange with t'coat wi' t'mandarin collar, t'jacket and that. But I suppose there was no harm in it 'cos I was t'only young lad in t'house. I'd been going a year to Leeds with him then and I used to go up to t'book shop for something to do. I used to walk up. It was down Wellington Street and I used to walk up to t'book shop 'cos he was in his office 'cos I was just sitting there like a 'nana. I used to go to t'work place and all at once I says to him, 'I want to come and work in t'factory Mr Coates.' 'Oh you don't do you?' Well he went on about it, he told his two sisters and they got on to me about it. 'Don't leave us, you're one of ours. You've no Mam and Dad you know, you're one of us. We're your family.' Of course I'd got it into me head 'cos I'd seen all these others going on t'train. They were men, you know, or seemed to be, and women, they were going to t'factories.. Then he says, 'All right then, what do you want to do? Cabinet making, upholstery or French polishing? I says, 'Upholstery.' Well I knew nowt about none on 'em but he says, 'Right, start Monday morning. I'll tell 'em. I'll tell the foreman to expect you but you're bringing me to work first.' I had to take him to work first and then go, so I wasn't going on t'train at t'finish. I had two days upholstering and I went to take him home at night and he says, 'What do you think to it?' I says, 'I don't like it.' 'Well what do you want to do then?' I says, 'I'll go for French polishing.' He says, 'Well stick to the damn job then and learn how to French polish.' Well I did. That were an accident but I did it. He says, 'Right then, you can start work at half past seven Dennis and don't bother about your train fare. Just give a note in at my office when you want your pass renewing and I'll renew your pass.' He says, 'And when it's dinner time, instead of bringing sandwiches, just come down to t'office,' which was only like from here to t'Swan, 'and have your meal with me.' That was a hot meal, you know, sponge pudding and all that sort of stuff. I did that for quite a while then I thought, it doesn't seem right.

(Well the men wouldn't like it would they?)

No, they were sniding about it. You know, I never took any snap and they were only Leeds loiners and they probably had jam and bread sandwiches and I used to go down and get a good dinner in t'office canteen. So I had a word with our Jessie and she said, 'Oh, I think you ought to stop it.' So I just stuck there a bit longer and I got fed up of going to Leeds and a job came up at Sherburn at White's, t'grocers. They wanted an errand lad and I thought I'd see about it. They were offering me as much money as I was getting going to Leeds and of course he was paying me train fare. Well I thought, 'Its only a mile to Sherburn so I can bike there.' So I went to work at White's till I were seventeen.

(Where was that in Sherburn then?)

It was a grocers. Did you know Grebby in Sherburn?

(No.)

He were a bus driver for Wynn's buses. That was in t'thirties. It was part of their house, right opposite t'milk bar in Sherburn. It was a proper grocer's shop. They were competing wi' Dickinson and Wards and all them. I was t'errand lad, then I had to help at back of t'counter if he were busy.

(Did you deliver on a bike?)

Yes. I used to go to Huddleston Hall and right down Aberford Lane to t'main road, where t'Tadcaster road goes across t'bottom.

The deaths of Denis and Joyce Hick and the wintry Easter weather has put a dampener on the start of the April 1998 cricket season. Denis was a lifelong stalwart of Milford football and a founder member of the Swan Croft Association which eventually purchased our ground. I shall miss our little chats way down Common Lane as he walked his dog - or the dog walked him.

The theme of this poem can apply to football as well as cricket and I think Denis and Joyce would approve.

Cricket Comes *(Colin Shakespeare)*

At the sea's edge, where the land begins,
On smooth, sea-drained sand
A father bowling to his son,
Family and friends field
And on the breeze the game starts to swing.

Cricket comes, collects its followers
And carries them through the summer,
And omens hoped the games may bring
No one can tell until it ends
The spin of a coin and how it lands.

Cricket needs its variations;
Its ups and downs, its fast and slows,
As this land flows in humps and hollows
Towards the horizon's boundary
Where the Pennines meet the sky.

On a scattering of grounds
Play sets the summer free;
It is as if someone above had sprinkled seed
And where it fell cricket grounds grew
To make each summer fresh, each summer, new.

102

CHAPTER 6

MONK FRYSTON

OLD JOHN – MR J. J. FOSTER

It takes a brave and intrepid Sherburner to write in a South Milford magazine about a Monk Frystoner, but if I can bring a few memories back of John Foster to those who knew him, or introduce this wonderful old character to those who didn't, I will risk my neck!

John Foster in Home Farm garden

John's night of glory was on 25th February 1972 when Bill Bowes, John Nash, Michael Crawford and other cricketing county big wigs, came to pay tribute to his record breaking sixty-five years as secretary of Monk Fryston and Hillam Cricket Club. Tickets were at a premium for the dinner held in the ballroom of Monk Fryston Hall. Wonderful speeches were enjoyed, and none more so than the chief guest, John Foster himself, who seemed relaxed and undaunted (at 83) by his illustrious and more practised opposition.

Dinner at Monk Fryston Hall - John Nash, Granville Heptonstall, John Foster & Neville Townend

Mr John Nash had done well for himself, having served Yorkshire CC for over forty years. He told us that 1906 was a historic year for cricket! He had been born, and George Hirst got his 2000 runs and 200 wickets. But most of all, John Foster started his record breaking stint. Yorkshire treasurer, Michael Crawford, read a message of congratulations from Freddy Brown, the President of M.C.C.

What especially endeared 'Old John' to me was his quaint old-fashioned way of talking, especially his pronunciation of his O's as in Bill Bowes, (another popular speaker) and bowling. They were pronounced as in Owl and not as in Dole, which really seemed to take him back to the 1800's.

Mr Bailey and his wife from Hillam Hall also attended and I seem to remember a television set was presented.

Granville Heptonstall was Chairman, and the whole evening was a credit to all concerned, especially for the lad, who had been a butcher boy, for Granville's father Tommy, on the day he got married!

Except for the first six months of his life and for three and a half years away in the First World War, bachelor John lived in the same cottage, handily placed for the old 'Chequers' pub and his cronies, and the domino school. His father was a railway man, and at fourteen he left school and joined the others of his family on the largish staff at Monk Fryston Hall, owned by the Rev. Benjamin Hemsworth, as a gardener. Brother Tom was butler and Uncle Raynor lived in the gatehouse.

In the war he trained with the K.O.Y.L.I.s but for some reason was transferred to the Royal Scots Fusiliers. After a spell in the trenches he very wisely became a mess waiter, and finished at Brigade H.Q. in 1919.

The friendship of the humble gardener and the land owning farmer Captain P. C. Thompson, later of Huddlestone Grange, Sherburn, began then, and carried on through many Selby Hospital Cup Competitions in future years.

John was lucky to retain his job on his return, as the staff was vastly reduced. He carried on until the estate was sold in 1946.

Mr. John Levitt who had died only a few weeks before the dinner, aged 94, had the title of Agriculturalist, and managed the running of the Hall, and its many attractions at that time, It was particularly famous for its collection of small birds and animals, and Mr. Levitt made frequent visits to Liverpool Docks to buy new specimens.

Before the First World War, Monk Fryston had a rugby team. The cricket team played down the common until invited into the Hall grounds in 1914.

Hillam and South Milford 1973 - Umpires Ken Walker &Bolt Wilson

Seated- Harry Lunt, John Foster & Granville Heptonstall,

Meanwhile in 1911 our friend played at the opening of the Hillam Hall ground against Mr. Lyon's Invitation X1. Monk Fryston and Hillam joined forces in 1945 and have played at the Hall ever since. John must have handled the delicate details of that very wise move.

John Foster with unknown friends

When I ventured to suggest that my friend David Grace must have been one of Hillam's best cricketers, John politely said that Frank Poole was useful and Granville not bad, and his father and Tommy Atkinson, and Joe Long, and etc..... - I didn't press the matter. I count myself lucky to have been given most of his old photographs, and to have him name and date them with very little hesitation.

Hillam CC 1910

Back - H. Laycock, T. Foster, A. Laycock, D. Ward, H. Furniss, A. Dickinson, T. Heptinstall, I. Atkinson, Chester, W. Long, W. Foster.

Front - R. Pickering, S. Robinson, R. Harrison, J. Foster, J. Long, T. Atkinson.

He died on 17th March 1979 aged 91; with what must be an unbeatable record of seventy years a cricket secretary! His simple headstone is less than a wicket's length from the imposing tomb of his kindly employers for forty gentle years. He would have enjoyed selecting two or three good sides from assembled friends at his funeral. It is said that characters aren't being produced any more. One like Old John will take some beating!

J.D.B.

MONK FRYSTON

(December 1998)

I have always been an admirer of Julie Christie, and it must have started with Dr Zhivago and Far From the Madding Crowd. Two weeks ago (May '98) her latest, 'Afterglow', was reviewed, and amongst the few days of publicity and interviews, she said she had great difficulty finding non-violent scripts that attracted her.

In the story of Monk Fryston, and the jovial squire, and his talented lady at the Hall, I think I have the perfect setting, supporting cast, and a period of great change in village and estate life from about 1890 to 1940 – just fifty years. Julie Christie would have to be the twenty-five year old Constance Mary Duke who married Reverend Benjamin Hemsworth JP on 5th September 1894 at Wilsford, Wiltshire. The reception was at her Grandfather's, Sir Edward Duke Bt's Lake House in Wiltshire, now the residence of Mr Sting and his film-making wife, Trudie.

Monk Fryston Hall

A better paid person than I would have to think of a gentle romance for Julie, as the world, its parishes, people and estates, rolled on through the Boer War, the Great War to end all wars, and ending after World War II with most of the principal characters gone, and the Hall becoming a famous hotel.

Benny and CM

Monk Fryston village has always been special amongst its more humdrum neighbours, with its solid stone houses and its thatched cottage looking over the square. The estate had been in Hemsworth hands since about 1680, and it shows. The earliest Hemelswards had come over with Danish Viking Prince, Thorgill Sprakalg. Much later they had fought in the Royalist army at the sieges of Pontefract, Newark and Sheffield. A spectacular family tree still has pride of place in the hotel, coming to a sudden end, when the Reverend Benjamin Hemsworth, MA, JP, died childless in 1923.

My interest in it all must have started when a retired gardener from the Hall, Mr John Foster, came to help my mother out half a day a week. John gave me his old team photos going back to 1902 and proceeded to name every one on them   including the vicars - mixing with their cricketing flock as they did in those days!! He looks to be captain of the 1910 side, before going away for the only time in his life, (except for the Scarborough Festival) when he joined the Royal Scots Fusiliers in the First World War.

I spent an enjoyable evening taping John back in 1966, with his old clock ticking away in his bachelor's cottage. His two uncles had worked at the Hall, Raynor living in the gatehouse. He also told me how many white alyssum and blue lobelia it took to plant up between the steps and the lake, and also about the huge decision to join up with Hillam, and move to Hillam Hall, where previously only the gentry in their funny caps and striped blazers had played. A few doors up was the 'Chequers' pub, and till its demise, John could be found from nine o'clock onwards, with his cronies, drinking halves and playing dominoes in the smog.

To the left of the road to Hillam is still the Heptonstall farmstead and house, but the buildings are empty, and the stackyard long since developed. Granville (known as Hepp), played a long innings as Chairman to old John's Secretary. He was an outstanding footballer and cricketer, having a county trial, and playing in the Bradford League in his prime. He tells a good tale on tape, one of being called from the hay-field, as a lad, to play against the toffs, and being rewarded with a previously unknown, untried drink called whisky! Hepp's father too was a sporting farmer butcher, and I have a wonderful photo of his slimline wedding day, and others taken over the years, as he became a good advert for Fryston beef, in cup and shield winning sides, as well as in choirs and on various committees.

The nearby Post Office and Stores still tries to compete, but the large chapel on the corner has surrendered, to be made into apartments. Mrs Earless and Old John had a long partnership here, Mrs Earless as organist from the age of fifteen onwards, and Old John for years as treasurer, fire lighter and stoker. She was born a Hemmingway, and her father was a railwayman, who also had a shop and sub-post office, then towards the Milford turn off. She went back to the days of tapping messages down the wire, before telephones, and delivering telegrams to local pea growers. She delivered them to the Hall

too, where Tom Foster, the butler, took them off on a silver tray as she waited for a reply. Julie Christie could make a watchable, gentle film of her life and times too. They sold postcards of the Hall and village, which were taken by a Mr Bramley who had a large old car. Her husband, Clifford, had the first Ford Model T lorry for his coal business. After leaving school, she lived weekly with her Grandfather, John Batty, a bearded old character, and seemed to be cheap labour in his grocer's shop in South Milford. On Bank Holidays the Hall grounds were open to the public. Mr John Levitt was in charge of the famous zoo of small animals and birds. He was born in Canada, and when a boat came in from South America or the Far East, he would go off to Liverpool on the train to buy new specimens.

Another cheerful character was little Harry Laycock who had a garage with petrol pumps at the footpath side. He would go out mending early tractors, and he too would have a part A previous blacksmith was a Mr Jamieson whose grandson, a Mr Oldfield, later helped to catch the Ripper. The best blacksmith around in my time was cheerful umpah umpah player Arthur Warren. As a young soldier from Devon, he camped in the grounds of the hall, whilst officers made merry inside. He met his wife from Birkin at a local dance.

Matt Gill, Harry Laycock & John Foster

But that is all too modern for our story and these are all bit parts in the goings on in village and Hall life. We will take liberties, and from now on call Reverend Benjamin Hemsworth, MA, JP, Benny, and his wife, nee Constance Mary Duke, CM!

Benny had gone to Harrow and Cambridge, took Holy Orders, but never had a parish, although he preached and stood in at church and chapel when needed. He is described as a character from Bunyan's Pilgrim's Progress, who 'did good by stealth'. How he came to meet CM (Julie Christie) is up to the scriptwriters, but her cousin Rashleigh Duke had been vicar for many years at Monk Fryston. As mentioned before, they married in 1894, and she came to Yorkshire to put her stamp on a small part of it.

She started a visitors' book which has come my way with dates, names, but no addresses. Amongst them Benny wrote interesting snippets of the times. ---

1900	Boer War	
1907	Rita Duke started as district nurse	
1916	Rev. W.M.C. Clarke left after 16 years	
Dec 1916	War becoming more intense	
Mar 1st	John Foster	}
13th	Wil Foster	}all left
Aug 1st	Tom Foster, butler,	}to
July 30th	W Goodenough, groom,	}become
April 5th	C Hill	}soldiers
Mar **1917**	We parted company with all indoor servants and started doing the work ourselves	
Mar 6th	Russian Revolution. Czar turned off throne	
April 5th	America came into war	
17th Jan **1918**	Michael Duke (Heir) came to see us - now 2nd Lieutenant	
29th Apr **1919**	Michael Duke m. St James Piccadilly - by Rev. B.H.	
1919	Drove 1400 miles in Blue Horse Caravan	
1920	Bought new motor car - been nearly all round England	
1921	Coal miners out Apr 1st - July 2nd	
15 - 23 June	Angel (CM) painted Bonnie Scotland in 7 days	

Sir Ernest George the architect had stayed and signed in January 1897. He was in charge of major alterations, including the addition of the ballroom, studio and billiard room. Stuck in and dated Jan 31st 1899, is an elegant folded dance card, with a yellow bow, and a photo of the front of the Hall. Inside is a list of dances with a space against each, for the gentlemen to sign as they do in old films.

1. Valse Mon Reve
2. Polka Bagatelle
3. Valse Toreador
4. Valse Blue Danube
5. Lancers Geisha

6. Valse Amour et Printemps
7. Polka Piccadilly Johnny
8. Valse Santiago
9. Lancers Artists Model

And it goes on to twenty altogether, with six more valses. So Julie's leading man would have to be good at valsing! The Ball was probably to celebrate the completion of the alterations. Lyons of London were the caterers 'and the whole affair was a great success' (CM has written in).

CM had two sisters who were both bridesmaids at the wedding. RJ (Rita) had been nursing in London, but was persuaded to come north to be the first district nurse. She lived in the Probendal House near the church. I only knew her companion Miss Strickland, who also had a companion in later years. When the Mouseman from Kilburn eventually replaced the ancient oak door I was amazed to see how the old knocker was nearly worn away over years of hard use.

I know very little about Nurse Duke, but at Church Fenton on February 16th 1975 I had typical beginner's luck with a borrowed BBC tape recorder from Ken Ford. My very first subject was Nurse Metcalfe, and listening to it again I am sure her life could easily be shared with Nurse Duke. For eighty-five pounds a year, she was an early Health Visitor, covering twenty-five villages on her bicycle. She occasionally enjoyed her sandwich lunch sitting on the little bridge halfway through Bishop Wood, surrounded by primroses. In 1900 the trees nearly met across the narrow road, but most were cut down in 1917 for fuel. Born in 1893 she had harrowing memories of nursing in Saloneka, and afterwards visited those who had been gassed in France.

I don't know for sure what Florence M. Duke did. I would like to think she was the photographer of the family, as an album of well taken, mounted, named, dated and numbered (e.g.409, 523) photographs also came my way after the Visitors' Book. Starting in May 1891 to November '94, these pictures give a wonderful insight into the lives and travels of the reasonably well-off. Four named wooden men-of-war are shown tied up at Portland Roads in September '92, which takes the camera back into Nelson's era. Holidays were taken in Holland and Bruges. More interesting is to see Victorian ladies in their long dresses actually lying on the sands at Skipsea, where their cousin Rashleigh was a vicar. There are many photos of Lake House, Wiltshire, and two young men racing round a lawn on bicycles makes me still more appreciative of the dedication of the long gone album owner. The one on the right is C.R.Duke, which puts a face to the artist of some of the one hundred and fifty paintings my father bought at the sale in 1946, and the twenty-five I was more or less given, when Probendal House was emptied and sold later. I assume C.R. Duke was a cousin as was Walter Medlycott another talented painter.

A.M. and C.R. Duke

Paintings by C. R. Duke - The Window in the Ballroom at Monk Fryston Hall and The Alpine Bazaar

Most eligible young ladies of those times would be adept at playing music of some sort, nature study, embroidery, poetry and art. Signing her paintings CMD to 1894, CMH later, after her marriage CM seems to have been gifted at most things especially sketching and watercolours, and various cousins shared her interests. Walter Medlycott Duke had exhibited in London, and had sketched some of the antiques in Lake House before it was burned down in 1906. I have a fine painting of a fireplace signed CMD, and until I was given the photo album with the same labelled 'at Lake House', I had no idea where it was.

Constance Mary Hemsworth (nee Duke)

No one seems to know what the Hall grounds were like before Benny's marriage, but certainly things happened after. I have mentioned the house alterations in 1899. Around 1900 seems to have been the time for the Lucerne Bridge to be erected by local labour, and the lake cleared out to make boating possible. Jeff Garnet, from South Milford, tells me his grandfather was in charge and as a bonus was offered either a bedroom suite or five pounds - he took the money! The bridge still stands, only a short walk through some trees and over two fragile rustic structures. Triangular paintings on wood in the roof sections by CM, of Coleridge's Story of the Shipwrecked Mariner, have weathered well, despite nesting swallows and present day hooligans.

Lakeside, Monk Fryston Hall 1991

Original Lucerne Bridge - Postcard

Lucerne Bridge built in grounds of Monk Fryston Hall

In a quarry to the west 'Bonnie Scotland' was created. The estate joiners erected a wooden hoarding against the face, and mountains were painted on it. In 1921 it is recorded in the Visitors' Book (by Benny I think) that 'Angel repainted Bonnie Scotland in seven days'. More of a mystery 'she also repainted the Swiss Scene (Lake Geneva)' but a clue to that is a water-colour I have, done by CDR, dated 1901, and titled Alpine Bazaar. There are many postcards of groups of ladies in fine hats standing on steps with a bothy nearby, and the mountains behind, all probably as near to Scotland as they would ever get. Heather was imported and sold by a young Walt Hill, and occasionally a pipe band played.

Fragile rustic bridge giving access to Lucerne Bridge

Nearby was an outdoor swimming pool, and farther down the Deer Park Mr Levitt lived, in his cottage adjoining the Alpine Tea Room and the Concert Hall. The tea room walls were hung with scenic paintings all done by CM. Walter Wainwright, a Sherburn butcher, tells of walking to weekly dancing lessons, and collecting other romantic adventurers on the way there.

Nearly five thousand pounds of Hemsworth money went towards major church repairs in 1891 - before CM's time. So in pre television days you would expect a good choir, and there was one. Not only that, there was a competitive choir conducted by school headmaster, Mr Morris, with thirty-six named, stylishly dressed people on a meticulously posed photograph. Sadly in April 1922 he was ill and a Mr Stout took over at the Yorkshire Choral Competitions, when with Benny as manager and CM as Hon. Sec., they won four first prizes, two seconds and two cups. There was also a good-looking Male Voice Singing Group, who raised a thousand pounds for the Comfort Tobacco fund in the war. They had a well-scrubbed look, with uniform of shiny shoes, best suits with medals on watch chains over waistcoats. Bowlers and billycocks were worn by the back row, flat caps are on the floor and the two straw boaters are resting on knees.

A hint of extra-marital romance could be introduced here for CM/Julie if necessary, but with so much going on I feel it might spoil the plot.

Life never seemed dull with tennis parties, Viennese and Gypsy nights, lanterns in the trees and parties invited over from Halifax for their annual treat, their charas parked in the square. Benny had been a curate there for three years and never lost touch.

It wasn't all joy. With all their indoor staff gone in 1917, July 30th 1918 saw a presentation to Pr Chapman (2nd Battalion Scots Guards) near the gate leading on to the terrace, by Reverend Benjamin Hemsworth MA, JP. It was on behalf of the Monk Fryston and Hillam Comforts and Tobacco Fund, in recognition of his having won the Croix de Guerre. There is a photo of the party in the guide book but it all ended too soon. He was killed in action October 12th 1918.

Benny died suddenly May 23rd 1925 aged seventy-four. There are four pages of tributes and obituaries stuck in the back of the Visitors' Book. The printed Order of Service for the funeral three days later at 3 p.m. is also there.

Hymn 165   O God Our Help in Ages Past

Hymn 184   Rock of Ages

Lesson   Corinthians XV, v.20

'The Times' wrote of his life as did the 'Skyrack Express', and in an appreciation thirteen years later CM graciously replied. There is so much more about this wonderful little man.

- his thirty-five years as a JP

- his opening of his quarries to provide stone after the Selby Abbey fire of 1906.

- his fine stables, although not a hunting man and his two sets of four to pull his coach

- his caravan tours

- his first car which CM drove (Bob Hoskins would play him)

Where to end the story is the big decision. CM ended her days in a wheelchair, and a lift was installed near the front door. (I wouldn't have Julie Christie end that way) There are fewer signatures in the Visitors' Book as the thirties came and went and none at all in nineteen thirty-nine. She died in May 1940 and there was no-one left to record her funeral details and tributes. There was no family.

The end of the Hemsworth family and the winding up of the estate may interest someone reading this.

Benny was the eldest of five children.

His only brother died in 1895.

His nephew Michael was heir to the estate but CM named heir for life.

Michael's mother was Benny's sister; his father the Reverend Rashleigh Duke was CM's cousin and had been Monk Fryston vicar 1884 - 95.

Michael died 1928 aged thirty-eight.

His son Peter Jack was only fourteen when CM died - still legally an infant.

His mother Mrs Frost from Hove appointed Trustee and administered the estate.

Peter Jack killed in action aged eighteen.

Benny's sister Mrs Woodhall died without issue.

Benny's youngest sister lived in Norfolk.

Her son killed in air raid 1915.

Had a sister, Dorothy Maude Wormald, second husband a retired Army Major.

Lived in East Dereham.

No desire to live in Yorkshire and decided to sell.

End of two hundred and fifty years of Hemsworths at Monk Fryston.

Sadly, until a few years ago the large Hemsworth tomb was almost overgrown with brambles. What faithful gardener John Foster, lying only yards away, would be thinking I hardly dare contemplate.

All the tenants and interested parties gathered at the 'Londesborough Hotel', Selby at 3p.m. on May 22nd 1946 for the sale. There is a photo of Granville Hepp looking pensive, and a few more. Others named were the Hathorns, George Goodenough, Hugh Batty, George Harrison and the ladies Laycock, Deeble, Smales and Neville. No problem finding names for characters in this story.

I have the catalogue with two coloured maps and photos of the house and grounds. Twelve farms and thirty-eight cottages are listed with the names of the tenants and the rents they paid. Better still, pencilled in by old John Foster are the new owners and prices they paid - they could have been snapped up for between £100 and £875. The Hall and grounds of 74.39 acres were withdrawn at £6750 - but Julie Christie wouldn't be drawn into this.

I conclude with an excerpt from a letter by the late J.L.Carr, the writer and schoolmaster, sent to his brother Ray in 1982. 'Excuse the paper. I tore it from the back of a History of England I brought to read. Well actually it is quite interesting, because I bought a set of five at Monk Fryston Hall sale in 1939 or 40, dragging them home by bus, and as they were published in 1757, that makes this notepaper quite elderly. It was a very hot day I remember. – Strange how one recalls the weather of fifty years ago, and forgets it a month ago'.

– I know the feeling!   J.D.B.

Haymaking Gang c.1900
Too many names! Team selected from: J Levitt, T Foster, A Ransome, J Lang, F Thornley, George Goodenough, Mr Foster's father,
R Furniss, J Beckitt, A Bradley, R Foster, G Crossland, F Kirkman, R Longbottom, H Foster, J Hall

Painting of Lake House by C.M.D - Pre 1894

Lake House, Wiltshire - Home of Sting

THE LIFE OF ARTHUR (WARREN)

(Interviewed 25th January 1991)

To-night is January 25th 1991 and it's day nine of the Gulf War. I am going on a taping expedition, one of the first I've done for a long time, to Mr Arthur Warren who used to be our blacksmith at Monk Fryston. Quite a character and I'd nearly forgotten about him until I met him in the old boys' school at Sherburn last summer with his euphonium, just going into a band practice when I was taking a lady round who is writing a book. I took a photo of him with his weapon and sent him it for Christmas. I've had a few chats with him and he's got a lot of stuff to tell me in a marvellous Devon accent. I saw an article in the Selby Times when it was his wedding anniversary and he evidently came to Yorkshire in the war. He was billeted in Monk Fryston Hall and met this girl from Birkin, married her and lived in the forge house, which was owned by Mr Alfred Watson, I think. He was his landlord and not the flavour of the month to Arthur. I knew he liked music because he was always singing as he worked and I'd seen him a few times at Castleford when he was working for the supporters club. He has a lot to tell me and I'm going there now.

Arthur Warren outside Sherburn School - 11th July 1990

I was born at a little village called Scoriton, which is approximately three miles from the nearest small town of Buckfastleigh. My father was a labourer but the smithing side is on my mother's side.

(What was his father?)

His father was a labourer, but on my mother's side it goes back generations. I'm the fifth and the last, the only one that carried on the trade in the Pearce family. My mother was a Pearce. As I say, I was born at Scoriton and then my father moved to a little cottage. We're going back to traction engine times now, and a traction engine set fire to the

house and burnt the bloody lot down. It had a thatched roof. We then moved to a thirteenth century house next to the church called Stairs Nest, which has a lot of history to it. That's the village that I know most about, Holne, where the smithy is and everything. My mother was the second of all the family. There were seven brothers and two sisters. My mother lost her mother after the other seven children were born. She brought them up, the boys and the younger girl.

All the brothers in their turn, as they grew old enough to work went to the smithy. What I want you to appreciate here Don is this, they all went to the smithy, every one of them but when a next one came on there wasn't enough work for them so they had to move on and get a job. They went all over. They had relations in Canada and they went all over because they just had to get a job. One, my Uncle Jack who I always said was the best smith of the lot; he ended up as the head locksmith of Dartmoor prison. He went into the prison service as a blacksmith and ended up the head locksmith. In the end, he got out of the prison service... you're not old enough to remember and I can only just remember, I think it was nineteen twenty-six or seven when they had a bad mutiny. My Uncle Jack got hit over the head with a few nails in a bag, a weapon, and from that day he never went back to Princeton. He hated the place. Have you ever been?

(No, I've never been near the place.)

You've never been to the prison? It's a lovely place but dreadful really. In those days - I'm going back a bit now - there was no such thing as tourism. Princeton was isolated and they got all the scum of the earth.

My Uncle Harry was the youngest. He can shoe. He used to shoe his own pony and his wife's pony but he went into the post office. My Uncle Fred carried on the business from my Grandfather finishing. Now then, I've got to bring this in because it's been part of my life. Both sides of the family were musical. My grandfather played the base fiddle in the chapel orchestra before they had an organ. One thing that has hurt me all my life is that the bass fiddle was hung in a mail bag and my Uncle Harry, the postmaster had that bloody bass and I always said it should have come to me. Somebody came in and bought it. My mother was musical, a singer not an instrumentalist. They were all singers, all the lot of them. They weren't a celebrated family but my Uncle Fred, as was my grandfather before him, was very bad tempered. They were very, very bad tempered people. Why I don't know, whether it was bred into them or what. Well going back to me being a bit of a lad, I don't know whether you've ever done it but we used to get little pieces of mirror and reflect the sun. Anyway there were a few of the lads sat on the school wall and my Uncle Fred was shoeing a horse and they were flashing the light onto the wall of the shoeing shed. Well he came down and walloped me. That's how ill tempered he was.

Anyway, when I finished school at fourteen of course I was told to go to my Uncle Fred. So I went and if any poor b... had a dog's life, I did because he moved with the times, as I did up to a point. The first things he got were two petrol pumps. - Oh but I'm over-jumping my tale.

When we lived at Stairs Nest my father was the sexton of the church and we were absolutely brought up church. Where were you if you weren't in church my father wanted to know. All the flipping lot were always in the choir, even as children. Well something happened. We had a lot of rain and under the house we lived in all of a sudden a spring came through the floor and we got flooded out. Anyway the house next door to my Uncle Fred - there were three houses, the post office, the house in the middle that we eventually had, and Fred lived at the far end. So it was a line of Pearce's and Warren's.

As soon as I started there with my Uncle Fred my job was to turn the flipping handle and pump the petrol. We had a tin box to keep the money in and tourism was beginning a bit then. If anybody stopped for petrol it was, 'Art, petrol.' Between our houses there was a lean-to with a corrugated dividing sheet, and he kept a stick there. If anybody blew for petrol, it didn't matter if it were bloody twelve o'clock or the middle of the night, Fred didn't go for petrol. He used to run this bloody stick across the corrugations and Arthur used to go and serve the petrol.

The man himself was a sheer genius. He was a wonderful blacksmith, a wonderful blacksmith. He kept up with the times, but obviously... We'd got to the acetylene welding stage when I went, but the man himself was a clever man. He made money because he was a clever man. Then he got a car and ran a taxi business and all things like that. But mean, he never gave me anything. I've said so in the pub and I'll say so again, and it can go on there, all the time I worked for him I had to be in t'blacksmith's shop, the shoeing shed swept up. You'll not remember what t'shoeing shed is - the shoeing shed was always where you shod and it all had to be swept up and the fire lit. You can imagine a young boy trying to light a blacksmith's fire 'cause there's no grates or anything. All that had to be done. He'd come out to me and he'd throw me a shilling. Now for that shilling I'd run well over a quarter of a mile to fetch him twenty Players. Every morning he'd just throw me this shilling and I knew what it was for and I went up to t'shop and back again. From me starting to me finishing, in those days twenty Players were elevenpence ha'penny, not a shilling - ten for sixpence and twenty for elevenpence ha'penny, and he never gave me the bloody ha'penny all the time I was there. He always took it off me.

Anyway him and his wife used to fall out and I used to be in between them. They'd go for months and months and wouldn't speak - just absolutely bad tempered! A good tradesman but very bad tempered. I can quote you one day... you'll not remember the old cultivators, we used to lay 'em and draw the teeth out. Of course being the lad I had to strike. I wasn't the blacksmith, he was. Well his wife was stood over there and I had to blow the fire remember with the bellows. You'll probably not even remember them.

(Oh yes, you'll have to tell me all about that.)

You pumped the bellows up, got the welding heat up, then you'd to dash round t'anvil, pick your hammer up because by then the anvil was ready for hitting. Anyway, I'm there hitting, and the blacksmith always tapped alternately to keep you in time y'see and to tell you where he wanted t'next hit. Anyway some'at got wrong and I'm bringing me hammer up and he's bringing his hammer down and I knocked t'hammer out of his hand. His wife was standing there and she laughed and he went and picked t'hammer up and he threw it straight at her - as evil as that! To the day he died he never gave me anything.

(So the blacksmithing, was it an arable area?)

Well not arable as you know it Don because you're among the hills you see.

(Harrows and ploughs and things?)

No, very few harrows. Ploughs yes. Down there I can remember we used to put iron on the bottom. They used to have a little tub and they'd plough starting at the top, and the rain would wash the soil down and every year they used to shovel all the bottom soil up into this little tub and pull it to the top, and start again.

There was a lot of cattle and a lot of riding horses. Fred Pearce was the only blacksmith around so we had a hell of a shoeing trade. A dozen horses a day was nought. There were two big estates joining the village with timber horses. You'll not remember timber horses will you?

(No)

They never walked you know Don. As soon as they took the strain off them they cantered. Timber horses were a sort of breed of their own.

(What was the idea of that then?)

Keep the weight going. The first horseshoe I ever took off, I'd just started, a lad of fourteen. It was a timber horse and it stood seventeen hands at least, it was massive. 'Take them shoes off.' Well the first thing you have is a buffer and a hammer to cut the clenches to get the shoes off. I'd watched them; I'd been brought up with the bloody job but never done it. You can imagine a boy of fourteen picking a bloody great foot up like that. Anyway I got 'em off in the end, and I can tell you the date I made my first horseshoe and that was the twenty-third of April, Empire Day, nineteen thirty-four. That's a long time ago.

We were very rural, oil lamps in those days. There was no electricity or anything like that, and if you worked late you used to stick a candle on t'end of t'anvil. That was t'only bit of light if you were smithing. Everything was hard work. If you drilled a hole you had a damn great drill with a big wheel at the top. There was only me to turn it, he never turned it.

(Was he a big fellow?)

No, a little fellow, a little wiry fellow. Never want to be big. I was t'wrong build. Anything to get under horses you want to be small.

There was only one horse down at Diddlecombe and this one was a bad one. I used to go down and fetch it, I don't know why, and I had to ride it back. Well I was never a rider and I had to give that bloody thing as much stick as I could up the hill to quieten it.

Going on a few months, one of the big houses at the other side of Scoriton bought the stables for a race horse stables. Of course, Fred down again, and me. We used to walk, he hadn't a car then, and they had a racehorse there, I'll never forget it. It was a black stallion called Jack Ketch, and if you dropped a nail you had to get out of the box because you couldn't go in any more. I used to be there to hand the nails, and he was terrified was Fred. The man himself was a genius. I've seen somebody come in for a bowler - we call 'em hoops - we used to make them out of quarter round and the man could just bend a round on the anvil with no aids at all, put the two ends in the fire and weld them and it would be round. Oh, the man was a genius.

(How much shoeing did you do when you came to Monk Fryston?)

Some, but I never intended to because I hated the job and hate it now.

(Do you do a bit now?)

No. I did Stanley's horse a time or two after I'd finished but that was all. Me starting shoeing was caused by ... do you remember Tom Hawley who was the blacksmith at Monk Fryston? Well we were sort of in competition. He either finished or died; I'm not sure which. Anyway Teddy Stoker and Edwin, they came into t'shop. 'What are we going to do about this shoeing job?' I said, 'Well I'm not bloody shoeing, 'cause I'd no tackle. I took Monk Fryston forge, not for a blacksmith's. I didn't take that for a blacksmith's shop at all. I took it to get a decent bloody house if you could call it a decent house.

Previous to the war I'd chance to buy a motorbike. It was fifty bob, that's two pounds fifty as it is today. It was an old Sunbeam and of course you had to tax and insure it and I could get it all for five pound. Anyway what had happened, Major Cook-Herald had hired a farm foreman who was a territorial Sergeant- Major. Of course he started work on us lads then. Some of them went in. There were six of us altogether...

(What year's this?)

We're talking about nineteen thirty-eight now. I'd chance of this motorbike as I say and I thought now then if I join t'Territorials — you got five pounds for signing on - so I thought I'd sign on and buy this 'ere motorbike you see. So I goes to Newton Abbott, and he takes me. This is in May nineteen thirty-eight. Then I buys my motorbike and I could go anywhere then. Up to that it was a bike and I only ever owned one bike....but we're jumping the gun. Let me come back again. Before that, going to school; my Uncle Harry who had the Post Office always wanted somebody to run telegrams. Telegrams in them days were big things. They're nothing now, they just ring 'em through, but there were a lot of outlying farms all around and I used to run t'telegrams. Anyway he used to come to t'school did Harry. He'd knock at school, 'Can Art run a telegram?' and they used to let me go and I used to get sixpence or a shilling. Well a shilling were a hell of a lot of money and the furthest one were three and a half miles. It was right over on the moor and we used to walk 'em you know. I hadn't a bike then. My brother had a bike but I hadn't, and I used to walk and it were all hills. Anyway, I'll tell you a little witty story; it's true but it's awful. I got a job previous to leaving school working in a garden for a lady called Miss Scott. Her father had been an eminent QC but I think they were just a bit down on their uppers and they moved out of Home Chase, a beautiful house, and went into another house. Anyway I used to work for her four hours on a Saturday morning from eight while twelve. Well at quarter to twelve Harry comes up. 'Telegram Art.' I said, 'You'd better go see Miss Scott.' So he goes to see her. 'Yes he can go.' Anyway I goes to Miss Scott for me wages, one and fourpence, that's all, and the lousy old Dutch she knocked a penny off for a quarter of an hour and I never stopped working. Yon old lass used to watch me from eight o'clock in a morning 'til I finished at twelve - never got a drink or anything like that. Nobody had any money. People don't appreciate what it was like. My father always had regular wages, a good job me father had, but there was never nothing to spare. There was a lady at Buckfast Abbey, a very very wealthy lady. Her name was Hamlin and her life was Dartmoor ponies. She used to show these ponies and Fred always shod 'em, but if he didn't shoe them he was always her right hand man. She thought the bloody world of him. Well we used to have to go wherever there was a show. We used to walk into Buckfast, get these ponies, walk to Buckfastleigh station which is another mile and a half at least and get these ponies on the railway. Fred was leading them and I'm behind 'em. Fred got ten bob but I never got a bloody ha'penny! That was a seven-mile walk and twice to the station and I never got anything. He wouldn't give me anything. The lousy rotten dog, he once went to a sale and he bought an old horse tedder and a two-furrow plough, which was useless where we lived. One of the first jobs he said, 'We'll go fifty-fifty on this Art, you do 'em and I'll give you half of t'profits.' Well the first thing I had to do was to cut one furrow off, and t'hacksaws in them days weren't like the hacksaws you get today, and I'd both beams to saw off. I messed about and painted 'em and did 'em all up. This tedder I did it all up, t'best way I could. I was no genius. Anyway when they were painted up he sold the bloody things to the Co-op. They'd bought a farm and he selled both to them but I never saw a bloody ha'penny. That's how mean he was! And all during the war when I came home … the meanest thing was, I always kept my motorbike there… after that I got a better motorbike and he even kicked my motorbike out. He wouldn't let it stop in one of t'sheds.

(Did he fall out with you then?)

He fell out with me father and mother. Me mother was a wonderful person, but me father, if ought upset him, well get out of the way quick! I can remember going home once as a little lad. We'd been playing. You know the oil they used to put on hooves, well two of us had been playing in t'shed. Fred wasn't there and I'd got some of this oil on me leg. Well I went home with it on and me father said, 'What's that?' I said, 'It's from t'blacksmith's shop.' He just went mad and he chased me with his belt - the bloody belt's still hung up in there now. It was the one he had in the First World War. Of course me mother always saved me.

Me father always started work early. He worked at a reservoir and me brother's job was always to get kindling - there was no gas stove or nothing - you just lit the fire and boiled the kettle on the fire. Anyway me brother had got wet sticks and they wouldn't burn so me father picks up the kettle and he kicks the bloody thing up the chimney. It was an open chimney with a chimney crook where you hung the kettle and he just picked the bloody kettle up and kicks it up the chimney. That's how bad tempered he was.

Me father and me brother were quite go-ahead and they decided they'd buy a wireless - this is a wireless think on. The one they bought was a Fellows and it had a trumpet like a gramophone that came down to a stand, and me father always loved to hear the clock striking in Paris. Well me brother's there with t'wireless trying to tune it in, me father's leaned over t'table with his ear against this horn, the trumpet, and me sister goes and puts her ear against me dad's bum. Course, what did I do? I laughed and I got a walloping for that. But me mother always saved me. Oh, he was a bad-tempered sod, but a good man. He never drank or anything like that and loved to go to church.

(How many did you get in church in those days?)

Oh, a full church. Me brother was a singer and me sister should have been a professional singer. She died in thirty-eight of meningitis. Me brother and sisters used to go round all t'churches. They used to sing these oratorios and Messiah's and all that. I wasn't old enough then you see 'cause I'm the baby, the youngest.

Me brother was good but he always took the Mick out of me because I was the baby. Well, he's coming home from work one day and there's a car broken down quite a way away. Anyway me brother says, 'Can I help you?' He had a motor bike then. 'Oh, no,' he says, ' it's alright. We've sent for the mechanic from the garage.' Of course I'm coming down the bloody road on somebody's bike. He says, 'Go down and look at that car.' I didn't know what was needed. Me brother shouts, 'Where are you going?' I says, 'I'm going down to look at this car.' And the lousy dog always told that tale, 'There was Art going down and he hadn't even a pair of bloody pliers.' But me brother was twelve years older than me. There were two girls in between and then me, so because I was the baby I was always sort of spoilt. Then when I was twelve me father worked at t'waterworks and it was Paignton waterworks up on the moor, the reservoir there. Me father looked after t'filters. Anyway someone had come up from Paignton from the council. 'There's an organ for sale.' Anyway he comes home and says, 'Do you want to learn t'organ Art?' I says, 'Aye.' So we gets this organ. It was an old American organ wi' t'pedals - no electric you know. We hadn't any electric then which would be nineteen thirty-two. Anyway we gets this organ. T'council lorry brings it and we gets it in. I had to practise every night wi' t'lamp, but the lady that taught me was the church organist, a lady called Mrs Sanders. But where she lived was, I would say, at least two and a half miles away and Sanders was the big timber man and she lived down agin' the big house, and I had a mile of wood to go through. Now can you appreciate a little lad of twelve-year-old in the middle of winter walking through this wood? I used to go straight from school, walk down and then she would give me a bit of tea. I can remember that. Then I used to take me lesson and play me piece, and then I had to walk home with the bit of music I had. You can appreciate a little lad walking through the wood. There were owls and I used to be terrified. Eventually I used to borrow somebody's bike but I still was frightened.

(Did you enjoy learning it?)

Oh, I loved it. I've never in all my musical career been good, never, but I've always loved music and I love it still. That was the start of my sort of musical career. I got on quite well actually. I used to play the church organ for children's services and anything to do with school. But the trouble was I always had - there were two of us.

There was another girl …. I was quite bright at school. Maybe I shouldn't boast about it but I was nearly always the top in exams. There was a girl there called Angela Honeywell. I could always beat her in exams but never at music. She never played the organ though. Well, to the war - you'll remember that on the 1st September general mobilisation was declared. That was before the war started. Anyway we all had a uniform of sorts, some had one and others had t'other because the scare had started in '39. Well, I rings the Drill Hall up …. Drill Hall's at Newton Abbott you see … 'You don't want me tonight do you?' 'No, you can come tomorrow morning, we don't want you tonight.' So me and another pal I was with, we decided we'd go round to t'pub and we might get a drink or two for nowt. I was nineteen then, still not a lot of money, but nobody had a lot of money then. Anyway we goes round to the local, a pub called 'The Church House Inn', a very old pub with a lot of history, and a bloody fifteen hundredweight pulls up outside. 'Where's Arthur Warren and a lad called MacTavish who worked at t'pub? In here, get your kit. You've to report immediately, we've come for you.' Course I had to go home and say goodbye but we didn't know where the hell we were going. Anyway that night, 1st September 1939, they didn't know where to put us and we finished up sleeping in a ballroom above a café in Newton Abbott. Before that I'd done a Territorial camp, but I'm jumping my tale again... One day I went to Buckfastleigh Carnival. They had a brass band and that day they were playing Colonel Bogey and I said, 'That's for me.' That was on the Saturday and by the Monday night I was in Buckfastleigh Band. My brother lived there then and that was the start of my band career. I can remember they gave me an old brass cornet, no case, and I took that home and practised. I had a good start because I could read all the music.

Well, to get back to when I was called up, when I went to t'Territorial camp, that was in the July. We went for a fortnight on Salisbury Plain. We were in the Royal Devonshire Yeomanry, which was a Territorial Unit. This Sergeant Major had been onto the other battery, which was in Exeter. 'I've got a cornet player here. Do you want him in t'band?' 'Yes, by god, aye we do want him in t'band.' So as soon as we got to Tilshead on Salisbury Plain I had to report to the bandmaster. I went there and rehearsed with them and played in the Officers' Mess. I didn't have a uniform or anything except a pair of trousers that fitted me. We played for t'men marching and that kind of thing, and that was the first rollicking I ever got in the army. The last day at Salisbury Plain, I'd been playing the night before and we were excused duties so we just used to get up and saunter down to t'band practice. Bloody Sergeant Major, well he was a Sergeant then, Truscott they called him, an engine driver by trade, looks in t'tent and I'm laid in bed. 'What are you doing in here?' I said, 'I'm excused duties Sergeant Truscott. As you know I'm with t'band.' 'Out!' and did he rollick me, and that was the first rollicking I ever got in the army and I never played in that band again because then war started. The first night they put us up in Newton Abbott and here was the first dirty trick. You can imagine it, there were about three hundred of us all crammed in and there was no way you could get out. If you had a blanket you just laid on the floor. Anyway somebody wanted to wee so he weed in his cup, and I'll never forget it, he just slung it and everybody got some! That was my first experience of army life. We were there at Newton Abbott for three weeks - nobody wanted us or knew what to do with us. In the end they sent us down under canvas near Plymouth and we were doing stevedores' work, loading stuff onto ships. The regulars were going to France and we were doing all the loading work. We were there right through the winter. We were under canvas on snow. Nobody really wanted the Territorials. After that we got posted to Tavistock, which is right on the moor. We'd to sleep on the floor. I never had a bed until I got to Crawley in nineteen forty some. We used to have what was called a palliasse and fill it up with straw wherever you went. I got diphtheria there and nearly died. I was very ill. I was in hospital for seven months then I got a month's sick leave and twenty-six pounds to come home on sick leave. I'll never forget it. I'd never had as much money in my life. I reported back to Horsham and we were going to France. I was still poorly, I couldn't walk properly but I'd to go back because my month was up. We were there waiting to go to France, just doing drill. Dunkirk started so what did they do with the Yeomanry then? We'd absolutely nothing, everything had gone to France. What did they do? They sent us to Eastbourne and put us on coastal defence. We hadn't a gun, if I said there were eight rifles between us I'd be exaggerating, and all we did was fill sand bags and make roadblocks. We stood to every night; we never took our clothes off. We were there right through the Battle of Britain. I have a picture taken at that time of me beside the first Messerschmitt that was shot down in one piece somewhere on the marshes. We were there all summer, bombed and strafed.

THIRTEEN was the unlucky number of this Messerschmitt 109 fighter, brought down near a South-east coastal town on Monday. By the marking on the tail it will be seen that the German claims four successes.

We'd bloody Gerry coming over and coming back and we got a right pasting. After that we were sent to Yorkshire for a rest. We didn't know where we were going because everything was done in secret. We were just told to get packed and off we went. We got on the train but hadn't a clue where we were heading for. Anyway the next day we lands up, we didn't know we were in Yorkshire. 'Everybody off!' You know what t'military's like. Off you got like bloody sheep and into these vehicles, which were waiting to take us away. Anyway, looking out of the back we were going through this town and we see these bloody black men. We'd never seen anything like it before and we got off at Askern and the shift was just finishing work. The pit-head baths were just in their infancy then so they went home to wash. We still didn't know where we were until we arrived at Monk Fryston. We moved into Monk Fryston Hall on 6th November 1940, everybody into the Hall and you slept wherever there was room on the floor. After a while they started to build some huts down in the park for us so that the officers could have the Hall. The Sergeants' Mess was in the old vicarage. These huts were like Nissen huts - they were in sections and bolted together and every bloody section leaked and they could never stop 'em leaking. Nineteen forty was a very cold winter and it was the only time in my life I've worn long johns. Think on we were southerners coming up here to that lot. It was dreadful - cold and snow.

When we were on coastal defence at Eastbourne they'd sent us four guns across from France. They were on wooden wheels French twenty-five millimetre and that was the only thing we had to stop Gerry. Nobody knew anything about them, then they sent us some ammunition so one Sunday morning we'd have a shoot, out to sea of course. They got all these guns lined up, I wasn't involved, I don't know what I was doing. Sergeant Wood laid this gun the best way he could - he'd no idea really and nobody else did. The first round they fired they blew up the bloody Duke of Cornwall's Light Infantry hut. They were in a holiday camp type of place and they blew the bloody hut up. Of course he got stripped. Well, when we moved up here we brought the bloody guns with us. Nobody really appreciated what a state we were in and everybody was in the same state. We had nothing, we bluffed our way through. If Gerry had landed at Eastbourne there was nothing to stop him except the bloody sandbags that we'd filled.

When we were stationed here at Monk Fryston, I met Lil here in t'early days, well then one day we were on parade and they shouts out, 'Anyone here with tradesman's experience?' So of course bloody silly Arthur steps forward and he says, 'What can you do Warren?' I says, 'I'm a blacksmith sir.' 'Report to battery office.' So I had to go the office and I filled a form in saying I was an unfinished apprentice. I never thought any more about it and carried on with my soldiering. I'll tell you my Grassington story now. One Sunday in the winter we went to Grassington to fire these guns again. They went by road and we went by rail from Knottingley station. The chapel's still there, I saw it not last year but the year before. They filled the chapel up with us; we'd no heating, no nothing. We arrived on the Sunday and it snowed that night. The Monday morning we started shovelling snow and we shovelled snow for a week. It took us that long to dig through to the firing range. We slept on the bloody snow that night, fired a few rounds the next day then dug ourselves out again. I'll never forget that, it was a very bad winter.

We used to stand on sentry post though why they needed a sentry at the back entrance I've no idea. Hobson the policeman was very good to us. When he came into the police house late at night he'd make us a cup of cocoa and it used to warm us up. They were hard times! Lil, whom I'd met when I was at a dance at Birkin, used to bring me some meat sandwiches. Three of us married girls up here. There was an article in the Selby Times about us a few weeks ago because it's fifty years since we came to Fryston. In the May we left here again. As usual we didn't know where we were going, but this time we went by road to St. Albans still with these bloody guns. We were on intensive training there. We got some more guns and even though we were field artillery they sent us to St Osyth, near to Clacton on coastal defence again. We were on parade one day and they shouts, 'Gunner Warren fall out and report to t'battery office.' So off goes Arthur boy to t'battery office not knowing what was what. Anyway I gets there. 'Pack your kit Warren. Here's your warrant. You're to report to Luton. You're going on a strikers course. If you pass this course you'll go into the Ordinance. If you fail you'll be coming back here. So I got all my kit, you only had a kit bag for all your stuff. I had a trumpet and I always seemed to be hugging it around. Anyway I gets there to Luton and found I was in private billets, in a house. The course was in a factory with an old blacksmith. Oh, I had six weeks of heaven because I didn't need a bloody striker course; it was born in me so I was there with the lads showing them how to go on. I passed straight away so then I gets posted to a place in Surrey waiting for distribution and from there I was sent to Crawley. That was a big civilian and military workshop. I got there, a wonderful place it was, and realised I didn't want to be a striker. I grabbed a CO and said, 'I want to re-muster. I'm not a striker, I'm a blacksmith.' 'Well, there's only one way we can tell. You'll have to have a trade test.' Well I can tell you what I made now; I made a step for a bloody trap. That was my third class trade test and I made this step, I was reasonably good then so I passed with flying colours. Then I was smithing with civilians and we were doing all sorts - tanks, vehicles, you name it. I felt I was wasting my time and needed to move on. Welding was the thing. My Uncle Fred had done a bit of welding and I'd a slight knowledge but not a lot so I thought, 'Now then Arthur boy you've got to be learning here.' So of course you had quite a lot of freedom so I started welding and did some studying and goes to see the CO. 'What do you want?' 'I want to re-muster sir. I want to be a welder.' He said, 'There is no such trade as a welder. You can be a blacksmith welder if you want but you'll have to pass a trade test.' Now, think on, I'd done a lot of welding. The man that gave me that trade test, well - you remember Harry Ferguson, the tractor man, well he was a genius. This staff sergeant that gave me the test had been a friend and worked with Ferguson. Well, do you know what he gave me to weld? Two pieces of one-inch plate to weld with acetylene. That was my trade test. Anyway I passed that test and from that day on I never looked back because I was always forward going and at just over twenty-one I was a full Sergeant in charge of this blacksmith's shop, the civilians as well.

Previous to that, I was always musical, even at Monk Fryston. I bought a trumpet and we formed a little band here and when we played in the big rooms there in the Hall we used to clear the decks and have a dance for the village.

(Do you remember the drawings on the wall?)

No I'm sorry I can't recall 'em. Well, back to Crawley, we had what was called a Regimental Officer and he worshipped me, I don't know why but he always liked me. He says, 'Sergeant Warren we have a dance coming up. How are we going to get some music.' So I says, 'We'll form a bloody band sir.' Anyway we had a pianist who played by ear. He couldn't follow music but he was brilliant. We formed a band and after that I couldn't do any wrong. I could have as many weekend passes as I liked as long as I was back for Sunday night to play for the dance. It was held in a little canteen and everything went right until the draft came from India and off Arthur went. I suppose I had a very lucky war but only because I made myself useful. I've always been willing to tackle any job and that's how I got on. Even after I left smithing and went to the workshops at Allerton Bywater I was well thought of.

Well I got to India on the way to Burma. We landed at Bombay in the middle of the night after a six-week journey. We got off and onto a train and finished up at a place called Kankinara, right out of Bombay, semi-jungle. We got there at night and were told we'd to form a guard. 'Go on then, I'll be guard commander,' says I. So I gets enough men to mount a guard and it's one of the most harrowing experiences of my life. I'd no need to stand guard but I was in charge. Everybody was frightened - it was jungle and we'd just come out from England. We'd just got our khakis, knees were white. When you got out there the old soldiers looked at t'knees, if they were brown they knew you'd been out for a bit. One lad would not go out, it wasn't the enemy we were frightened of, just the animals, snakes and things. One time we were sitting in a little picture place they'd rigged up for us - most of them were Indian films - and a bloody snake went across t'stage in front of t'screen. Oh, aye, it was jungle country. Gracie Fields came there and entertained us and I'll never forget it. She was lovely. They didn't know where to send us and I got posted to a place called Kallian, seventeen miles out of Calcutta. That meant getting on a train by myself back down to Bombay, four days and four nights on the same train with the same engine and wooden seats. That was some journey. It was crowded and they were all lousy. As soon as the seat got warm the lice used to come and bite your bloody legs - we wore shorts of course. Anyway we were on this train, we stopped every so often to eat, and I lands up at these Indian workshops in an old jute mill on the banks of the Hooghly, which is a part of the Ganges, doing engines up. I wasn't an engine man but I just dropped in and got on well.

Sergeant Warren and indian friend

The Colonel, a Colonel Foreman, a very fine man, says, 'How long have you been a Sergeant, Sergeant Warren?' 'Three years Sir.' 'Well you're a WO1 as from tomorrow morning.' That was as high as I could get. I gets on with this engine job. The workers were all Indians, we were just supervising. I geed them up and got the production up and up and did very well and I was there until my de-mob number came up. The war had finished and I'd seen very little of it. When the time came to come home I couldn't get into Bombay because the riots were on, the Indian Mutiny. I got a phone call, 'Do you want to fly home?' 'Aye,' I said, 'anything to get home.' I had to report to Calcutta. I was told I had to go to Poona so I had to get on a train and that's no mean journey! Gets there and was told, 'You're homeward bound. There's a plane in the morning. When it came it was an old Dakota. It took us up to Karachi, which was a big airport. We'd to stay there for the night and leave the following morning. That plane was a York, it was the same as a Lancaster bomber but the inside had been taken out and seats put in for troops. The first drop down was Shriber and as we landed one of t'bloody engines packed up as we were landing so we had to stop there for a week until somebody flew an engine out from England and put it into this plane. By it was hot. We then dropped down into Lidda in Palestine for a week. That was to cool you down, to acclimatise you after the tropics. We got there just as the oranges were ready. I've never seen anything like it. There were oranges, lemons and bananas. We'd a lovely week there. We were then picked up by another plane, an American Liberator, to fly home with refuelling stops.

We were sitting in the bloody bomb bay, no heating think on, nothing like that. We dropped down into Tripoli and we stayed there for a night. Well I used a cutthroat razor. You couldn't get razor blades and my father had given me a cutthroat razor and I used it right through the war and I left my razor strap in Tripoli. We were off the next morning and we stopped at Marseilles to refuel then we landed at night somewhere around Cambridge. They took us from there to Northampton, which was a demobilisation centre. We got there at night; I don't know where we slept. Next morning we went round this big place and we got our demobilisation. It was the 28th February 1946. You were allowed to keep your uniform but you'd to give your great coat in. You could have done with it coming out of the tropics. We lived at Beal then. T'wife had got a little cottage. We'd married before I went in 1941. I got to Doncaster all right but getting to Beal was another matter. I got off at the Horse and Jockey and had to wait for a bus. I was frozen. In those days the essential works order was still on so you couldn't work where you wanted you had to work where you were sent. Anyway after a month you had to report to the labour exchange to be told where you'd to go to work. Anyway I gets there and was told I'd be starting work at John Harker's shipyard at Knottingley on Monday morning as a welder. Course I'd done all sorts of welding but not like it was at t'shipyard. I didn't realise such welding existed but I'd to get stuck in or I'd be on my way. That was where I got all my positional welding but what a horrible job in winter. There was no protective clothing, nothing. We just wore a boiler suit, which you had to buy yourself. We used to go in t'tanks, icy cold and we'd to weld all positions and that's where I got all my basics at welding. Learning to do positional welding, that's everything except ordinary welding, that is vertical and overhead it gets very tricky. Those days have gone; it's much simpler now. I didn't like the job. It was a rough job. We used to get old barges in and you'd be lying on your back trying to weld and there'd be tar dropping on you. I decided I wanted to be out of there. Anyway I knew there was a job with Steven Toulson so I decided to go to see him because it was only at the top of t'hill from Beal. Jack was the boss at the workshop. He said, 'I'll start you lad, but not until you've shown me what you can do.' He says, 'Can you gas weld?' 'Aye,' I says, 'I can gas weld.' 'Well let's see you do some.' They had an old American Ford lorry there with a split in t'wagon. He said, 'Weld me that up. Let's see what you can do lad.' Anyway I welded it up. It was a doddle.' 'Oh,' he said, 'you can start.' I said, 'I can't start Mr Toulson, I'm sorry. I'm at t'shipyard.' You couldn't get release you see. On the 1st January the essential works order came off and I put my notice in at t'shipyard and I finished on the 7th. I started at Toulson's in 1947 and I'd been there only about a fortnight when we got all that snow. It took two hours to walk from Beal to work because I had to walk backwards but you had to go because nobody had any money so you had to work no matter what. When I came out of the army after six-and-a-half years service I only got ninety-three bloody pounds. While I was in the army I'd been getting twenty-six shillings a day, which is a hell of a wage, I've still got my pay books. I was at Toulson's three-and-a-half years. It was a wonderful job. They liked their pound of flesh but they were good people and your money was always there and everything was right. Ben Collins from Hillam used to work there and he knew John Willy Watson. He said, 'There's a house going at Monk Fryston, t'blacksmith's shop.' He says one morning when we were working. 'Does tha want it? I can put a good word in for you.' Anyway I comes home to talk to Lil. We were living in a one up, one down at Beal with a ladder as a staircase and no water except a pump outside.

Blacksmith Warren

(Had you any family then?)

Aye, we had David. We paid half a crown a week. So me and Lil went on t'bikes to look at this house and we decided we'd have it. We contacted John Willy Watson and he came to see us at Beal from Tadcaster. He said, 'Will you carry on the blacksmithing young man?' I said, 'I will if you want me to,' but we took it for the house not the blacksmith's shop. That's how we got to Monk Fryston. Dick May had a sale of blacksmith's tools and John Willy Watson said, 'If you want any money Mr Warren just see me and I'll lend you some money,' and he lent us a hundred pounds and I paid him four percent on that money but it got me started. John Willy took to us and the first thing he said was, 'You can't go into that house like that. I'll put you a bathroom in and a new Yorkist range and hot and cold water.

It was like heaven! We stripped the walls and there was newspaper on the walls dated 1838. I wish we'd kept it. There were three houses there and ours was the middle one. John Willy Watson, I'll praise him until I die; he was a gentleman to us. He said, 'Will thirty shillings a week do me lad?' There was no business think on, just the blacksmith's shop as Dick May had got out leaving two pairs of bellows that nobody wanted. They couldn't even sell 'em at t'sale. I bought an anvil and a few other things. Anyway when we got the house we stripped it out and cleaned and painted it.

Think on we were biking from Beal every night and fitting in all the overtime at Toulson's. You never knew what overtime was until you worked at Toulson's. I've even been asked on a Sunday afternoon if I'd be going back for a bit at night. They had a hundred wagons when I was there so you can imagine the work that was done. I was the only blacksmith but I had a striker, old Ben Collins. Well we got the house cleaned then we moved from Beal lock, stock and barrel. Of course then I'd to bike every day from Monk Fryston to t'topside of Beal where Toulson's was. It was no problem; I'd be about twenty-eight and a big strong lad so it didn't worry me. Poor old Mr Smales had a milk round and a little farm in Monk Fryston Hall, Parkside Farm, and the first job I did was for him. He brought a cartwheel round, a thick hoop, and with an ordinary breast drill which was all I had I drilled five holes in it and counter sunk them and put countersunk bolts in it - all with a bloody hand drill - for half-a-crown, sixpence a hole. How many would do that today? From the money John Willy lent us I bought an electric drill. I hadn't a welder, I couldn't afford one. I did get a gas welder but gas welding has its limitations so somehow or other I had to get an electric welder. The work started coming in, lots of jobs, but all welding because the other chap, Tom Hawley, all he did was shoeing. I got a nice little job going at nights, not full-time and I started to do a lot of work for Hartley's. Sometimes I used to work all night and think nothing of it but eventually I told Lil I couldn't carry on at Toulson's, I'd have to pack in. Well poor old Jack was as broken-hearted as me. He said, 'Oh, you're never going to leave me are you Arthur lad? What am I going to do?' Anyway I left Toulson's the best of friends and we always were. Then a chap called Philip Simon came to see us. He was with the Yorkshire Rural Industries. Anyway we got talking and he said, 'If you want a welder we can lend you the money.' I got this welder, I think it was ninety-eight pounds, and I had three or four years to pay it back. Well of course once I got this electric welder I was made up. Everything went ahead. I did a lot of smithing, no shoeing but plenty of harrows. Eventually through the same people I got a power hammer, which was great, until I came to sell it then nobody wanted it. I never made a lot of money but I gave good service working night and day. We used to be up at five in a morning.

(You put that turnip chopper in for us. It was hanging off the side of a wall and you put an angle in to hold it. I think you were a bit upset because you said, 'Now Mr Bramley, that'll see us out.' Then he put a chain on just in case it went and I think you thought he'd insulted your work a bit.)

Turnip choppers were always a bit of a bogie to me.

(Well it's still going after all these years.)

When old John Willie died we went to his funeral, poor old lad. He always got his money on time, mark my words, and the interest until we got it all paid back, and believe me that hundred pounds took some paying back. You see there was such a small profit margin. Nowadays they charge what they want, they've no scruples. I used to charge two bob to lay a bloody harrow tooth, that's taking it out, welding a piece on out of the fire, drawing it out, putting a point on, putting it back and straightening it - that was all in!

(Had Mr Watson bought it at the sale?)

After the sale, they couldn't get a buyer for it so he bought it after, and also Miss Duke's house opposite the church and the one next door and the policeman's house. When he died Alfred took them. He wanted us out. We had been going to buy the property. We put a hundred pounds deposit down then he died. What had happened was that the council had been and condemned our house because we'd a back door and a front door but they were both at the front, and if you hadn't a proper front door and a back door in them days your property was condemned. Anyway he wanted £1100 for it. It was a bloody big yard think on and I was going to get the yard, the house and the shop - not the other houses. Anyway I went to see t'bank manager. Well first I went to the council because I'd to get the order revoked because it was condemned. Anyway we decided we'd buy it - Salisbury was the solicitor for Bromets. They started drawing up the papers then we got a letter from t'solicitor asking us to go in and see him. We thought he wanted us to sign the contracts - I'd made arrangements for t'money to be there and everything. Well we went in and decided we'd have a bit of dinner in Ponte while we were on t'job to celebrate. When we gets there he says, 'I'm afraid we've some bad news for you Mr Warren. Mr Watson has had an offer from the Duke of Rutland who intends buying the property.'

Of course we came home very upset, we never expected anything like that and I don't think we'll ever get the truth of it all. Stanley Atkinson was a great friend of ours and I was telling him and he said, 'Now look Mr Warren, I'll ring the Duke'. He rang the Duke of Rutland at home and said, 'What are you doing turning our blacksmith out of his home?' He said, 'I'm not, the blacksmith can stop there for ever.' But whether it was him that upped the offer or not I don't know, but Alfie kept pestering us and we didn't know what to do about money or anything. In a way he was right because we were paying a little rent, only thirty bob a week, but the property was dreadfully dilapidated and cost a fortune to put right. I couldn't see any way that it was worth any more and so we got at cross purposes and in the end we fell out. He told us he wanted two thousand pounds and I said, 'I haven't got that kind of money,' and he said, 'We could put a lot of folks in here.' He couldn't get us out, I'd seen to that. We could still have been there. Anyway we got to know about this place so we bought it and got permission to carry on blacksmithing provided we put some cover up. We were going to be allowed to put a shed up. Anyway one day I was talking to Lil - this place had neither water, sewerage nor electric light. We paid five hundred and fifty pounds to get electric brought here.

(Who lived here before?)

Joe Wells and Mrs Wells - they said he always wore Wellingtons, even when he went to t'Yorkshire Show. It belonged to Mrs Wells. She'd originally come here as a servant girl to Asquiths from Castleford. When she died her sister let us have it, two and a half acres altogether. Well Lil didn't want me to start blacksmithing again. She said she didn't want all this lovely place cluttered up with tractors and rubbish so I decided I'd finish and I got a job at Allerton Bywater workshops.

(How did you get into Castleford rugby then?)

I got involved through our David. He's always loved sport and we started going to Castleford rugby with Lil going shopping in Castleford whilst we went to t'match then we'd pick her up on t'way home. She must have been very patient because she used to hang about even when we went to away matches.

(Was that during Hardisty's time?)

No, it was before that when Kenny Pye and all those - Albert Lunn, gaol kicker, I finished up a great friend of his. Then one thing led to another and we got to know several people. We were never on the committee, only the supporters club but we did a lot for them. We raised a lot of money through running bingos and all sorts of things. We were there in their heyday, both Wembleys. I can remember Hardisty playing and several more. They were only boys when they first came. We have all the rugby league programmes and we went on both trips to Wembley.

Reg French (2nd left) leads Labour Party May Day Parade down Gowthorpe (with clock), Selby
Aurthur Warren behind him

Sherburn Brass Band
Rear Left to Right - Wally Cockerham, Bill Kendrew, Raymond Henry, Charlie Lund, Don Bowler, Dan the Dane, Eric Wilkinson,
Geoff Chilton, Teddy Crossley, Basil Sheppard, Victor Henry, Ivor Cooper,
Jim Thompson, Frankie Fenton
Front Left to Right - Ronnie Kitchen, Jim Stokes, Joe Beal, Cyril Wilkinson (Band Master), George H. Wright (Founder), Bob Baker,
Denis Dawes, Walter Ellis, Arthur Warren

CHAPTER 7

FAIRBURN MEMORIES

My father's parents died before he married, so I had only one set of Grandparents, the Roberts, who more than made up for my loss. Mother was the middle child with brothers Fred and Hubert. They all lived at Fairburn, a village now looking over water filled ings, which were grazing and hay meadows in their young days. Skirting the backside of the village, traffic rushes at great speed to unknown destinations along the two-lane carriageway, now the A1, but in those days the Great North Road. Stone des res houses have been ingeniously built in odd corners over the past ten or twenty years, but mostly on the sites of at least four farmsteads, all with superb views. Fairburn's mining, farming hey day of vibrant pubs and much feared football and cricket sides has been replaced by a semi ghost town of commuters in executive houses, and the sport struggles. Sadly it is not on its own but a few stalwarts try to keep things going.

Mother with brothers Hubert and Fred

As far as I know, and I hope I am wrong, no one has recorded or photographed these changes. I have a selection of old postcards and various Roberts, Bramley and Makin photo albums. I have some good slides from the river across the Ings and one of Pinfold Farm with Arthur Hunter's ice cream van in the foreground, coming up the road. In total it is a poor record of a massive transformation. A written pot pourri is more of a challenge and a worthwhile alternative to the cosy armchair and the dreaded telly on a winter's night. Happily in 2001 a Historical Society was founded and is making up for lost time

It is as an eight year old in the early days of the war over fifty years ago that my memories are frozen, in a world before supermarkets and of farms with horses, cows, calves, pigs, hens and geese, etc., with men passing on their skills to the next generation as of yore!

Where to begin is the question!! Probably by paying a rare visit in those petrol scarce days and with a bag of urgently required calf nuts in the back, in case we were stopped. Through Lumby was the least risky way, over the Selby road and past the wood on the left which is now a substation with pylons scattered to and from it in all directions.

Uncle Dick's Pollum Farm was inland to the right, and fields the rest of the way to the old North Road seemed to be shared amongst Fairburn's farmers who were all Bramleys. Except for Grandfather Roberts who had put a barn up, all other produce had to be led home and over that busy road even then.

There was a memorial garden of rest to the left of the crossroads and some years later, following Granddad's coffin to my first funeral service, I saw all the old men sitting there, stand to attention and take off their caps. He had paid for their seats.

The 'top pub' or the Wagon and Horses was across to the right. Going left was the school, where succeeding generations were taught the three R's by an assortment of teachers. It faced on to the road, as did Milman's Garage, where cars, tractors and motorbikes had been sold and repaired since first invented. Milman and Dressers first bus to Castleford started from here.

On crossing the road and going down to join the Castleford road, Farmer's Row Cottages were on the left and Uncle Guy's Crag Farm was on the right, with his cattle in the fold at the end having a fine view over the water and the cross beneath blocked by a high stone wall. Guy retired early but kept his hand in by growing peas with us at Sherburn, and ploughing out Brotherton Marsh for the first time. He was the only cricketer amongst the Bramleys at Fairburn and in return for certain favours supplied John Nash, the Yorkshire Secretary, with the odd bag of our peas. His transport manager, Harry Hobman delivered Lock Lane pullers in his cattle wagon and was no sport. 'I would rather lean on that gate and watch them there taties grow than watch thee play cricket,' was his philosophy.

On the left corner is now the excellent Wild Goose Gallery, which at that time was a sweet shop belonging to Newhalls. Past another pub and Arthur Hunter's fish and chip shop and ice cream parlour was Uncle Tom's Bay Horse Farm. He had married Florence Makin, from a big farming family at Beckfield, near where the swans are now fed. In 1906 my Grandfather Frank and family had left this farm to take over Home Farm at Sherburn from his brother James, who went off to Huddlestone Grange.

Frank Bramley and Family at Bay Horse in 1906 before move to Sherburn

The church and cricket field is farther along here. Before getting involved at South Milford cricket club I had a spell at Sherburn. In the first team, one Saturday at Fairburn I found myself poking about nervously as Grandfather watched from his usual solitary spot from over the wall near the North Road. My partner was Ken Powell, ex Somerset, and I stayed with him for at least twenty minutes. I was quite pleased with myself - but no comment from Grandfather. Years later, with Grandfather gone, I had no trouble charming Grandma into lending me their snazzy Morris Minor for courting trips to Leeds. A large house at the very end called Aire Cliff, which is now the Bay Horse Pub and Restaurant, also belonged to a more distant, non-farming relative. Uncle William was a Company Secretary at Fryston. Mother used to say they were a bit superior to the rest, and it was the only house where she had to knock when delivering the parish magazine.

So back to the junction and nearly opposite, and still there, is Cross Farm, home of bachelor Uncle Joe, eldest of the six sons and headquarters of Joseph, the pea growing king of the 20's in that area. Four of them served in the First World War and Fred is still in France. Jim, the delicate one, died in the 'flu epidemic that followed and was first into the new church-yard that he'd helped to prepare. Besides Joe; Dick, Tom and Walter at Burton Salmon were all put on farms of their own, and a whole book could be written about this family and those times. Walter (Uncle Wally to me) had an accident with a corn drill and retired early in life for a farmer.

Jim Bramley at Cross Farm

Tom Bramley in pea field at Ledsham 1912

He and Auntie Alice had been lucky enough to furnish some of their house with things from the sale at Byram Hall, the parkland of which came up to the nearby hamlet of Poole. He spent a lot of his remaining years helping us at harvest and potato time, and sometimes to thresh. Ireland was his favourite place and he liked nothing better than travelling round the fairs with our cattle buyer for as long as he could afford. Auntie Alice appreciated the peace and a smoke free house!

Going down the hill which I dreaded then, as it seemed so steep, in our old Morris, there was a craggy cliff on the right with a door into a mysterious, but maybe functional prison cell! At the bottom was the Institute where Granddad, in his foresight, had helped set up an early sort of youth club, below the original school. The old chapel was opposite and long gone now.

Residents of Bellwood's Yard with Jim Bellwood, His Mother and Grandma on extreme right

A little farther on the right, three other cottages formed Bellwood's Yard, the home of another ancient relative, Aunt Mary, and her husband Mark Bellwood, a retired carter and wagonette owner. Aunt Mary, who was Grandfather Frank's sister, lived to a good age. She made an annual visit to Sherburn where she supervised the making of a suet jam roll in a muslin cloth, with white sauce. Mother used to quote her as saying, 'When the conversation turns to ages I withdraw!' Their son Jim worked over forty years for no-one but Bramleys. He was most unlucky, and remarkably unresentful, in that if his mother had been a male Bramley he would certainly have farmed for himself and done well. Jim kept Joe going until he married a widow late in life. Joe's new wife took over, and fell out with Jim, so he came to work for us.

Uncle Arthur and Maister Sidney

Uncle Arthur lived round the corner going down Cutt Lane to the river. He also was only slightly related to the rest, and had been better educated, in that he spoke better, and was more of a gentleman, but could swear like a trooper when riled I am told!! He was captain of the local Home Guards, and practised frequently on them. When his wife, Aunt Sadie, died long after him at Halifax, his twin daughters Betty and Jean brought their mother back to Fairburn and the younger generation toured the village for probably the last time to be shown where the Good Old days took place. Family tradition was kept up after the funeral, with a sit down lunch at the Bay Horse and I came away thinking that owd Arthur and Sadie would have been quietly proud of their brood! My mother was fond of quoting one of the Miss Bramleys who kept a shop. She liked funerals better than weddings 'as you hadn't to wait for an invite and the food was often better.'

Miss Mary Bramley, Nancy Bramley, Grandma Roberts
Mrs Alfred Bramley, Edith Bramley and Miss Harriet Bramley

At the other side of Cutt Lane, also with a bad get-out on to the busy road, was Well Trough Farm where Uncle Sidney lived with his family of Mary, Nancy and George. 'Maister Sydney' played the stock market and, at a good age, liked to carry a hoe when out walking to impress anyone he met. Stone built houses now cover this site, and the farm moved to Manor farm and a better situation nearer the A1. Nancy was my mother's bridesmaid, and in all her photo albums is a real beauty. Sadly at an early age she started with arthritis and must have had a painful life. Latterly her wheelchair never cramped her style. She was always the life and soul of the homes in which she resided, backing horses and playing cards etc and never a complaint, or short of visitors!

View back from the Cutt 1999

Mother and Father at Wedding Reception

Well Trough Farm on left, Pinfold Farm on right - 1920s

Before leaving the Bramleys for the Roberts's at Pinfold, I ought to mention another early pea growing brother of Joseph, George Latham of Waller House. Sadly hailstones at the wrong time finished George Latham. His son Claude, remembering this, started a round selling buns and teacakes before disappearing to Harrogate and becoming a grocer. He married in 1919 and didn't mix with his farming cousins until he thought himself reasonably successful in the fifties. He was invalided out of the First World War and hobbled about the village with a stiff leg held out in front of him by a chain round his neck. Being back to normal in time for the Victory Sports he was given many yards start in the hundred yards. As the gun went off he scuttled over the line in a cloud of dust, and never looked back again!

I think that covers most of my namesakes around that time farming in Fairburn. The only two others not related were part-timers Ben and Walt Wright whose homestead was at the top of the very steep (at that time) Cawdle Hill. Over the wall from them was the home of my Grandparents and Uncle Hubert, at Pinfold Farm, my favourite place then, and through the mists of time, still is!

Sketch of Pinfold Farm

It was a lot quicker to drive there then in our second-hand Morris 12 (BAH190) than it has been to write this, and at the age of eight getting to know all my relations and their goings on was to be an interest for the rest of my days! Later, in a free art period at school, I would draw Pinfold as you see it (still) coming down the hill, and as it thrilled me on every visit, with my dear Grandma waiting to fuss and spoil me and later send me tuck parcels and the Green 'Un when away at school!!

The stone house was end on to the road, but with the bend the room windows looked back up the hill. In summer it was often dark inside as a climbing white rose covered the front. What made it more unusual and adventurous for me (from flat Sherburn) was that the whole homestead was built into the hillside and Well Trough over the road carried on down to the water. It is still a sort of farm but it has been smartened up. The rose has gone; the walls of the house damp proofed and the yard concreted and tidy. Worse still, and like most farms, there is no livestock at all, just their ghosts and my memories.

Tea Outside at end of house looking up the Street

131

At that time they milked three or four cows and had two or three horses, so it was best to park close to the cowhouse which joined on to the house end. A flagged path, fronted by a flat topped wall, led to the front door, but more important to the hand milkers, also to the kitchen at the other side, where buckets of warm milk were carried to be poured into the hand turned separator. Various coloured cats lurked on the wall to have their thirsts quenched from milk poured on to a hollow stone. Is it still there? Who else knows? We always went round and in at the back door. At all hours people collected their E Coli green top milk in jugs and cans from there, and Hunter's ice cream was made from Pinfold milk. One Christmas a teenage carol singer was invited in to sing an encore of South of the Border, and we all joined in with the Aye Aye Aye Ayes.

Geoff Wilkinson, a boy of my age, was my playmate and carried on as boy and man and like Jim Bellwood kept the place going to the end of Uncle Hubert's days and was left it in his will. So there is one happy ending in the middle of this story. I only got to know Uncle Fred while visiting him in Seacroft Hospital after major heart surgery.

We had rugby and Scandinavia in common and I would have loved to have compared notes especially about Scandinavia. I do know he signed for Hull Kingston Rovers for £100 from Brotherton St John's and bought a motor bike with the money. Later Billy Batten flattened him in a cup-tie and he didn't play again. There is a photo of him looking very relaxed in Sweden visiting the Johansons whose son and friend spent some time working at Pinfold in the 1930s - so an early exchange visit!

Uncle Fred on Motor Bike - Sweden

Where there were cows there were flies, and I was the chief flit man, going round blasting them, but always careful of their tails, legs, etc. and squirts from the milkers. They faced away from the house and were fed from the turnip house next-door, through holes in the wall into their mangers. Work study is no new idea, and using the slope behind, the whole turnips were tipped down through a hole in the back wall near to the chopper, frost free amongst the thick walls.

After milking Geoff and I followed the cows to the top of Cawdle Hill, then right along a track to various fields beyond a row of miners' cottages, which stretched from the main road up the hillside. There was a shop at the bottom and ash pits and dry toilets at the backs. Officially they were called New Row, but were known by all as Shagam!! Mine to know the reason why came later. There were gates on fields and gardens then, and the cows and the horses too, knew their own way. We led the horses by their halters, and were told to turn them towards the gate before we let them go, thus avoiding a back heel before they galloped off. Once when there was a poorly cow, we were banished from the proceedings, but watched the long-armed vet, do what Herriot did in every other episode on TV, from the loft above.

The hen hut was a smelly, itchy place at the other side of the house backing on to Wright's wall. But other hens laid their eggs in nettles and straw stacks all over the place. My favourite was a Sussex Cross that laid her speckled eggs in a hollow under the granary steps, just beyond the cowshed. She didn't peck when I felt underneath her for my daily treat, and they don't come any fresher than that!

Tomatoes and cheese with vinegar, pepper and salt, and brown bread was another Fairburn treat that, until then, we didn't have at home. I seemed to have more freedom there and learned things - at only seven or eight, I was allowed to drive the Fordson tractor on between stooks at harvest, and return home feeling very important. I was also allowed to go to Castleford on the bus with Geoff and saw my second film (after Lassie) - 'One of Our Aircraft is Missing' - all about Wellington bombers, and flying has interested me ever since.

I can't remember anything about the granary. The stackyard was at the top of the hill, round a bend, which must have been tricky for the old threshing machine and steam engine to get to, unless they could get in from the top end. It would have been a long way to carry eighteen stones of wheat from there even though it was downhill.

Uncle Hubert, Mother, Grandma and Grandad in Top stackyard

The granary was better sited for the days when corn was flailed and tossed in the wind in the solid barn opposite the house, with a fold yard at the back. This yard continued round between the bottom end and the roadside wall, and I would think have been mucked out from the road. The stable, the hub of any farm especially to lads, was at the end of it. The horseman would come back after tea to give a final feed and brush up, and the village lads would gather to offer help. But at Pinfold I'm told they played darts, dominoes, mouth organs, and the squeezebox - yet another early youth club!

Pinfold Farm in reecent times

Loose boxes for calving cows, stirks and pigs were situated at the top of the yard with a stone horse trough near the way through on the left. Home made straw barns and bullock folds rose above each other going up the hill. Once up there, a panoramic view over the rooftops and ings to Brotherton, Fryston and Castleford could be enjoyed. There is a modern barn up there now, but in the he-men days it was the stack yard where all were individually built, and skilfully thatched. ' Far from the madding crowd' could easily have been filmed here.

Going down the grass hill at the other side, past an abandoned car in nettles, through a door in a wall, and the bathroom window was on the left. It was a big thrill to secretly climb out from there, and escape à la Just William. Walking down to path level and round the house and we have done a full circular tour, our car is near the cow shed, but there is still lots to recall.

Granddad Roberts

Granddad, known to all and sundry as J.P. was an early Farmer's Union pioneer. In the days before paid secretaries he did the job for the Pontefract Branch for forty years, and travelled to meetings in London throughout the war regardless.

So to help him, but mostly his other half, they had got him a hut and placed it just across from the back door, to do his union work in. He was a great pipe smoker. I only went in once but couldn't see much through a fog of Redbreast. Amongst his various retirement awards was an autograph book, with a letter of appreciation from the President Sir James Turner, and a list of friends who had subscribed to a generous cheque, but no autographs. To make up I have nearly filled it with new sets of postage stamps from the last twenty years, and I hope he doesn't mind.

To the left of his hut, and above the main road, were a wash house, coalhouse and other dark holes. Opposite, and best of all, was a whitewashed loo, a wooden two-seater, where I learned to appreciate other sorts of quality papers and earthy scents. And so, having vaguely toured the village and farmstead, I'll try to envisage that favourite old home from the long ago and far away.

If the yard looked really blathery, mother, sister Kay and I would get out at the gate, and walk along the footpath and up four steps, under a clipped privet arch at the house corner. I'm told the village bobby watched the world and his shady mates go by, from under its shelter, where it hung over the wall. There was a small lawn between the house end and the wall high above the road. Very askew box Brownie photos of family groups, most of them minus the bride and groom, are the only ones of my parents' wedding reception held there in 1932.

Mother and Father's wedding group minus the bride and groom

So to recap, going up this path and straight on would take us to the vintage loo, just to the right J.P.'s office, behind and across the slope the hen hut. So round the corner to the back door, which was in a flimsy lean-to porch, and then left into a long low kitchen, where everything seemed to happen. This also was cut into the hill, as the window on the left looked on to a six-foot wall. A glazed square sink trough was under the window, and to the left, on a thick stone slab, was the milk separator of mysterious workings. But my favourite thing, above the door, was the little man and woman, who came out of their wooden house to tell us of the day's weather prospects long before TV - one for rain and one for shine, but I can't remember which was for which!

All the plates, cups, saucers, pots and pans must have been in a large pine cupboard against the wall with drawers at the bottom. A door to the cellar was just beyond this, and then another door into a long living room, with a view over the yard at the far end. The top of the cellar steps was shelved, and did as the pantry. The steps down would be called dangerous today, and sadly, I understand, it has now been filled in. But they were worth risking then, as a good selection of pop from Hey Brothers lay below, including Dandelion and Burdock, Ice Cream Soda and Cherryade. Hams and bits of bacon hung on hooks from the curved brick roof. It must have taken some digging!. On one occasion I took a bottle of pop next-door to David Wright's. His mother supplied two rugs and a clotheshorse and we camped for the afternoon on Mount Everest, in the meadow above their farm.

The kitchen at Pinfold Farm

The cooking, eating area was at the far end. An open fire, that had to be lit every morning, and an oven, that had a Friday black-leading, was the centrepiece. The food came straight on to the table on the left. Grandma, who I seem to think did everything, sat with her back to the fire. Uncle Hubert sat on a wooden bench against the panelled wall. If I sat too near the end, he would stand up and I would finish on the floor, but only once. I squashed flies with total freedom on the panelling, as their blood and remains were wiped off cleaner than on wallpaper in the rooms. Granddad J.P., when at home, sat opposite us and, I suppose, did all the talking. He would talk to anyone anywhere, especially on his train journeys. My father was the opposite, and would never be first to start a conversation, although he knew more than most. So they got on well together, talking the night away, with me soon asleep on the sofa to the drone of their voices, and in a haze of pipe smoke. I have no memories of the journeys home. However I do have recollections of a mouth-watering cake they said I had won in a Red Cross raffle. It was deep sponge filled with jam, cream and custard, but I don't remember eating any.

There was always a good fire in the snug. On either side of the mirror above, in the mahogany surround, were portraits or photos of Grecian style ladies with feathers and roses in their hair and low cut dresses - my first pinups. The table in the left corner near the window had the telephone on, (Knottingley 110) and was covered in books and papers. When the sad day eventually came, and everything sorted out or sold, the old table made nearly £300!

The cold, damp far room was arrived at through the snug, and by crossing the front door hall, with the stairs going up on the right. A large three-piece suite, an unplayed, out of tune piano, and a mahogany sideboard were the main items in here. On the walls hung a panoramic view. In later years I recognised it as Stockholm, which must have had connections with Uncle Fred's visits. Father's oil paintings hung round the rest of the room, and whether they were Christmas presents, peace offerings, or part of the dowry will never be known. Before the days of radiators, it must have taken some warming up in winter and was rarely used.

When I stayed, I was thrilled to be in mother's old room, and it was colder still even with a hot water bottle to warm the huge feather bed and in summer. Two large, draughty windows offered magnificent views over rooftops and water, and I still admire what must have been an expensively tinted photo of her sitting cross-legged on a stool, in her Pontefract High School uniform. Just getting to school must have been an adventure. She had to walk two miles to Burton Salmon station, by train to Baghill and walk again. Uncle Hubert had a very plain little bedroom next-door that smelt of socks and sweat the odd time I peeped in. At the other side of the stairs my Grandparents' room whiffed of humbugs and mothballs. Their only window had a view over the yard, which was handy to see the horses going out, and the cows coming in.

Two steps down at the other side led to the bathroom and, as aforementioned, an easy escape in case of fire. Running water and electricity must have been a bigger boon to them than computers are to us now. Mother says in her days at home, they had a tap in the house, but water had to be heated on the fire, and carried in buckets across to the washhouse on Mondays and into the tin bath in front of the fire on bath night on Friday. Mother, being the girl, got first go at the clean water. A big improvement was the purchase, at Byram Hall sale, of a hipbath, which held two buckets, and was wonderful - but sadly she didn't explain the finer details.

When the cosy little bathroom was built I don't know. It only had a bath, sink and airing cupboard and of course running hot water, but I seemed to have more time and fun there with Grandma in charge than at home! Mother attended a sort of dairy/cooking school at Garforth, and learned milking and butter making, and how to look after and kill, pluck and dress hens, ducks and geese.

Mother leaves home for better things

During the war we killed a pig in the garage on a Saturday morning. On Sunday morning it would be cut into hams and sides, which were laid out in the cellar and salted later. I predug the hole for the guts and intestines and eventually got organised for Jack Bradley to drop them straight into my barrow, which helped a lot! I can't say I looked forward to the occasion, but when Grandma Roberts came, a few days later, to render the fat into crispy scraps, and make juicy pork pies, it was all worthwhile. I also had the lucrative job of delivering frys to Farrars next door, and to one or two other people, who later would kill their own pigs and return the favour. Sixpence was my usual tip!

I suppose the weekly cooking, feeding, cleaning programme in farmhouses remained the same for generations until recently. With us it was a big fat joint of (most likely) beef on Sunday, cold on washday Monday with rice or sago pudding. Cold on Tuesday, and again on Wednesday, unless made into Shepherd's pie. Thursday was big baking day for bread, cakes, pies and meat and potato pie which father called forty to one. He always complained that it was better on Friday warmed up, and never got his way, to have it made on Wednesday and warmed up twice! Fish day was Wednesday teatime, when Fred Wood, an up and coming corn merchant, usually joined us, and talked me into being a Wakefield Trinity fan.

Granddad Roberts died on August 23rd 1953. I think he was the first close relative to do so. He had been kicked by a horse and developed pneumonia. I hadn't seen him for some time till he called one day. I watched his fidgety hands toy with his unlit pipe, and worse still had hardly any chat, and his clothes hung on him. I remember crying all the way down the Horse Paddock field and staying out till he had gone home! Grandma died on January 1st 1964. She had kept going bravely by looking after Uncle Hubert, who never married or went off far. They were very generous, lending me their hardly used Morris Minor for jaunts into Leeds when father had preference on ours. Uncle Hubert went on for another twenty years, looked after by Geoff and various friends and my mother, but he had a sad, slow end.

Now, as I said before, Fairburn is another dormitory village. Farming has moved on and nearly all those people mentioned are now in the churchyard amongst the people they grew up with. Bennets, Greens, Walkers, Dudleys, Cotterils, Kelseys, Sutcliffes, Bellwoods and Wilkinsons are also familiar names, but the Bramleys of old seem to dominate. I usually join them for half an hour on New Year's Day, after a look in the Goose Gallery, and a walk down Cutt Lane and along the river bank.

The dearest spot a good man finds on earth

Is that where he, a prattling child, first knew

The tender care a gentle mother gives:

First saw the roof that held him from the storm,

And learnt the worth of a kind father's hand:

The spot where o'er his grandsires' graves he strayed,

When all was fresh and beautiful to him,

And innocent.

Anon

Three Friends - Mr Willie Brumley,
Butcher Wainwright and Mr Frank Bramley

Beneath those rugged elms, that yew-tree's shade,
Where heaves the turf in many a mouldering heap,
Each in his narrow cell for ever laid,
The rude forefathers of the hamlet sleep.
The breezy call of incense-breathing morn,
The swallow twittering from the straw-built shed,
The cock's shrill clarion, or the echoing horn,
No more shall rouse them from their lowly bed.
For them no more the blazing earth shall burn,
Or busy housewife ply her evening care:
No children run to lisp their sire's return,
Or climb his knee the envied kiss to share.
Oft did the harvest to their sickle yield,
Their furrow of the stubborn glebe has broke:
How jocund did they drive their team afield!
How bowed the woods beneath their sturdy stroke!
(Extract from Elegy Written in a Country Churchyard - Thomas Gray)

POSTSCRIPT or EPITAPH

Today, May 23rd 1998, I called in at Pinfold Farm to find Geoff Wilkinson tending his garden, defended by a dog who wasn't to be fondled. I hadn't been there since Uncle Hubert's funeral, and not round the buildings for years. They were very much the same. The cow house is filled with son Peter's joinery equipment, and the turnip house still has a good chopper there, but buried under other bits and pieces. The stone barn is as solid as ever and should be worth a small fortune with planning permission. Tidiness is what has happened most, with plants growing on top of walls and in corners.

No hen lays under the granary steps, although there are some penned on the hillside at the back. Now that his cockerel is starting to crow, Geoff is waiting for his first complaint from one of the three houses built tight to his top boundary fence. Of course the house and surroundings can only remain as it was in memory and has really been brought up to date. The old stone surface has been smartened by pebble rendering, and a large porch extends over the path the milkmen took. The wall is altered, and with a dog like that, I suspect cats keep well clear.

The steps from the road are the same, but there's no friendly shelter for Bobby Johnson under the clipped bush hanging over the road. Going along the house end, and round to the back door, (with the dog locked up) you realise that gardening is also what has happened. Away have gone the wash house, the coalhouse, the two-seater loo house, the henhouse along the wall, and Grandfather's office. The whole slope with greenhouses at the top is cropped across its width, and down to the road wall.

Inside, the house is almost unrecognisable with a new entrance, modern cooker and kitchen. The table is in the same place however. Outside, tons of soil have been dug away from the walls to prevent dampness, and it would be a brave youngster who would try jumping from the bathroom window today.

Going through the gate, the surface of the hillside is tidily grassed and mown, where clumps of nettles used to hide hens' nests. Neighbour Peter Halls can't spend too much time enjoying the view, as his patch of garden is very much up to standard, and a lot more level than Geoff's. Although I haven't been in, his house looks light years away from the Wright home I knew. The stable and boxes down the yard are also someone's mansion now. The old grey mares are dead and long gone in this part of Fairburn, but there are no weeds round these ranch house doors.

Geoff told me David Wright had called the other day for some wheat for his hens. He said he could remember everything. We'll have to get together some day.

David died in 2002 and sadly, as far as I know, all his memories will have gone with him - a double tragedy!

Joseph Bramley pea pulling at Ledsham about 1912
Harry Perry, Alf Mathers With Horses and Wagon, Old Bill Stephenson With Fork Behind Women

First wide angle team photo 1912? - Including Joseph Bramley (left)
and Tom, Joe, Dick and Old Bill Stephenson

ICY COOLLY

A long time ago, when none of us had watches, and three or four weeks were spent boringly hoeing sugar beet and turnips in all weathers, the sight and sound of the five to five express steaming up from Selby, brought welcome relief to tired arms and watery eyes. Other trains crossed at ten and three to mark morning and afternoon drinking times, and a red bus conveniently went to Pontefract at ten to twelve and warned us of dinner. But on hot summer days, and farther back still, the hoot of Arthur Hunter's klaxon horn and his call of 'Icy Coolly, Icy Coolly' brought a thrill of expectation for a cornet or sandwich of his very own home made ice cream.

Mr Hunter's base was a fish and chip shop, where he also made his own special brand of ice cream, in Silver Street, Fairburn next to the 'Three Horseshoes' pub, and I suppose he did his various rounds every afternoon. His mode of transport was something special, even then, and old customers will be pleased to know it is still going strong today!

'Arthur Hunter' outside Pinfold Farm, Fairburn

The ice cream vehicle (or float), which is the only way to describe the gaily painted mobile shop asking you to 'Stop me and try one', and boasting of 'One Quality - only the best', and 'Pure Ices'. In 1924 the original body was coach built for Mr Hunter to go on to a Rover Eight. In 1926 he purchased a Singer Saloon and changed the body around between them for winter and summer use. But in 1936 Arthur Hunter bought a 1930 Morris Cowley Continental two seater tourer with dickey. The tourer body was removed and the ice cream body transferred to the Cowley chassis, and that is how most of us oldies will remember it.

It was taken off the road during the war time, but was soon out and about when hostilities ceased, and worked faithfully for son Billy until 1964, when it was pensioned off as its reliability was becoming suspect. Enter Peter Dawes.

Peter too had loved the ice cream cornets at 2d or 3d each, and 'Arthur Hunter', the vehicle, when he lived in Church Hill. Later, as a bank manager in Cheshire, with a passion for vintage cars, he still had lingering thoughts of the red and cream ice cream car and (evidently) its distinctive exhaust note, as it left him licking happily.

His campaign to find its whereabouts entailed phoning all Hunter numbers around Fairburn, and his fifth call had Arthur's son Billy on the line, who told him it had been put into an old stone barn twenty-four years ago and not touched since! A visit was arranged, and to Peter's delight, a mutual price agreed, with Billy happy to know it was going to a good home.

WX 2644 was in remarkably good condition. Old dripping cartons had protected the roof, and an old mattress the bonnet and radiator from twenty-four years of grime. To everyone's surprise the brakes were free and the tyres successfully inflated to 30 psi. Half the village turned out, with mixed feelings, to see it depart, with Peter secretly hoping to have it restored for Mr Hunter's sixtieth anniversary in 1990 — in three years time.

'Arthur Hunter emerges after twenty-four years

The trials and tribulations of restoration are well recorded in an article by Peter in the August '92 'Automobile Magazine'. After a frenetic three years of hard work, family team work, and total commitment, Mr Hunter passed its MOT with no trouble, and took to the road for the first time since 1964, maximum speed thirty-five miles per hour.

Harewood House saw it leading the parade and winning a trophy, with Billy Hunter and family thrilled at the reunion. Billy donned his smock and boater and soon slipped back into the routine before recorded jingles, — 'Never mind your mother - have another', 'Icy Coolly'.

Billy Hunter at Sherburn Gala in 1992 with Arthur

I have further interest in the Hunter ice cream business as my grandparents used to supply the milk, and one of my mother's early jobs was wheeling the churn up the hill from Pinfold Farm every day in summer - not an easy task! I first met Peter when Sherburn Gala was honoured by Arthur's presence a few years ago, and promised him a photo of it in front of Pinfold in 1958. In return he sent me more photos and tales, so this article has been very easy to write. Happy Days! Icy Coolly!

J.D.B.

140

JIM BELLWOOD AND THE POLLUM FIRE

(Recorded 15th August 1982)

Jim Bellwood was unlucky that his mother was a Bramley and not his father, who was an ex-pitman and waggoner. Farming was in his blood and consequently he worked all his life for his Bramley cousins instead of being a Bramley farmer himself. Jim spent forty years as our foreman at Sherburn and never expressed any resentment. He taught me a lot and I don't think we had many wrong words, although he must have held his breath at times. This tape is about his early days at Pollum Farm, which is for sale at the moment, as it was then when we explored it with son Martin, a tape recorder and a camera to store away Jim's memories.

Jim Bellwood with Martin Bramley and tape recorder

It's August 15th 1982. There's been rain during the night that's stopped us from combining the oats across the road. Martin has come in to tell me that Jim is here. We are going round Pollum Farm, which recently belonged to Mr David Cooke and is to be sold at Brotherton Fox Hotel on September 7th at 6.30pm. I showed Jim the sale brochure and fifty pounds wouldn't have given him as much pleasure. We've now arrived and Jim keeps saying 'Good God, good God.' He's not been here for forty years or so.

There've been vast alterations here since my time. I came here in the winter of 1919. There was only one man, Harry Perry, who'd been here twenty-five years. He lived on his own. There's three cottages and he'd lived in them all twice. When I came he and his wife lived in the stockyard cottage, but it's a lot different now to when I started.

Pollum Farm Yard - skilful work and outdoor poultry

Happy Days with the binder

I was only thirteen and had to bike from Fairburn, which is a mile and a half away. In them days there were four horses plus twenty cattle in the fold in winter. The horses led turnips and ploughed through the winter, but in spring they'd bring three pairs from Fairburn to drill. We'd set to with three sets of harrows in front, one drilling and one harrowing in behind, and the field went in in a day. That's how we'd carry on.

In 1920 Walt and Dick were at home in harvest time. I'd ride a spare horse up and Walt came on his bike. I drove the horses, and Walt was on the binder. Two Irish men lived in the spare houses for harvest. They'd get about £2 and drinkings twice a day for the harvest month, no extra for overtime! Any wet days you still got drinkings, but if harvest wasn't done in the month, you worked for nothing till it was. It was a grey mare I brought up, but Walt'd leave me to take t'dinner and drinking things, and all t'rabbits we'd shot, back home on its back, whilst he jigged off courting to Knottingley on his bike.

In December 1920 Dick got married and his Dad decided he'd come up and live here. He'd been gassed in France. They were both in the Veterinary Corps but Walt never went abroad. Dick married Adelaide Woodall, who'd been a nurse, from Brotherton. Her brother farmed at Cliffe. Walt was married to Alice Masterman and they bought Hall Farm at Burton Salmon from the Ramsdens of Byram Hall to start on. The other brother, Tom, had lived at Pollum before I started, but went to Bay Horse Farm in Fairburn, which they rented, in 1914. His first son, Ted, was born at Pollum.

Bramley Group including Bill (second left), Dick, Adelaide & Joe (on right)

Cross Farm, where I originally set out from, had set three sons up on farms. Joseph had three more sons. Fred the eldest, got killed in France in 1915, and Jim died in 1918 on holiday at Blackpool in that 'flu epidemic - the worst of all time. It was one of the wettest harvests too. They hadn't finished when he went off in October, and they were starting tattying. When they made the new churchyard at Fairburn they had to alter a wall as the road corner was too sharp to get round. So Joseph's men and carts did the job, but sadly his son Jim was first to be in it. (Funeral report from local paper below).

A Well-known Fairburn Family Bereaved

Readers of this paper will remember that in our report of the opening ceremony of the new Cemetery attached to St. James's Church, Fairburn, mention was made of the efforts of Mr. Joe Bramley and the several members of his family in the work done. Sad to relate, the first to be buried in the new Cemetery is a member of that respected family. On Wednesday last were laid to rest the mortal remains of Jas. William Bramley, the fourth son of Mr. And Mrs. Bramley, who while staying at Blackpool developed influenza, and pleurisy and chronic bronchitis supervening, succumbed on the 19th inst. He was accompanied by his fiancée, Miss Maud Woodall, of Brotherton, who also was a victim to influenza but has been brought home and is reported to be improving. The deepest sympathy with the family and Miss Woodall is felt by the villagers and residents of the district. The deceased was of a quiet but genial disposition, and was held in the highest esteem by all who knew him. In his teens his health was not of the best, and prevented him following his strong inclination for engineering, his efforts in this direction being confined to the farm engines and his steam models. Gardening in summer and fretwork in winter were his hobbies. He was a fretworker of no mean order. The Lord's Prayer, in a beautiful design, which hangs in the village church, where the deceased was a regular attender, is admired by all who see it. This was worked and given by the deceased and his eldest brother, Private Fred Bramley, of the Hampshires, now reported wounded and missing. His brother, Private R. Bramley

(Trench Morters) home on leave from France, has had a sorry home-coming, but arrived in Blackpool to be with the deceased in his last hours - as were also his parents.

At the interment the services were taken by the Vicar of Ledsham (Rev. G. E. Warlow), assisted by Mr. Wellburn, of Hillam, who is conducting the church services in the absence of the Rev. J. H. Thomas (Curate). The chief mourners were the parents; Mr. and Mrs. Tom Bramley, brother and sister-in-law; Privates Richard and Walter Bramley, brothers; Mrs. Fred Bramley, sister-in-law, and Private Joe Bramley, brother, victims to influenza, were unable to attend. In addition there were present numerous other relatives, the village people en masse, and sympathisers from neighbouring parishes.

Wreaths were sent by "His Father and Mother"; "Tom, Florrie and little Teddie"; "Joe, Richard and Walter"; "Maud, with dearest love"; "His Sister Susie"; "Uncle Ben and Family"; "Aunt Ann and Family"; "Aunt Lizzie Powell"; "Mr., Mrs. and Jim Bellwood"; "Mrs. Woodall and Family"; "Mrs. Bramley"; "Arthur, Percy and Miss Jowett"; "Mr. and Mrs. H. Dickinson"; "Mr. and Mrs. Wm. Bramham and Family"; "B. and M. Ash"; "Annie, Ted, Annie, Herbert and Sarah"; "Hannam and Rose"; "Mr., Mrs. and John Webster"; "L. and M. Howarth, Blackpool"; and "Mrs. Kellet and Barbara". The coffin was of polished oak, with brass mountings. The funeral arrangements were in the able hands of Mr. Jenkinson of Burton Salmon.

Another brother, Joe, was in partnership with his father at Cross Farm and he stayed there. It was about 120 acres. Joseph had taken on Pollum Farm from William Bramley who lived at Scarthingwell. The Bay Horse had been in the Bramley family donkey's years because Joseph and his brothers William, James, Benjamin, Frank and sister Polly had all been born there. Their father was Jonathan. In 1906 they had all gone bar Frank. His brother James had been at Home Farm, Sherburn, but left to go to Huddlestone Grange, and, on May 1st that year, Frank went to take on Sherburn, and I was born next day!

A chap called Thomas Hirst took over Bay Horse. He was a bit of a big head, and was going to show Bramleys how to farm, but he had to sell up in 1914, so Joseph took it over again, and Tom went to it. In 1923 the Palmerston Estate was sold and they bought both farms.

In 1929 we'd finished harvest and Dick and family went off to Blackpool on holiday. By the end of September we'd done a week's muck leading, three carts, two Irish men filling, two emptying in the field and I was driving. On Saturday 29th September I was staying whilst they were away, and Ernest Halls was living in the stockyard house. The Irish men were going off tattying to York. I was looking through the kitchen window and down the yard, when I saw sheets of flame on the straw stack and the end of the Dutch barn. The barn was full with five stacks nearby and three of hay and pea straw. I was in a terrible sweat and didn't know what to do – both Dick and his Dad were away, with only Joe at home. I biked to Fairburn, but someone had seen it from the road and had phoned the brigade. Eventually there were seven engines in the yard, but they had to pump water nearly two miles from the reservoir and were hampered with burst pipes.

Pontefract fire engine in attendance

They had it under control by twelve, but Dick came home from Blackpool and the first he saw was the farm well and truly alight. Things never looked up after that for him, as they found out they were under insured, and had lost a lot of money, especially after such a good harvest. Everyone rallied round. It took all day Sunday to get it damped down, and we had three horses and carts tipping the smouldering remains in lines in a nearby field. It wasn't a pleasant sight every time you went past, all the years' hard work burning in t'field. They'd saved the hay and pea straw by putting sheets on and watering them down. I will say t'firemen worked very hard. None of t'buildings got on fire, which was a great achievement 'cause t'barn was, what, only about twenty yards off.

Pollum Farm from the air in the 50s

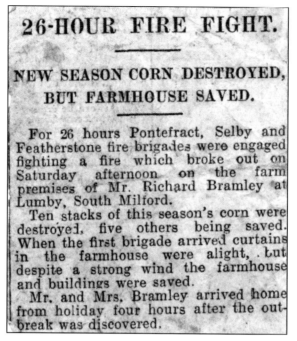

Report on fire from local paper

We hadn't any cattle whatsoever that winter. We only had horses. We'd nothing to do, no threshing, no cattle – t'main job was ploughing and t'cleaning t'stackyard up and getting ready for another year. Walter at Burton Salmon gave us two or three loads of straw and I fetched some from Adelaide's brother at Cliffe. I went twice for bedding for t'horses. It upset Dick so much that I came and stayed for about two months – slept here too, it was such a shock. It was a shock for everybody. I'll never forget a day like 29th September – and that put an end to a lot of things.

Joe and Billy were born. Joe on 24th January 1922 and Billy in February 1924, I think. We'd two men living there then in t'cottages besides Dick. We ran three pairs of horses and the pony and trap, which was the only way of getting to Fairburn other than walking. We didn't get any help from Fairburn. Each son as he took on his farm had to manage his own difficulties.

In 1926 there wasn't many tractors about. That was t'same year as t'strike. One of t'chaps that sometimes brought letters and t'papers was a mechanic from Monk Fryston. Harry Laycock 'ad done a course at Fords at Dagenham for tractor mending and that sort of thing. There wasn't any new ones except t'old Titans that had come from America in 1920. During the war years the Americans had brought a lot of small Fordson tractors over, very much like Fergys are now. In fact they went in partnership for a while. Harry knew of a chap that had had one stored away from the end of t'war or just after. So he went and had a look at it and bought it. That was 1926 and we thought we'd won the World Cup. Bindering and no horses to take and bring home at night and feed up – glorious that!

Then we got to ploughing. That was a bit of hitting and missing and slipping sideways in them days, but we got through all right. Unfortunately that year, 1926, was t'second time t'miners came out completely. They started in May and didn't get back till October. The one before was in 1921, and funnily enough both years were hot ones, very hot, and a lot of corn got scorched and peas burned off.

We had a threshing set at Fairburn belonging to Joseph that used to go round to Cross Farm, Pollum, Bay Horse, Burton Salmon, Woodalls at Brotherton, Arthur Bramley's and more. Walt had been t'driver, but there was no coal. So it became my job to go with this Fordson, which had a pulley on it and gave them all a session after harvest. Well in those days every farm in Fairburn except one belonged to a Bramley, so if you went you had to know which one you wanted.

There was another one related to Joseph, and he had a son called Guy. Well they'd bought one of these old tractors and they had a machine and he did for himself and his Uncle Sidney who lived at Well Trough Farm. So I'd a bit of a problem that back end, and I wasn't very old either.

There was a fellow called Tom Mollar (Morley maybe) who used to drive t'old steam engine on threshing and grinding days. He'd been with engines all his life, and knew them backwards, but was past his day. It was portable, this engine then, and we had to pull it around by horses. When we fetched it to Pollum we put three horses on, and four to get out on to t'top road – five if it was bad weather.

This Tom Mollar used to go to Walt's a lot. He came down when we were threshing there and couldn't believe his eyes to see this little tractor, which only weighed fifteen cwt, buzzing along driving t'machine and tying straw batons too. Nobody stoking up and just a bit of greasing!

Actually Pollum is in Fairburn parish but has a South Milford address. The reason for that is they had such trouble getting the post from Fairburn when the Milford postman went past the lane end to Lumby and Ledsham. So common sense prevailed and it made it a lot easier.

Dick and Adelaide in later life

Dick's lads were growing up, times were getting better, and we'd more tractors, but in 1935 Joseph Bramley died. I must say everyone used to call him the Old General, and what he said was law. Never mind what anyone else said, Tom, Dick, Walter or anyone, if he said something, that was it, and everyone knew it. I'll tell you this, it was the biggest funeral that had ever been in Fairburn, for t'simple reason he grew peas all over - Ledsham, Brotherton, Burton Salmon and all over. Brotherton pullers must have been amongst the best in t'country. In them days we'd pay a penny a peck (8lb) and we'd put 'em in ten-peck bags (80lb). Then they went down to half bags and I've seen us with more pullers in the field than anybody else, and we'd be paying a penny and they'd be paying three halfpence. The simple reason was law and order. What he said counted. If they didn't do as they were told - out - and no messing, and everyone knew it. When t'miners were on strike he wouldn't allow any foreigners in t'field. He only had pullers from Fairburn or Brotherton, good times and bad, no one else! At his funeral three parts of the women of Brotherton were there. The road was lined from farm to church. The church and churchyard were full - the biggest funeral ever!

That was in 1935. Well in 1937 there was nobody to manage Cross Farm again so I left Pollum on my birthday, as I'd started on it, and stayed for fifteen-and-a-half years before moving to Sherburn for the rest of my time.

Jim Bellwood with Cup for Forty Years' Service presented at the Yorkshire Show

CHAPTER 8

WARTIME ESCAPADES
OF FLIGHT SERGEANT SID DUDLEY 1480232
1944-45
EX FAIRBURNER

I have only got to know Sid in recent years. He seemed to know all my Bramley relatives at Fairburn, and my mother when young too!! Getting it all down on tape gives me a kick but his flying and prison days and that harrowing, hungry, cold walk was an added bonus in my cosy study.

This is Sid's account of his last raid over Germany on November 2nd 1944. To date his time as a POW is not down on paper, so a transcript of our taped chat on 13th June 1996 follows with Sergeant Ben Couchman's diary of the forced march fitted in accordingly.

Flight Sergeant Sid Dudley

November 2nd 1944

6.30 a.m. We were called by the tannoy system to report to the mess, to have our pre-op meal by 7.30 a.m. At 8 a.m. we were to report to the briefing room, Everything pointed to a possible take off time around half past nine to ten o'clock.

Sometimes on our way to briefing we would ask our ground crews how much petrol they had put in the tanks, hoping to give us a clue as to how far to the target. No luck this morning though.

On entering the briefing room we were told that, due to bad weather over the target, there would be a delay. Eventually it was to be twelve Noon before we actually trundled down the runway and were airborne.

The target today was to be a synthetic oil refinery at Homburg, situated on the eastern side of the Ruhr Valley. Homburg, being a small town, was situated on the opposite side of the valley to Duisburg. A target we had bombed a few days before, a maximum effort up to a thousand bombers, it was heavily defended but still must have taken a severe pounding. We bombed Duisburg twice in twenty-four hours, first time at 9 p.m., the second at 7.30 a.m. Both raids took place on 14th October 1944.

The Ruhr Valley was known to Aircrew as Happy Valley and Death Valley. Some named it 'Angels' Paradise'. Targets in the Valley were dreaded by all. It was so heavily defended with 'Ack Ack Crews' and fighter squadrons of the enemy, because the German war production factories were mainly there. We fully expected a very hot reception. Tension was running very high and nerves as taut as bow strings, apprehension being the key word.

So back to the briefing — Upon entering the briefing room, the Red Ribbon showing the route to be taken was duly pinned on the maps. The Intelligence Officer gave us the information where to expect flak and fighters. I must stress they were not always correct, as were the meteorological forecasts, though odd times they did get it correct.

It was a surprise briefing today; firstly the Squadron Commander was to lead the Squadrons (115 & 195) in the second wave. Squadron Commanders were not usually allowed to fly on missions except the odd daylight mission. Biggest surprise of all, we were to fly in formation - this would give better and more effective protection against the enemy fighters. This was the first time ever for Bomber Squadrons. Everyone thought it was a stupid idea. We had always flown as individuals, and furthermore the Squadron Commander was to fly as Second Pilot, which meant he was flying with an inexperienced crew, maybe their first or second operation. This gave rise to concern to Bruce our Navigator. Supposing the leading A/C Navigator got it wrong, no-one could tell him as there was to be full radio silence between a/c. Orders to be obeyed (ours not to reason why).

One job today for me was to drop the window through the flare chute at so many seconds' interval upon entering the target area. 'Window' was the term used to describe the long metal tinfoil strips. When dropped the reflections on the enemy radar screens became blurred and distorted, thereby confusing his predictions of the height of his target - most important the numbers of aircraft. We were to learn later, the Germans had learned to counteract our ruse and had learned to use our 'window' as an aid to predict very accurately our height, speed, etc. with serious consequences for us.

Sid in flying gear

After questions at briefing were answered, we proceeded to the 'Parachute Room' and collected our chute, then to the 'Crew Room' and changed into flying gear from our locker. We put our 'valuables' into a canvas bag, labelled it and handed it to our Padre. Some of the chaps also handed him a last letter to home or girlfriend. If the crew failed to return the Padre would post the letter next day. We also collected our flying rations - one bar of Fry's Milk Chocolate, two packets of Wrigley's Chewing Gum, and six Barley Sugar Sweets. If it was to be a long haul, we were issued with 'Wakey Wakey Tablets' to prevent falling asleep. We also collected our 'Escape Kit' This was a collection box approximately six by four by one and a half inches. It contained a compass and detailed maps of Germany, Belgium, Holland and France printed on silk, which were excellent. Also forged money in Marks, Francs and Guilders currencies, Horlicks tablets, water-purifying tablets, a fishing line and hooks. Also about two energy tablets which enabled you to run at great speed for and up to twenty minutes, so before the twenty minutes was up you must find somewhere to hide because you fell asleep for two hours solid (could do with some now). There were various forms of compass one could carry, and then it was out to the perimeter track where the crew bus took us to dispersal and our aircraft. We stored our gear and rechecked our various instruments, then climbed back out, had a chat with the 'Ground Staff' and a last cigarette before climbing back in and settling in to our various positions.

Finally the engines were started and warmed up and, at the allotted time, taxied down the perimeter track to the end of the runway. On being given the 'Green Light', the throttles fully opened, we sped down the runway and were soon airborne.

Lancaster A4H with crew
From L. to R. - Sgt. Paddy Flower (Mid-Upper Gunner), Fl. Off. Frank Major (Bomb Aimer), Sgt. Noel Price (Flight Engineer), Fl. Off. Bruce Lumsden (Navigator), Fl. Off. Peter Funk (Pilot), Fl. Sgt. Sid Dudley (Wireless Operator/Air Gunner), Sgt. Jerry Kenny (Rear Gunner).

We were to rendezvous at 8,000 feet above Reading. Our position was to be number two at the head of the flight. On arriving over Reading, the squadrons we were to rendezvous with were nowhere to be seen. We circled for two or three minutes and Bruce decided we could wait no longer, so we set course. We were already four minutes late. It was a bad start, and to me bad omen. Four minutes late meant we were disobeying orders - a Court Martial Event. But things were to get worse. Instead of the leading aircraft increasing speed, he actually lost speed. He had a dickey engine but could not communicate as we were under a strict radio silence. Consequently on crossing the enemy coast we were actually eight minutes behind schedule - this was annoying Bruce who worked strictly with his wrist watch and log.

On crossing the enemy coast, the Squadron Commander feathered his port engine, stopping it and bringing the propeller to a position where it would not windmill. Then, by means of an Aldis Lamp, flashed to us in Morse code the signal to take over in lead position. This now put our pilot in a bit of turmoil, and after discussing the position with the navigator, they both decided that we should increase speed and try to make up lost time. At this time we were about thirty minutes from the target. The rest of the stream decided for some unknown reason to stick with the Squadron Commander and soon we had opened up a gap. Presumably the pilot thought he would catch up the first wave, which we could see way up ahead. (No chance!)

I left my desk and stood up at the astrodome and looked around. It was a lovely sight to see the stream of bombers way behind, and a trio of American Lightning fighter planes crossed overhead. Today they had given us fighter protection but being out on our own left us vulnerable, especially to the radar controlled ack ack. We were to pay a little later for our mistake as the enemy radar could very accurately home in on a single aircraft, they could predict our height and speed most accurately. In about ten minutes or so we turned on our last short leg into the target. Up ahead the first wave were on their bombing run. The flack seemed heavy and concentrated over the target, and shells were bursting at the correct height - just over 20,000 feet. This did not worry us unduly, we had seen it before and we had survived twenty operations. One might forgive us for feeling maybe a little complacent and perhaps 'cocky'. Anyhow we always thought and indeed wished that it would be another crew, not ours, that failed to make it.

Just before 2 p.m. we started our bombing run. I switched from the wireless over to the intercom and heard Frank, the bomb aimer, giving instructions to the pilot - right, right, steady etc. The target was coming up between the two wires on his bombsight. My thoughts were, 'Soon have bombs away, push the nose down and get the hell out of here as fast as possible'. This was our usual routine. Seconds later there was a loud, muffled thud - must be very close to be able to hear it above the noise of the four Merlin engines. I decided to go up into the cockpit and see just what was happening. The starboard inner engine was hit; black smoke streamed back over the wing. The cooling system and fuel tanks were also ruptured and petrol and antifreeze were streaming backwards, fanned by the slipstream of the propeller. It was like a very heavy mist. Part of the nose was blown off. A small piece of shrapnel teased across the back of Frank's (b/a) right hand. I returned to my desk and as I passed behind Bruce I noticed a hole in the fuselage. I picked up a lump of shrapnel, about three inches in diameter, intending to take it home as a souvenir, but it was very hot, so I dropped it on Bruce's desk. Still busy working out our homeward course, he gave me a grin. He did not know that had it come through six inches more to port, it would have hit him in the back.

I dropped back into my seat and plugged into the intercom system, to hear Jerry, rear gunner, cursing. His turret would not rotate at all. Meanwhile another shell burst close by. One could smell cordite from the bursting shells. Pete, the skipper, told us he could not hold the aircraft steady, and he thought we should have to abandon the aircraft, so I climbed into my parachute. By now we had three engines stopped and feathered and we began to lose height. Frank dropped the bombs and we tried to maintain height. We turned into our homeward run. My thoughts at this time, we could maybe make it back as far as friendly territory and then jump. I told Jerry I would come back to the rear of the aircraft and help him get out of his turret, so I took off my chute again, carried it back and dropped it near the door. On passing the flare chute, I hurriedly picked up the last bundles of window and pushed them down the chute one after the other, no pausing or counting the seconds - knowing it would not help us but would help the boys behind.

I then slid on my stomach down the rear fuselage to the rear turret and saw Jerry, our rear gunner, desperately trying to crank his turret round by hand. I could not operate the 'dead man's handle' as there was no hydraulic pressure or electrical power. Both these facilities were provided by the port engine, and this was dead. I suggested to Jerry, keep cranking. I will go forward and get the fireman's axe, which was stored behind the navigator's position, and try and cut a hole in the side of the turret and pass him his parachute. He could then clip it on and fall backwards out of the plane. It would have been a futile exercise as he had partly turned the turret so he could not fall out as planned or get back into the fuselage either. His doors had to be positioned either on to the beam or into the fuselage. His was halfway between; nevertheless I was going to try.

I slid back into the fuselage and plugged into the intercom above the door. Pete was shouting into his microphone, 'We are going down. Jump. Jump.' So I clipped my chute back on, kicked the catch on the door with my boot. It immediately flew open and swung off its hinges and fell into space. I jumped out feet first. It seemed to be a long way to the ground. The air pressure caught my chute and gradually somersaulted me backwards, until there was a loud clap and the chute opened and steadied my fall. It was then a peaceful sensation, I could breathe again, it was so quiet.

I then discovered I was completely lost, did not even know the direction I was facing and did not even have a clue as to where I was on the Continent. I looked up and saw four more parachutes above me, which was reassuring to me. Down below the fields and hedges, the woods and lakes fooled me into thinking there was no war on down there. But then the enemy started firing at me with rifles and machine guns. It was nerve racking until I hit the ground with a thump. We had been instructed way back in time that as soon as we hit the ground we should hide our parachute and harness, run from the site as fast and far as we could. This was not to be.

As soon as I hit the ground I released my harness and chute, stood up to take stock, only to find myself staring down the barrels of five German rifles. I immediately threw up my hands and surrendered. Within five minutes the other four had joined me. We had dropped in the German Front Line. They hustled us into a Dutch farmhouse until dark, then by truck into Germany; into a stinking prison cell somewhere. We had become reluctant guests of the Third Reich.

In Conclusion

Looking back over fifty years, talking and reminiscing with a few ex RAF pals at the 'Flying Club', I can only conclude that five of us out of the Crew were very lucky to escape with our lives intact. Unlike Jerry, our rear gunner, and Pete the pilot, who eventually paid the ultimate price. Jerry never got out and went down with the aircraft and was interred somewhere in Belgium. Pete, I understand, eventually did jump but was too low and suffered severe injuries. He was picked up by a British Tank Crew. He was eventually flown home to Canada and died from his injuries soon after.

Our bad luck was to be taken prisoner, to suffer humiliation, degradation, starvation and, at times, harsh treatment. (That's another story!)

RELUCTANT GUESTS

Bruce the navigator had a passion for accuracy and punctuality, and timed his descent at eight minutes. Sid was first down, caught, and soon joined by his other four crew members in a Dutch farmhouse. Later he regretted not eating the despicable food generously offered. They were all keen to get away as soon as possible, but a search found their escape kits, and they had not a lot of idea of their whereabouts.

After dark, they crossed a river to a barn where German soldiers were billeted. There they found their bomb aimer looking pale and shocked with a gashed hand, from shrapnel, which Sid bound with his handkerchief. They were then moved by lorry to a civilian jail, and all five shared a stinking cell.

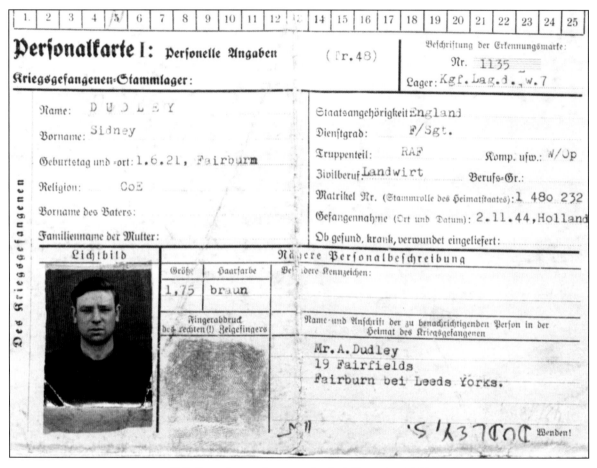

Sid's first prisoner of war record - 2nd November 1944

Bright ideas of escape came to nothing, and no wonder. Plan one by Bruce was to crown the jailer as he brought in the food and grab his keys. Sid volunteered to be hit man, but was foiled by a young blonde girl delivering five apples through the pop hole. Next night they 'dined' in an army canteen on fried pig potatoes, sauerkraut and Ersatz coffee. Bruce and the bomb aimer departed and the rest moved to a private house for questioning. More was required than name, rank and number on the questionnaire, and although the high-ranking, friendly ex-pilot plied Sid with cigarettes and promises of better accommodation, his negative answers condemned him to a solitary underground cell of eight by four feet. All their clothes were taken away to be searched. Sid lost his watch and his prized white polo-necked sweater, though he got his watch back much later. The heat was either at maximum or minimum, but after ten days still saying sorry, the officer seemed to have all the answers he wanted, and Sid assumes somebody squealed!

At a transit camp, welcome Red Cross parcels and overcoats were issued, before a two day rail journey, forty to a cattle truck, took them to Dulag Luft Vll, with a population of eleven to twelve thousand men. This was to be home for nine weeks. Frustration, boredom, hunger, humiliation, degradation and horror were just a few feelings that readily come to mind even now. Horror was when the duty detail for collecting soup, left his billet before the all-clear sounded, after a raid on a nearby town, to be first at the cookhouse door, and was shot by a guard. His last words were, 'Get that bastard.'

Dulag-Luft. Kriegsgefangenenkartei.		Gefangenen-Erkennungsmarke Nr. 113	Dulag-Luft Eingeliefert am: 11.12.44 L.

NAME: DUDLEY	Vorname des Vaters:	
Vornamen: Sidney	Familienname der Mutter:	
Dienstgrad: Fl/Sgt. Funktion: W/Op.	Verheiratet mit:	
Matrikel-No.: 1 480 232	Anzahl der Kinder:	
Geburtstag: 1.Juni 21		
Geburtsort: Fairburn	**Heimatanschrift:**	
Religion: C of E.	Mr. A. Dudley	
Zivilberuf: Farmer	19 Fairfields	
Staatsangehörigkeit: britisch	Fairburn bei Leeds Yorks.	

Abschuß am: 2.11.44 bei: Holland	Flugzeugtyp: Lanc.
Gefangennahme am: W.O. bei: W.O.	

Nähere Personalbeschreibung

Figur: mittel		Augen: braun	
Größe: 175 cm		Nase: gerade	
Schädelform: rund		Bart:	
Haare: braun		Gebiß: gesund	
Gewicht: 8 kg			
Gesichtsform: voll		Besondere Kennzeichen:	
Gesichtsfarbe: gesund			

Sid's prisoner of war record - 11th December 1944

Sid still has a small New Testament Bible, which helped to keep him sane. He says he's not religious but is a Christian. Those who know him wouldn't argue with that!

The Russians were advancing only twenty-four hours behind, and it was vital that prisoners of war were not taken by them. So when people complain of a poor holiday, with no sun, or a bad few hours flight to Florida or Hongkong, they should try to remember the stamina and endurance of Sid and his half-starved mates - two hundred and twenty-seven kilometres, walking through the snow for twenty-one days in a Polish mid-winter!

Coming from the land, Sid knew what to look for and where to find it to survive. Once he found a few handfuls of barley in the bottom elevator of a threshing machine in a barn. Raw sugar beet was delicious!

SGT. BEN COUCHMAN'S DIARY OF THEIR 227 KM MARCH - JANUARY 1945

Sergeant Ben Couchman POW kept the following pencil-written diary during the forced march from Bankau in Poland to Luckenwalde near Potsdam during January/February 1945.

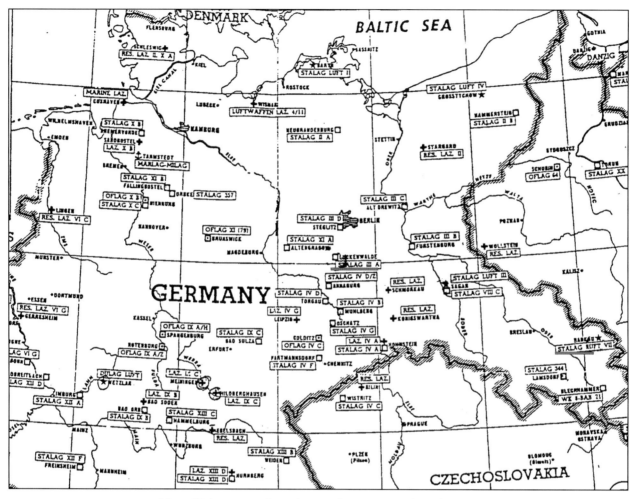

Map of Prison camps (Printed in Sunday News March 25th 1945.

Start of March (Bankau Stalag Luft 7) and End of Train Journey (Luckenwalde) are indicated in red

January 17th 1945: Bankau Stalag Luft 7

Things went as usual until about 11 a.m. when we were given orders by the Germans to leave ahead of the Russian advance. Then the panic started. Food that was likely to be left was eaten. Headquarters, stores and cookhouse were ransacked.

> Rumours were plentiful:-
>
> 'POWs unable to walk would be left behind.'
>
> 'During the march for every man who escaped or tried to escape, five would be shot.'
>
> 'We were outflanked by the Russians and there was no hope of the march succeeding.'

There was a roll call at 4 p.m. and we were told that probably the march would commence early the next morning, at the latest mid-day.

During this day there had been a continuous line of trucks, wagons and carts carrying military and refugees, proceeding west along the road passing the camp.

About 6 p.m. the Germans ordered 'prepare to move' and issued marching rations: 1/2 loaf, marg., honey and pieces of sausage. At 10 p.m. ordered to go to bed.

January 18th

Woke up shivering, as my blankets had remained packed overnight. Soup 8.30 a.m., roll call 9.30. Formed into three parties and told this would be our marching order. The road was full of lorries, horses and carts and refugees from the Russian advance.

> Latest rumour:- 'We were marching to Stalagluft 3 Sagan, which was 200km. away.'

At 4 p.m. in the afternoon another roll call ordered and we were informed that the march was postponed for two or three days. Half an hour later we were ordered to parade ready to leave. We waited for about an hour and then drifted off to the billets. The German guards were as confused as we were. Food was becoming a problem but a further raid on the cookhouse produced some oats and treacle. The air raid warning sounded while we were preparing the watery porridge, and all the lights went out. After which all 'non-walking' POWs were shipped out of camp to travel with civilian refugees. We were told to parade at 4 a.m. the next morning, and so to bed.

<u>January 19th</u>

Lights on at 3.30 a.m. Paraded 4 a.m. Stood around in the cold snow until 7 a.m. when we trudged out. That day we walked 28 kms. With the longest stop being half an hour. As we proceeded, the POWs had discarded in the roadside much of their possessions that were impossible to carry through the snow. Marching with an accordion was impossible for one POW and it was tossed into the snow with a lot of other possessions.

At night we were lodged in barns, I slept (?) sitting up.

<u>January 20th</u>

Awakened 4 a.m. and started marching about 6 a.m. Gerry said that Kreuzburg, that we went through yesterday, had fallen to the Russians and that they were now 10 kms. behind us. Gunfire could be heard all day. The marching was difficult in soft snow and the POWs threw more of their kit away. The guards picked a lot of it up.

Reached Karlsruhe shortly before noon and were put in a brick factory. Received cups of acorn coffee from the field kitchen. At 7 p.m. we were back on the road. The bridges over the Oder River were to be blown up by 8 a.m. the next morning and we were to be over the river by that time.

<u>January 21st</u>

We had walked all night through the snow and crossed the Oder River at dawn. We were told there would be rest and accommodation at a village 5 kms. Ahead. We heard the explosions of the Oder Bridge as we marched.

When we arrived at the village there was no accommodation for us. We walked a further 8 kms. And found refuge in barns. During the night some men dropped out due to the intense cold and fatigue. The only food we had during the past twenty-four hours was three slices of bread, a spoonful of bully, a small bag of biscuits and a cup of coffee, and we had marched for fourteen hours through the snow.

To bed, and the name of the village is Buckette.

<u>January 22nd</u>

Roused by Gerry at 1.30 a.m. who said we had to move quickly as the Russians had crossed the Oder north of us. There was an argument with Gerry before we marched another 20 kms. We sheltered once again in big barns. We received one biscuit between two and a pound of margarine to last five days. We dug in the frozen earth and found pieces of potatoes, carrots and peas and made ourselves a cup of soup, and then to our blankets. We had two blankets and slept fully dressed with every bit of clothing we possessed. The village nearby was Jenkwitz.

<u>January 23rd</u>

We were called at 6 a.m. and were on the road at 8 a.m. Promised better billets and a good meal when we arrived at our next destination. However, when we finally arrived it was more big cold barns, a cup of tea, a cup of soup, we found a few spuds, and then to bed.

<u>January 24th</u>

The village we were in was called Wansen and we were told we could rest all day. Made a fire and roasted a few spuds, supplied with two half-cups of soup and quarter loaf of bread from field kitchen.

<u>January 25th</u>

Wakened at 1.30 a.m. and on the road at 3 a.m. Weather warmer but walking through the slush more difficult. We passed through Strehlen and later in the day we put up in a barn at Heidersdorf, having walked 30kms. Issued with a cup of soup and a fifth of a loaf. French POWs said that the Russians were nearer to Sagan than we were.

<u>January 26th</u>

Stayed all day. Scrounged some spuds and beans and made some stew. Issued with two half-cups of soup from field kitchen and a seventh of a block of margarine. I went to bed.

<u>January 27th</u>

Awoke at 8 a.m. and, as there was nothing doing, stayed in blankets until 10 a.m. Issued with half a loaf of bread to last two days. Started marching 11.30 a.m. Roads crammed with civilian refugees. Rested in barns after walking 20kms.

<u>January 28th</u>

Wakened at 3.30 a.m. and on the road at 5 a.m. Walking easier as the snow had hardened. Walked 25kms. Many of the boys had frostbite in their feet. Arrived at the barns at 1.30 p.m. It was very cold and no fires were allowed, so I went to bed.

<u>January 29th and 30th</u>

Stayed in blankets until soup was served. Other rations were seven biscuits, 1oz margarine and one tenth of a tin of bully beef. At 4 p.m. ordered to prepare to move and started off at 5.30 p.m.

A blizzard was blowing and at times walking was tough, as the snow was two to three feet thick. Transport littered the roads, stuck in drifts and in the dark we had to walk single file to get round them. Reached our barns at 4 a.m. We had walked 21 kms. And Gerry tried to crowd us into two small barns. Then they opened up a small loft. It was 7 a.m. when I crawled into my bed. A tragedy hit me when I had to go outside for two minutes and someone stole my blankets.

January 31st

Woke up about 7.30 a.m. but stayed in bed until about 11.00. Roasted a few spuds I had scrounged from a Polish girl, and made a brew of tea. Gerry made us parade when he counted us, after which we marched to Goldberg where we would get transport ration from the field kitchen; half a cup of rolled oats, a little coffee, a tenth of a block of margarine and a small piece of bread. The weather was much colder; I cooked my oats and went to bed.

February 1st

Awakened 6 a.m. and on the road by 8 a.m. The roads were clearer of refugees. It had rained during the night, melted the snow and there were puddles everywhere. We stopped at some barns about 8 kms. from Goldberg. There was little room in the barn. I slept at a cowshed further down the road, after fencing off the cows and spreading straw over the dried cow dung. Gerry rations two fifths of a loaf, half an ounce of marg. and half a cup of oats.

February 2nd

Awakened by chaps getting water. Cooked more oats and a couple of spuds. Cows escaped and so we turned them outside.

February 3rd

Woke up fairly late, finished off my oats and drew half a cup of barley from field kitchen. Gerry issued rations - half a loaf and a quarter of a pound of margarine to last three days. Let the cows out just after dark.

February 4th

Had to get up at 8 a.m. to let the cows back in. Ate some bread and a cup of soup. Went to bed at 11 p.m.

February 5th

Cows broke loose at 2 a.m. and trampled all over our beds. We managed to get them out but were awakened at 4 a.m. and were on the road at 6 a.m. Arrived at Goldberg about 9 o'clock and were loaded into railway box cars which were thirty feet long and eight feet wide, thirty-six men to a truck. There was not enough room for all to sit down so we took it in turns. Travelled about 100 kms. And stayed the night in a siding.

February 6th

Train moved off at 6.30 a.m. and stopped about every fifteen minutes. Travelled about 100 kms. Finished off my food.

February 7th

Hardly slept. Train moved about 5 kms. during the whole day. Issued with one cup of acorn coffee. Train moved about 25kms. during the night.

February 8th

Everyone awoke very weak and shaky. About 10 a.m. the train stopped and we got out. Walked very slowly 11/2kms. to the camp at Luckenwalde. We were given one cigarette each, after which we had a hot shower and a cup of soup and spuds. It was our first food for nearly three days.

Bankau	- Winterfield	30km.
Winterfield	- Karlsruhe	20km.
Karlsruhe	- Pugwitz	41km.
Pugwitz	- Grosser Jewitz	20km.
Grosser Jewitz	- Wansen	25km.
Wansen	- Heidersdorf	30km.
Heidersdorf	- Plaffendorf	20km.
Plaffendorf	- Peterswitz	21km.
Peterswitz	- Praunitz	12km.
Praunitz	- Goldberg	8km.

		227km.

SID'S STORY CONTINUED

The survivors finished up in a camp at Luckenwalde with many thousands of all nationalities and abilities. Of the twenty in Sid's hut eighteen of them had flown Halifaxes. All thoughts of escape had gone. A radio was shared out between them for safety and eventually, when assembled, they heard on the Middle East wave band that General Montgomery was winning his desert war.

A Gerry guard who was in charge of roll call, or appel, had a small diary with a map at the back. Every day he would mark off and show them where the Allies had got to and the Russians too. The British were supposed to be at Leipzig twenty-six kilometres away.

With the end of the war in Europe only days away, camp guards were more relaxed but worried about their future. Some left and some just ran away. Sid and his three crew friends Bruce the navigator, Paddy the gunner and Frank the bomb aimer just walked out and headed west.

At about eleven o'clock, walking through a wood, they hid from a unit of marching Germans with their guns at high port, which means ready for action. Later they broke into a deserted cottage by a crossroads looking for food, but no luck. Up in the loft Sid found a German officer's uniform with a five hundred-mark note in the pocket, which he later disposed of in case it might lead searching Russians to think him a German with disastrous consequences. Whilst still up there Frank called him down to talk to four youthful Germans. One, with a white blanket round his shoulders and a mauzer underneath, spoke perfect English and asked to be taken to the British lines. Sid said they could tag along but throw their guns away as there were Russians about too. It was very scary as many more came out of the bushes. The situation was so frightening that Bruce went off back to camp, not wishing to get shot having come so far.

That afternoon they came to a farmhouse and stopped the night there. They hunted around for potatoes and turnips to boil up as they hadn't anything else to eat. Next morning they set off again, having lost the Germans. A young woman approached going like the clappers in a pony and trap. They stopped her and piled into the back and she took them into a town, which could have been Mulderdorf. There a Russian dragged her away, probably to rape her.

There was a bridge over the river with a Russian guard on with instructions to let no one over. They decided to walk so far down river and build a raft, but it didn't come to that. A young girl of about fourteen or fifteen came up on a bike. She spoke perfect English and understood their problem. She told them to wait and get across when the chance came. She rode up, gave the soldier her bike and he went off on it, which seemed like a miracle. The Russians were illiterate peasants, most of them were half-sloshed and this one had probably never had a bike. So away he went. They ran like hell over the bridge and didn't stop for half a mile.

Later they came across a broken-down Russian tank with an all woman crew. They made signs for something to eat and were given some slices of fat bacon and tubes of creamy cheese. They weren't allowed to light a fire to cook it, so they had to eat it raw like they did, and it wasn't bad. Further along they came on a Red Cross station in a village with only a woman there, who said she had been raped four times that day! She wanted them to take her with them but they had to refuse. She cut the blisters off their feet with scissors and put stingy anti-septic on them. She also gave them cotton wool pads as they hadn't socks on.

Going along a mainish road through another wood they came on eight German soldiers digging a big hole with two Russians in charge, who actually saluted them. They assumed the Germans were digging their own graves and quickly moved on. After another mile they decided to have a rest on top of a bank with a ditch behind, but when they looked in the ditch it was full of dead German soldiers, all laid head to toe, fully dressed for battle. They must have been shot too, so feeling queasy they hurried on.

Coming to a guesthouse seemed too good to be true, but they could only offer shelter for the night. However upstairs, occupying the beds, were Italian soldiers whose officer had a gun, so there was no arguing there. Sid slept in an old-fashioned armchair with his feet on a stool. Next day there were some Italian gypsies, probably slave labour and walking home. One woman gave them their first taste of macaroni, and Sid really enjoyed it boiled and with sugar on it. Then they jumped on a cartload of loose straw. Underneath something hard turned out to be a can of minced meat, which Sid put in his rucksack, made from an old towel. Later, when warmed up over a fire, they took it in turns to dip in.

They then came to a river, which Sid assumes to be the Elbe, with a plank and rope across it next to the blown-up bridge, and the Yanks and Russians at either side. The Russians were stopping people going over but not coming back their way. Sid shook hands with the guards and set off across, expecting a bullet at any moment. It never came and they were to be greeted by the Americans who made a big fuss. A jeep took them to their camp on an aerodrome. They had a medical, a light meal, cigarettes, and three baths in one day as they were lousy. They stayed there for three days, with others rolling up all the time, and then were flown in Dakotas to Belgium.

There were thousands of aircrew there and they were all given another medical, a meal of steamed fish, which was the only item on the menu for two days so that their stomachs could cope. and a bottle of wine. There were more hot baths and de-lousing, with DDT powder in every corner. Sid is amused that it is now banned. They scorched the bugs out of their clothes with matches. They were there three days then they flew back in an Australian crewed Lancaster of their old squadron into Wing.

On the desk, in the hangar checking them in, was a chap who had hidden in the roof of the brick factory with two others on the long march and had been left behind. They had been fed and chauffeured by a Russian tank crew, and handed over to the Americans when they met up. A much easier journey to freedom than Sid's gang had. They were confined to camp and the Sergeant's mess, were allowed one pint of beer and could send a telegram home. Eventually they were kitted out with clean new kit and sent home on a month's leave. After a week, reaction set in and Sid went back farming, helping George Bramley at Fairburn when he felt like it.

More paid leave followed as they were being kept on, ready to help out in the Far East. Much to Sid's relief the atom bomb solved that situation and Sid drew over £300 in back pay to start out in Civvy Street.

Sid spoke with feeling of missing the squadron and even prison life when he was first discharged, and describes it well. Squadron life consisted of ops. and checking instruments every day. If they didn't fly they went for a bash, and seemed to move in cliques of navigators, wireless operators, gunners, pilots, etc. and made as much nuisance as possible. If money was tight, and they couldn't get into Ely, they would strap it up in the Sergeant's mess. Sometimes, in more sober moments, they went into the cathedral, to listen to the organ and think, sometimes for two or three hours, to pass the time. Saddest times were when friends didn't come back and then they would drink to them on another bash. Sid's best friend, Don Swaine from Micklefield, had also trained as a wireless operator in front of him. Tragically he was missing on only his second trip laying mines. Two other Fairburners also joined the RAF. Frank Wilkinson, wireless operator/air gunner and Dennis Barker, navigator, but sadly, like Don, who was my wife's unknown uncle, they too disappeared without trace!

Sid left his glasses after our taping session on 17th December 1998 and I delivered them back to his trim bungalow in Riccall in the afternoon. As we stood in the conservatory extension surveying his immaculate lawns and tidied up flowerbeds, he said that he enjoyed having his breakfast there and reading the paper at leisure with a coffee. 'That's what I call retirement,' he said. Having had the privilege of hearing his story I said I would prefer to call it SURVIVAL!!J.D.B.

Sid Dudley
At Home Farm ploughing match 2001

SID'S ACTIVITIES PRIOR TO 2ND NOVEMBER 1944

Before he embarked on what was to be his final operation, Sid was involved in operations with 115 and 195 Squadrons flying from Witchford, Cambridgeshire.

List of Operations with 115 Squadron, Witchford, Cambridgeshire.

Date	Duration Day or Night	Aircraft No.	Duty	Aircraft Lost	Details from German Records
08.08.44	5.10 (Night)	AF4	Operation Bremen	10 Lancasters	Bombed in front of Allied Troops
23.08.44	1.30 (Day)	SND900	Air Test		
25.08.44	8.55 (Night)	A4H	Operation Russelheim (Diverted to Methwold)	13 Lancasters 7 Halifaxes	Opel Motor Factory 9 Killed, 31 Injured
25.08.44	0.25 (Day)	A4H	Return from Methwold		
26.08.44	5.20 (Night)	A4H	Operation Kiel	17 Lancasters	134 Killed, 1002 Injured
28.08.44	1.05 (Day)	A4H	Air Test		
29.08.44	9.30 (Night)	A4H	Operation Stettin	23 Lancasters	1569 Houses Destroyed, 565 Badly Damaged, 32 Industrial Premise Destroyed, 23 Damaged.
03.09.44	3.10 (Day)	A4E	Op. Eindhoven Airfield	1 Halifax	Raid Successful
05.09.44	3.10 (Day)	A4B	Operation Le Havre	No Losses	Bombed German Positions, No Details of Casualties.
06.09.44	3.15 (Day)	A4B	Operation Le Havre	No Losses	German Fortifications. Good Results.
08.09.44	3.30 (Day)	A4C	Operation Calais	2 Lancasters	German Positions
12.09.44	5.25 (Day)	A4B	Operation Frankfurt	17 Lancasters	One Troop Train Destroyed, 469 Civilians Killed.
20.09.44	3.10 (Day)	A4F	Operation Calais	1 Lancaster	German Positions
23.09.44	4.00 (Night)	A4B	Operation Neuss	5 Lancasters	617 Houses and 14 Public Buildings Destroyed, 289 Killed, 150 Injured.
25.09.44	3.05 (Day)	A4B	Op. Calais – Abortive		
26.09.44	2.25 (Day)	A4B	Operation Cap Gris Nez	No Losses	German Defence Positions
27.09.44	1.45 (Day)	A4J	H2S X-Country H.L.B.		
30.09.44	2.20 (Day)	K0B	H2S X-Country		
05.10.44	5.45 (Night)	A4H	Operation Saarbrucken	3 Lancasters	5882 Houses Destroyed, 1141 Damaged, 344 Killed.
06.10.44	5.15	A4H	Operation Dortmund	2 Lancasters 2 Halifaxes 1 Mosquito	191 Civilians Killed, 418 Injured, 38 Missing.

List of Operations with 195 Squadron, Witchford, Cambridgeshire.

Date	Duration Day or Night	Aircraft No.	Duty	Aircraft Lost	Details from German Records
14.10.44	3.55 (Day)	A4H	Operation Duisburg (Day Attack)	13 Lancasters 1 Halifax	Intensive Damage to Property, German Anti-Aircraft Overwhelmed.
14.10.44	4.20 (Night)	A4H	Operation Duisburg (Night Attack)	5 Lancasters 2 Halifaxes	9000 Tons of Bombs Dropped in Forty-Eight Hours, Large Number of People Buried Alive, City Wrecked
19.10.44	5.40 (Night)	A4H	Operation Stuttgart	6 Lancasters	376 Killed, 872 Injured
22.10.44	4.20 (Day)	A4H	Operation Neuss	No Losses	65 Killed, 175 Injured
23.10.44	5.35 (Night)	A4H	Operation Essen	5 Lancasters 3 Halifaxes	607 Buildings Destroyed, 812 Severely Damaged, 622 Killed, 569 Injured.
02.11.44	App.2.49 (Day)	A4H	Operation Homburg	5 Lancasters (including A4H)	Synthetic Oil Factory Destroyed

Sid's Operations

SHOWPIECE....LANCASTER

I dream now of another time,
Of soaring wings and slipstream whine,
Of airscrew arcs and engine drone,
And cloudy canyons I have known.

Once we were many, and we knew,
The love of thousands, our aircrew,
So many lovers, past recall,
Yet we were faithful to them all.

When towering columns split the night,
With brilliant beams of searching light,
Then in just moments we became,
Small insects, round a naked flame.

And with us then, our young men knew,
An eighth, unwanted, crewman flew,
He whispered, taunted, often near,
Unseen but known, for he was fear.

Time after time, we saw the cost,
To all who fought so well, yet lost,
For them a fiery plunge through space,
In another time, another place.

For you old lovers, youth has gone,
Relentless, time is moving on,
With arms outstretched, with measured pace,
To take you all in cold embrace.

Time has not marred my grim old frame,
To your fading eyes, I am the same,
Look well, all strangers standing there,
For I am the mighty LANCASTER.

Walter Scott, ex 630 Squadron Royal Air Force
(East Kirkby)

Bomber Station 1943? Actually East Kirkby Jan 1991 (Brian Goulding)

CHRISTINE AND SID - CATCHING UP (Christmas 2000)

I always knew that my quarter cousin (plus) Christine Bull (nee Bramley) and now living in Queensland, had had a much travelled and exciting life, and by acting as a kind of 'go between', I have come to know quite a lot about it.

I first met Fairburner Sid Dudley on a Sherburn Aero Club trip to East Kirby, and later I wrote up his flying experiences. As a lad he had worked for Christine's father (my Uncle Guy) at Crag Farm, and evidently must have expressed doubts at the suitability of nursing as her choice of career in a well-remembered conversation way back in 1948.

On a recent visit I suggested a surprise phone call would make Sid's day and they could review their last fifty years. Sid had an eventful war, up to being shot down, and sadly was the only one of five Fairburn flyers to return.

True to family letter writing tradition a six page summary duly arrived to be forwarded on to Sid, but is now back with me to be typed up, to add to Sid's adventures. Between them they have logged up a few air miles and memories.

J.D.B.

3 Myoora Place, Jindalee, Queensland,
Australia.
17th December 2000

Dear Sid,

It was good to talk to you when I was at Don Bramley's in June. I am sorry I wasn't able to get to see you again - maybe next time I am over there.

Don had given me a copy of your RAF adventures and I found it most interesting reading. You had a lucky escape when your aircraft was shot down.

After our conversation over the horse trough at Crag Farm (1948) I went to do my general nurse training at Leeds General Infirmary. It was hard work as you predicted but I enjoyed it. After becoming a State Registered Nurse I went to St Thomas's Hospital to do my midwifery training. I then returned to L.G.I. and did a year, mostly on night duty, mainly in Casualty. That really was hard work but I learnt a lot, especially on Friday and Saturday nights when the drunks came in and we had a policeman on duty all night. We used to stitch them up on the floor, as they tended to roll off the trolleys!

In 1954 I joined Princess Mary's Royal Air Force Nursing Service and worked in RAF hospitals at Halton, Cosford and Wroughton. From Cosford I was posted to the troopship 'Devonshire' - a Bibby Line ship, which sailed out of Liverpool. We did two short trips to Malta, Cyprus and Port Said, then a long trip out through the Suez Canal to Aden, Colombo and Singapore.

From Singapore we took the Fijian Regiment home to Fiji - they had been fighting the Communists in Malaya. They were interesting and friendly people and we were invited to the welcoming home ceremonies in Suva. The other sister on that trip was trained at St James's in Leeds.

After Fiji we headed for Christmas Island with the first troops to set up for the atom bomb tests. It was a lovely island then and I've often wondered what it must be like now. From there we went on to Honolulu and spent a pleasant few days there. The U.S. Immigration officials were amazed to find females on a troopship, and we were checked out thoroughly before being allowed ashore. We were only allowed $3 per day for expenses, so we had to take packets of sandwiches from the Devonshire and bottles of Liverpool lemonade to sustain us on Waikiki beach...!

We had an almost empty ship back to Singapore, where we picked up troops and families, then after Colombo we had to divert via Mombassa, Cape Town and Dakar as the Suez Canal had been blocked. We arrived back in Liverpool one cold November morning after a wonderful ten-month tour of duty.

Shortly after my return to Cosford I was posted to Wroughton and from there did Casualty Air Evacuation. We flew to Germany, Malta and Cyprus in Hastings aircraft and returned home packed with four layers of stretchers. Going to the Far East we used the Comet 2 aircraft calling at Aden then Singapore. As the Comets often had supplies to take to Woomera at that time the medical staff (usually 2 Sisters and 4 Orderlies) were left in Changi, where we went on duty at the hospital. I really enjoyed that time as we had a good social life and I got to know Singapore.

The hospital there was very primitive and poorly equipped, but we were quite busy treating Caltex employees and local Indonesian families. After a month there I was sent 80 kilometres up into the jungle to open a clinic with an English doctor in the oil-drilling area. Being right in the middle of the jungle there wasn't anywhere to go - no shops, cinemas, etc., but we did sometimes go further through the jungle to the coast, where we water skied. I had a pet monkey called Henry and he used to sit on my shoulder and hang onto my hair when I skied.

I met my husband, Tony, there. He was from Birmingham and was working as a surveyor doing exploration for Caltex. We were married in Singapore in 1960. When the Indonesian government stopped exploration we returned to England in 1961 and our daughter, Jane was born in Scarborough.

Early in 1962 we went to Nassau in the Bahamas, where Tony had a job surveying. It was very pleasant living there and we made lots of friends. Peter, our son, was born there in 1962, and our younger daughter, Susan, in 1967. Having small children I didn't do any nursing there but I helped out at a kindergarten for eighteen months before we left in 1971.

We spent a few months living in Yorkshire before coming to Australia in 1972. The man helping to find Tony a job quickly organised me into nursing again. I worked for twenty-two years in an aged care nursing home run by Italian nuns, and spent the last four years as Assistant Director of Nursing. All our children worked there when they were in high school – weekends – and it was very good experience for them.

I retired six years ago when Tony retired, but we still lead a busy life doing voluntary work and travelling. I work at a special school for disabled children and help with hydrotherapy. Tony does meals on wheels and also helps out at a local private radio station.

Jane now works for Quantas and flies round the world, as does Peter with British Airways. Jane is based in Sydney and will be in Los Angeles for Christmas. Peter is based at Heathrow – a very convenient base for us when we go over to the UK – and will be in San Francisco for Christmas.

Susan's husband, David, is an Army Sergeant and has just been posted to Pukapunyal north of Melbourne, after eleven years in Adelaide. We are joining them for Christmas and expect lots of fun with our nine-year-old grandson, Joshua.

After my father died in 1985 my mother came here to live with us. She had always wanted to travel and we had a wonderful stopover together in Singapore. Unfortunately, she only had seven and a half months here before she passed away, but I'm glad to say they were happy months. Auntie Wyn, Don's mother, sent me a letter that mother had written to her telling her how happy she was here

Christine and her mother in Singapore

Now I only have the Bramley cousins to visit in Yorkshire but we have good times together. Two years ago Don organised a family reunion and there were an awful lot of Bramleys there, including Betty and Jean – Arthur Bramley's daughters.

Bramley family reunion

So you see what a life I have had after your discouraging words, which I think made me more determined than ever to be a nurse!

My best wishes to you and your family for a Happy Christmas and a prosperous New Year.

Christine (Bull)

HARRY RAWLING AND THE RAILWAY OF DEATH

Dining near to four Japanese recently, and briefly noting their easy use of knives and forks compared with my hopeless and once only attempt at chop-sticks, my thoughts turned to Harry Rawling whose funeral I had attended on September 24th 1999.

As many people fly off on exotic holidays all over the world, worrying about knee space, jet-lag and airline food, with a standard of living and way of life as never before, Harry's mystery tour of Thailand and his experiences there may be worth telling, but won't be easy reading. Harry had started as a lad at Page's Mill, Tadcaster and finished as a director. We didn't do much business with him, but nevertheless he was always most helpful and friendly. I can't remember how I came to know about his war, but eventually I persuaded him to come and talk to our discussion group at Selby Fork. Luckily I taped him, and this is his horrific story.

Harry Rawling - Glad to be here

Don's been nattering for many years for me to talk on this subject, but it's a lot of years ago gentlemen, forty years ago, and the memory, thankfully, fades. This story starts in late '39 in Page's office at Tadcaster. War broke out in September and I was earning a pound a week. Wheat had got up to ten pounds a ton, Woodbines five for twenty and a pint of beer was fivepence halfpenny.

I was twenty-three and all the lads my age couldn't get into the forces quickly enough, so I went down to Lady Lane in Leeds to the recruiting offices. Everyone wanted to be among the glamour boys in the RAF, so I went in there. The chap said, "What do you do?" and I said, "I'm a clerk in an office in Tadcaster." He said, "That's not much good to us is it? Can you drive? Have you a public service licence?" When I said, "No." he said, "You're wasting my time. Your sort are ten a penny. We've no room for such as you!"

I was that annoyed I went straight down to the army office. "What regiment would you like to join?" the sergeant asked. "West Yorkshire," I replied, but he said they were full. The next I could think of were the Duke of Wellington, but no vacancies there. "So where can I go?" I said and I signed on the dotted line for the Royal Corps of Signals, which I'd never heard of. Three weeks later came a letter to report to 760 Great Cambridge Road, Enfield, which turned out to be the biggest garage I'd ever seen. It was January nineteen forty; fifteen degrees of frost, and every place to lie down occupied, except near a draughty sliding door. I had arrived at eleven at night, in my best blue suit. The stores were shut, no blankets, palliasses etc. and I sat on my case thinking I shouldn't have been in such a hurry to go to war.

January and February 1940 was a pretty keen time and I trained as a wireless operator. After two months basic training there, we moved into Norfolk for five or six months defending the perimeter of a 'drome now called Coltishall, but known as Scotto then, where the 242 Squadron of Canadians were commanded by Group Captain Douglas Bader. Also we were supposedly defending the East Coast against a German invasion. We had guns but no ammo, so it's a good job they never came. Then we hardened off in a Scottish winter, came back to Staffordshire, and were then earmarked for embarkation.

On the thirty-first of October 1941, half the Division went to Liverpool, and the other half to Glasgow, and we set sail into the unknown. I was on a boat called Orcades. The convoy joined up somewhere west of Ireland. Things were grim, sea support was limited, and we were told the first three or four days out would be the riskiest, as we would be in range of French based Stuka dive-bombers. Our only escort was one cruiser, HMS Calypso. Just before dawn there was a lot of aerial activity and we thought, "This is it. Here comes the Stukas," but it was the North American fleet coming to take over from

Calypso, with one aircraft carrier, two heavy cruisers and nine destroyers. And remember this date gentlemen, October thirty-first, 1941, six to eight weeks before the United States joined the war!!

We thought we were due for the Middle East but they escorted us to Halifax, Nova Scotia, and there we got on to American troopers (USS Westpoint). This boat was only a year old, had done one consular trip to Spain, and carried then sixteen to eighteen hundred people. Needless to say they put nine thousand troops on her. Bunks were twelve high in the hold.

Next stop was Port of Spain in Trinidad, but no shore leave there. We were still sure we were making for the Middle East. Three days out of Durban we deviated through the Roaring Forties nearly to Antarctica to avoid a large German raid. On December seventh the Japanese bombed Pearl Harbour, the Yanks came into the war, and on December tenth we arrived in Cape Town. We had a wonderful four days shore leave there. The locals couldn't do enough for us.

The American fleet left us and the Dorsetshire took over, sailing up the East Coast of Africa. Just off Mombassa another big boat went off, we found out later to Singapore, and we changed course to Bombay. We always thought that British troops were sacrificed politically in Malaya, because of the vast numbers of Australian troops struggling there. We stayed three weeks in Bombay whilst the powers that be saw how things were going in Malaya, and it wasn't very good. Two days out of Singapore our escort asked for all available air cover to see the large convoy in. Three bi-planes were all that were left. The Japs bombed the convoy but only got one ship, which was beached successfully without many casualties. We knew Singapore was doomed before we got there!

We arrived January 31st , and the capitulation was February 15th , so after all that training and travelling, my active service lasted just sixteen days, and it was complete chaos. It was supposed to be impregnable. No one knew who was in command. The locals didn't know there was a war on, and were wining and dining up to the night before surrender. Heavy fifteen-inch guns from HMS Elizabeth had been placed pre-war facing the sea. Other guns had no ammunition. The mile long causeway linking up with the mainland was blown up at the far end, and easily repaired by the Japs. The reasons for surrendering by the GOC, were no food, no ammunition, and no water, which came from the mainland along the causeway.

Our problems started on February 15th. The Japs had never heard of surrender, and we were the lowest of the low from the word go, and only in retrospect can we understand how they treated us. During the Malayan campaign 140,000 Allied troops were involved, of these 30,000 were killed, 90,000 taken prisoner and 20,000 wounded. The Japanese casualties were 10,000.

I finished up in the regular army area barrack blocks in Changi, most of which had been bombed. We didn't have many guards, as there was nowhere to go. Changing from army rations to a handful of rice and a few vegetables played hell with the constitution. Malaria and dysentery took its toll, and morale got very low. There was nothing to do, and about 70,000 in a tiny area. After about three months, I volunteered to go and work on the docks as a coolie, loading ships and living in the warehouses, which was a great change from stagnation in Changi. We found some army rations in a corner, and quietly mixed a bit of bully beef with the rice. But the Japs were dead against looting, as we soon found out. We hadn't been there long, when one of their army drivers had been caught flogging petrol to some local Chinese. His officer executed him there and then in front of our working party, with a great two-handed samurai sword. We hadn't been happy to start with, and that didn't help!

Their favourite punishment was to put you into a sort of cane box. You couldn't stand, kneel or sit. You just had to crouch, and seven days without food or water was a very long time! Also standing holding heavy weights above your head in front of the guardroom was another punishment. We thought hard before looting with those sorts of punishments!

About this time the Japs thought we should be paid, and they came out with a cardboard currency in cents. My rate was about fifteen cents a day, being a sergeant. One egg from the Chinese cost about $2.50 - a fortnight's work.

In December we were told we were going off to a land of milk and honey where the food and conditions would be a lot better. We had worked hard on the docks, and this was to be our reward. Thailand and some reward it turned out to be!! The British had laid the railways in Malaya and supplied the rolling stock. I had loaded sacks of corn into those iron box wagons with sliding doors before the war, and that was our transport - thirty-five in each. During the day it was unbearably hot, and at night terribly cold. All we had was our few personal belongings. They only stopped once a day for a handful of rice and a drink of water. Fifty percent of the lads suffered from dysentery, which is more or less permanent diarrhoea. Hanging out of the sliding door, over the chain, was the toilet system. What a state we were in!

The journey took five days, and we arrived in a place called Banpong in Thailand. The grapevine had it that the idea was to join a railway from Bangkok to Rangoon. Bangkok to Banpog was already built. We were actually on the stretch between Banpong and Mulmain. The Germans had surveyed this jungle in 1936 for the Thais, with the idea of completing the line, but had said it was absolutely impossible. The Japs intended tackling it, and all they had was rolling stock in Malaya, and lines that were to be ripped up and moved to Thailand. They had an unending supply of labour, Allied prisoners-of-war and natives.

We got there and were dumped in bare jungle, just one mass of bamboo, which we chopped down for huts and shelter. The only consolation for us was the temperature was reasonable. As you may have gathered, we were underfed and under clothed. We had hardly any medicines, and no treatment for malaria or dysentery. In our poor condition the slightest scratch from a bit of bamboo produced festering sores, which spread and often led to amputations. I was lucky. With a small leg ulcer, I could see daylight past my shinbone and was beginning to think of amputation. But a pal of mine came back with some carbolic acid from the cookhouse. The doctor said it might do the trick, if I could stand the pain. He plastered it for three days, and eventually it healed.

At first, when we had anaesthetics, doctors asked for volunteers to keep the flies off, but later in cold blood we had to hold people down. At one camp there were about two hundred with something or other off. We used to time various surgeons - six and a half to seven minutes was about the best for a leg. In the early days one or two tried to escape. Eventually they were caught and brought back. Everyone was paraded after work to watch them dig their own graves, and if they were lucky shot, if not bayoneted into them.

But back to the railway. It was purely chopping down the bamboo for various uses. Stretchers were made by putting two poles through either side of a bag, and with a man at each end were very efficient. The Jap engineers would come along and put levelling poles up, and then we were either digging a cutting, or building an embankment. We worked eighteen hours a day. The rice ration was eight ounces per man, and if anyone was sick, meaning they couldn't work, their ration was stopped. Eventually we got so many bags of rice for so many yards of line, and no more 'til it was completed.

I've seen men carried to work, lying at the line side breaking stones. There were no excuses, and the Japs were the same with themselves. If a soldier was injured in action, the next senior had to assess if he would be any further use, and act accordingly. And every morning, wherever he was, a Japanese soldier would take his hat off, bow to the sun, and mutter something like, "Emperor, I'm sorry I didn't die for you yesterday, but I'll do my best to die for you today."

So you can appreciate our situation. They were madly fanatical. All the supplies came up the river, and as we got up the line, illnesses got worse and more people died, but replacements kept coming up from Singapore plus more native labour. As long as the work rate was acceptable, they didn't care how many died, and it was no use complaining.

Well the line was four hundred and fifteen kilometres long the total casualties were 116,000, which works out at one death every eight yards. It took three and a half years to build. Two thirds of the way along we ran into cholera, which is a painful disease, and you can be dead within twenty-four hours. There was a special camp called Konkri. Sixteen hundred British troops went in and twelve hundred died, mostly from cholera, At this time we never expected to survive this railway line. You were always suffering from something, and less food and no medical supplies, and then came the monsoon. Three months rain, very little clothing, and we worked right through it on a handful of rice. There were a lot of accidents too, but I suppose some of us believed in miracles, which might get us through, and one happened. They dropped the bomb.

It was a pretty grim time. We never got any news, and it was all rush to finish, because they wanted to use it. Eventually it was completed at a place called Konkuita where both ends met up. The Japs actually used it for five or six days bringing up troops and supplies. They were so unsure about the bridges that one driver walked across first, the other set it off and got out, and his mate got in at the other side to stop it. Then the RAF set about it from the Burma end and demolished it in six weeks. To try and stop this the Japs moved lots of prisoners-of-war to strategic points and lots of lads got killed by our own bombs.

The order went out that we had to be graded. Those unfit for work to stay in Thailand and the others back to Singapore. I had weighed in on joining up at thirteen stone four, and at this time I was down to six stone five pounds and passed fit for further work. In due time we were hauled back, and the change was amazing. They were very anti-British after the capitulation, with Japanese flags coming out from under the beds. Three years later there was a complete change of attitude. They had had enough of them, as they had plundered and shipped everything back to Japan. One of the most welcome sights to me was a four-engined US plane bombing the docks, which were about derelict anyway.

Then we found out we were bound for Japan, to work in the salt mines. For three weeks we lived off rice and horrible fish stuff and nothing else till they took us to the docks. We'd had a pretty rough time on the line, but the next three days was about the worst! Eight hundred of us were stuffed down the hold of a little coaster. You could neither stand, sit nor anything, just one human heap at the bottom of a boat. They pulled the hatch covers over, and took us out waiting for a convoy to form. After three days without food or water they took off the covers and we pulled out thirty-seven dead.

Eventually a convoy of about eleven boats set out, containing three oil tankers, three destroyers and coasters including ours full of prisoners-of-war. Around dusk on the third or fourth night out there were a series of terrible explosions, and the same again at dawn. We learned later that two American submarines had sunk them all bar ours, and Chinese spies had saved us.

They dare not go any further towards Japan, so we went to Saigon, which was French Indo China, and very friendly towards us, and the food improved. Then eventually we started building an aerodrome, nearly on the border of China, at Phnom Penh in Cambodia. It was then June/July '45, and the Japs were very touchy, as things went very much against them. They told us they expected an invasion of Malaya, and possibly parachutists. We were set to dig a large moat around the camp as defence against them. We found later it was for our own graves, but fortunately it didn't come to that because the atomic bomb was dropped and the Japs surrendered. They still carried on with their atrocities, and thousands were murdered in out of the way camps. We were lucky being near Saigon, and US planes were soon dropping leaflets telling us and them what to do, and what not to do. A fortnight later a regiment of Ghurkas came in and sorted them out. There were thirteen hundred prisoners in our camp, and the quinine ration had been nine tablets, enough for one person for one day. The day after the bomb dropped, they brought in twenty thousand bottles! Their excuse had always been there wasn't any! They did start treating us a little better, but it was too late then for many.

In due course, we assembled on Saigon airfield, and some old Dakotas came in. After surviving the last three and a half years I didn't fancy them, but quickly got on, when told the alternative might be an extra six months. We flew to Rangoon via Bangkok, where we were screened and went through an army hospital unit. Lord Louis Mountbatten met every consignment that came back. They wanted evidence of all the ill treatment we'd had, names and witnesses, and he was keen that anyone, who so wished, could stay behind and witness the executions. We were happy to say our bit and get out. Doctor Derrick Smith from Barwick-in-Elmet was in Singapore, and one of his jobs was signing death certificates. A lot committed Hari-Kari but not many of the guilty ones got away.

We left Rangoon on a boat called the Orduma, calling at Columbo and Port Suez. We got our first mail for three years at Gibraltar, when I found out that my father had died two years before. We were occasionally given postcards to send with five things to fill in - I am well, I am working, I am ill, and I've forgotten the others. The only ones sent off had to be I am well or I am working. Two of mine got home but took three years. On October 31st, 1945 we arrived back in Liverpool, the same place as we had set out from so long ago.

A few weeks ago there was a letter in the Daily Telegraph from a chap called Stan Cherry of West Moors, Dorset, who I was with for quite a while.

Harry (left) at Sledmere on York Birthday Club Trip - also Ben Blacker, Arthur Blacker, Jim Barton,
Alf Watson, Doug Elliot, Stanley Bayston, John Barton and Nigel Sampson

LETTERS TO THE EDITOR

ANNIVERSARY OF A RAILWAY

Sir -- Forty years ago, on Oct.17, 1943, a ceremony took place in the middle of the Siamese jungle. The present anniversary is one that not many former Far East prisoners-of-war would care to celebrate joyfully, even if they remembered it, and indeed there is a far too rapidly diminishing number of them still around to do so.

All the same it was on Oct. 17 that the two portions of the Burma-Siam Railway met, at Konkuita, the one coming up from Thailand totalling 265 kilometres and the line from Burma 152 kilometres.

It would be amusing to record that the two ends missed by half a mile. Perhaps presaging Japan's rise as an industrious engineering nation they met exactly, whereupon a copper rail was laid and secured with a golden spike -—quickly removed by the Japanese before the prisoners could get at it.

Probably more to the point as statistics are the numbers of Allied prisoners who built it: 30,000 British, 13,000 Australians, 18,000 Dutch and 700 Americans. Of them 13,000 died. At the height of the Japanese "speedo" we were joined by an unknown number of impressed local labourers, of whom 90,000 died.

On a 250-mile railway line between us we had shifted 150 million cubic feet of Siam and Burma and counting the local labourers, had left one dead body for every 13 feet of track. As an exercise in managerial ability it was abysmal; as a way of reducing prisoners it had proved first class. What can one say now about such figures and such an enterprise? That the railway was built against the rules to provide a sea/land link for the Japanese armies fighting in Burma and for the eventual conquest of India: that it was built in not much more than a year, from June 19, 1942, when the 600 prisoners of "B" Battalion under Major R.S. Sykes, RASC left Singapore, until that day in October, 1943: that it was to figure hugely in "The Bridge on the River Kwai", and that there never was such a Colonel on either side, nor such a bridge, come to that: that the boys who built it have never been quite the same since and in far too many cases are now either dead or pre-maturely ageing men; that when the "Railroad of Death" had been finished there were still almost two years of captivity to go: that when the war was over – an unkind cut, this – the unhappy railway was deemed not to be viable and for the most part was pulled up.

My reason for adding to all that has been written is the hope that my letter will be a reminder to those who care to listen that while the mainstream of hostilities ground on inexorably during those years, something much worse than they can possibly imagine was also going on, in a backwater of the war, an undeveloped tropical wonderland with almost every tropical disease in the book, and probably some that weren't.

We were young, and had been fit, at the beginning. I was young, Royal Signals (Territorial Army) and about as young and fit as it was possible to be, at the beginning.

It is now "40 years on". I hope there will still be some of us around to remark the 50th anniversary. Rather sadly I feel there will not be many.

But those who did come home came with something more than a disinclination to love their late enemy or when they grew older to buy his cars. They had been together up that famous creek, without any paddle, and come through.

Their lives may have been shortened, but there wasn't much that could be done to them in the years ahead that hadn't been done already. Three-and-a-half years of deprivation and misery, sickness and tears, and the occasional laugh, had been traded for a marvelous feeling of "we made it" that we shall carry with us to the end. Or maybe it is because we were young and those times now seem great because it is our youth that we look back upon with envy.

We left too many good men behind in the military cemeteries at Chungkai and Kanchanaburi, and others still buried in jungle graves with the great trees their only memorial. And the ones who came home, and are now wearing out – if your readers know one who needs a helping hand, please give it.

As for me, I would like to have three wishes. One is that the young of today will peer at us, all of us who came through the Second World War, and resolve that Britain must remain strong: another is that we must try never to be so colossally stupid again. The third? Of course, to go back to see what is happening to our railway.

STANLEY CHERRY
West Moors, Dorset.

P.S.

PS. Stan Cherry had written such a good, moving letter back in 1983 that I couldn't resist the temptation to see if he had survived to the fiftieth anniversary. Helpful directory enquiries gave me three S. Cherry's in that area. Number one, no reply; number two, a fax; number three, please leave your message after the tone. The message left went, 'If you are the Stan Cherry, ex Japanese prisoner-of-war, who wrote a letter to the Telegraph in 1983, please phone this number.'

At ten o'clock next morning, seventy-nine year old the Mr Cherry is on the line for a helpful and interesting chat. The following morning, as promised, a copy of the letter, various snippets and useful facts about the Railway of Death are in the post.

Although I have had the odd bad dream just writing about it, this has been a worthwhile exercise, and Stanley Cherry's presence on the phone, and in real life too, makes for a Happy Ending.

THE ONE THAT GOT AWAY

At long ago Drax Old Boys dinners, I used to admire the good fortune of a few Worthies, who gave out their years as 1914-18. Back in February, I was in a similar situation, talking to a class at Hungate school, on my war memories!!! As my well-behaved and attentive audience of eleven year olds were of my age when the war ended, I had to confess I hadn't many first class experiences to pass on.

I could tell them that Dad's Army isn't over exaggerated, having spent Sunday afternoons, Just William like, spying on their drilling and mock battles. In the days before computers and of hand hoeing sugar beet for three or four weeks, I heard every year the same stories of Uncle Arthur's platoon at Fairburn. Their exercises usually ended with his words, "Now lads, another cock up!" — but it was the best time of Jim's life.

Memorial to Ever Young Elder Panton Brother

I proudly accompanied my father on his fire service duty night at Sherburn pictures, sitting in those two seats at the top of the aisle and in the 1/9's free! Afterwards we looked in at their headquarters behind Mills' shop before walking home.

Mother's apple pies and cakes were taken to hungry soldiers guarding the aerodrome, in exchange for trying on their hats and swivelling their guns. It was the same towards the end of the war with German and Italian prisoners in exchange for badges and buttons. But it was the aeroplanes of that time that thrilled me, and still do. I knew most of them by sight and sound, made balsa models, and got innocently high on the sniff of dope, glue and the sticking on of transfers.

I will always be thrilled with the stories of those times, I get a special tingle mixing with and talking to the brave people who took part and were lucky enough to come back! Anyone similarly afflicted will enjoy Lincolnshire Aviation Heritage Centre at Earl Kirkby near Skegness. Farming brothers Fred and Harold Panton are the unlikely owners of a Lancaster bomber there, which they are patiently restoring. Their wives and daughter run the Naafi and shop, and it is all a wonderful memorial to their elder brother who didn't return. His youthful portrait (19 years old) holds pride of place amongst the prints, paintings and memorabilia.

I was there on a bus trip from Sherburn Aero Club May 8th 1996, with a few young at hearts who had, it seemed to me, spent their best years servicing Lancasters. Bill Bell had actually baled out of one fifty-three years ago and spent the rest of the war behind wire. His explanation of the life and escape route of a rear gunner didn't attract me to that job.

Bill Bell

We were unlucky to have picked the wrong day to hear the two working Merlin engines fire up, but the still lively wives had no problem charming Fred and Harold to slide open the many doors and have 'Just Jane' trundled out, and have the traditional team photo taken in front.

Buying my flying guru Digby Lamb the video, instead of £15 bus fare, proved good value too, and very informative. The bomber had been built in 1945, and so too late for any action. It was in Australia, and flown back in 1965 to be put on show in Blackpool. It was sold privately in 1972 and was for many years outside RAF Scampton, home of the Dambusters, before eventually coming into Panton ownership in 1987. It took eleven men thirteen weeks to remove it to East Kirkby.

Digby Lamb & J.D.B. at East Kirkby

The engines had been idle for twenty-two years. Two ex RAF engineers took up the challenge and after seven hundred and twenty-eight man-hours on the job, one engine finally spluttered into life. Four months later and number two was working, at a cost of £7000 each. The finance involved in restoring the rest of the plane makes it extremely unlikely that 'Just Jane' will ever fly again. But when you consider what two Lincolnshire chicken farmers have achieved already, and the pleasure they have given along the way, it wouldn't surprise me at all if it did!!

If you know of any veterans from those stirring days, talk to them and learn from them. Like those fellow Old Boys of long ago, they won't be here for ever!

Flight Lieutenant Henry George DFC was guest speaker at a Draxonian's Dinner in December 1994. After listening to his story we realised how lucky he was to be with us. Most memorable however was his recitation (plus actions) of a poem he had written looking back at an airfield, and the excitement and thrill of setting out on a raid and, for Henry, coming back.

J.D.B.

REFLECTIONS

For all of us here gathered, our thoughts are just one,
We've passed our youth and halcyon days, life's journey nearly done.
Our tread may now be slower, our actions more sedate,
Our reactions not as quick now, as when we played with fate.
But to each and all our memories are more vivid at this time,
Memories compiled and gathered when we were in our prime.
Our journey down the motorway has closed a gap in years,
And stilled a recollection and an eye too damp with tears.
Amidst a derelict airfield, in neglect and in decay,
Flights of fancy overpower us, gently take our thoughts away.
Transported on a magic carpet, back through the years back into time,
We see this and other airfields as we saw them in our prime.
Battle orders quickly posted early in the day,
Petrol bowsers and bomb trolleys to each aircraft make their way.
Guns are harmonised and loaded, equipment checked for wear and tear,

Engines run at rated boost and revs to get them there.
Teleprinters spell the target, spell the route and spell the time,
Wanganui or Paramata, details come in endless rhyme.
Then the lull before the briefing, the airfield quiet and still,
Many thinking, many resting, some the time in writing fill.
Dusk approaches, stars are showing, the sun already set,
Briefing room already full, one can sense the sweat.
Red tapes show the route to target, slight alterations here and there,
Long and deep the penetration, through the dark and still night air.
Eat your meal in subdued silence, each and all in silent thought,
Of parents, homes, friends and loved ones, not of the trip with danger fraught,
Then by crew bus to dispersals, laden down with all our gear,
Start the motors, test equipment, feel the tension, feel the fear.
The airfield now has full vibration, noise that splits the still night air,
Nav lights gleam, exhausts flashing, as each bomber takes the air.
Gradually the sounds subsiding as the squadron moves away,
Fainter now the sound of motors, nav lights slowly fade away.
Now the lull before the landing, the airfield quiet and still,
Ground crews resting, meals preparing, leisure now the time to fill.
Light of dawn is now approaching, the airfield again will come alive,
Flare paths glowing, chance lights gleaming, to dispersals transport drive.
The airfield again has full vibration, noise that splits the morning air,
Tyres on tarmac cause a screeching, pyrotechnics fill the air.
Tired and weary are the warriors, dark of eye and pale of face,
Men who through the hours of darkness, saw death's spectre face to face.
Gone those ghosts of past reflection, in the present time we stand
Near an airfield now forgotten, except by us, this Crispin band.
Crumbling and decaying buildings, a squadron block which is no more,
Hangers filled with junk and rubbish, straw and dirt on mess room floor.
Where are the men who fought the battle, where are the men who led them there?
All are older, most are wiser, most look back in quiet despair.
Others they are marked by crosses, where the Rhine and Elbe flow,
Bathed in summer by the sunlight, covered by the winter snow.
Memories only can sustain us, solace sometimes found in tears,
Past comradeship essential, in the autumn of our years.

Flight Lieutenant Henry George DFC

Sid Dudley, Fred Panton, Harold Panton and Bill Bell Amongst Still Glamorous Ladies on Aero Club Trip

NURSE METCALFE

The late John Sands who drove the library van fixed up a night with Nurse Metcalfe. She was my second victim with Ken Ford's borrowed BBC tape recorder. She was a hardy lady who didn't wear stockings, and with mottled legs that had been too near her fire over the years. Her house, the old vicarage at Church Fenton, was a living museum and there was always a bottle of beer and fruitcake when I called.

I went to her funeral five years later in 1980 and would have loved to have had her poker, knowing its story, but it wasn't to be, and where everything went I have never heard.

This meeting takes place on February 16th 1975. It has been a dry mild winter and the lawns have already been cut. These are troubled times with inflation, unemployment and rising prices; revolutions and bombs in Ireland. Mrs Thatcher has defeated Mr Heath.

Nurse Metcalfe at WI Slide Show

I was one of the early health visitors under the WRCC and I had twenty-five villages and Selby to visit. I got £85 a year, £3 for a bicycle and £5 for uniform. Biggin, Little Fenton, not Church Fenton as it went in with Tadcaster, Hambleton, part of Gateforth, Wistow Lordship, Cawood, Drax, Drax Hales, Hirst Courtney and Temple Hirst were some of the villages.

Once I was biking along the riverbank at Newlands when the bore came down the river, rushing along. The river was deep down and the next moment it was washing the bike and me. I dropped it and fled to a cottage and one of the men there went and retrieved it.

In the forty-seven floods I went to the gate with the intention of going to Mass at Scarthingwell and the water got deeper as I got to the gate. As a general thing I didn't usually wear stockings so I took off my shoes and waded out. Water was flowing down the road like a river, and I was past the White Horse before I could put my shoes on again. I got to Mass and begged them for one for the water to stop, because it was really frightening to see it flowing all over the fields and gardens. Father said he couldn't because he'd already promised it for Mr Atkinson who lived down at Tank House by the railway line.

When I got home I bethought myself of an old lady who lived at Holly Cottage, two doors away from me. So I paddled there and she was shouting, 'Help, help,' from the bedroom window. There were some youths and men opposite sitting on a wall watching the water, not taking the least notice. She had a lot of rose trees in her garden and my poor feet suffered. I said, 'Please come down Mrs. Clarke, I'll get you out.' She said, 'I can't, it's over the kitchen table.' She brought some dry shoes and socks and eventually we got the door open and out she came. I shouted to those wretched men to come and help us out of the rose garden, which they did of course.

There were floods before in 1893 but I wasn't here then. This house has never been flooded because it's on rising land. They knew where to put them when it was built.

(We're enjoying this nice warm fire. Can you tell us something about it?)

The two Mr Sunderlands from South Milford wanted it for York Museum but my mother said, 'No.' There are some steps up the chimney and before this range was put in it's thought it was an escape route in the time of the persecutions. There certainly is a hideaway in the wall, which you can see before you go. The range itself is two hundred to two hundred and fifty years old.

Fireplace at The Old Vicarage, Home of Nurse Metcalfe

(Tell us about the clock that's ticking away. You say there are only two of them.)

Yes, they are in the clock books. Rono Rollison made them and this one is dated 1720. The other one is in Scotland. It was made for my father's uncle, a Doctor Day, who practised around Halton, this end of Leeds. The spinning wheel and desk are of the same period and I think they came together.

There are five tree trunks supporting that wall behind you Don. I had it stripped and re-plastered. It's a good two feet thick.

(What's the brass thing there with the glass on top?)

That's a shell case from the Battle of Jutland that my brother brought home. He wasn't supposed to but he did.

(And the poker?)

This is a bayonet from Salonika. Really it was picked up above Kramien in Yugoslavia for me to get a little more hot water from a wood fire, when I was there with a casualty. It's four-sided and experts have said it's Turkish.

(Said clock strikes ten.)

(Time flies at this job. Tell us please about some of the big houses you visited.)

Scarthingwell I know best and I well remember the Duke of Norfolk, who has just died, coming there as a young boy of about sixteen or seventeen. He came quite often from Everingham because his Aunt, Miss Louisa, was his mother's sister and Mr Arthur was his Uncle, and their young daughters and son were all very friendly. These were the Maxwell Stewarts. The house and gardens were beautiful. They'd a tennis court and a gorgeous lake with swans and yellow and white water lilies. Mr Arthur loved his swans and water lilies.

(Have you seen it lately? It's a swamp.)

I know. It's sad! There's a beautiful chapel at Scarthingwell. It used to be half full of maids, servants and outdoor staff when I first remember it. I'd go sometimes in the evening for nine o'clock prayers. They'd be playing tennis but we all went in for prayers. Father Bray was the priest and Father McGirke came after him.

Lotherton was my next love. Colonel and Mrs Gascoigne were so kind giving recommends for the miners and any other people from Aberford, Barwick and Garforth to go convalesce at Bridlington, Harrogate, Ripon, etc. The hall had enormous vases around when you entered. The old Colonel liked to be in there. It had a huge settee in front of a roasting fire, even in summer. There were big easy chairs and chests and these huge Chinese vases, eight or nine feet high, standing about.

It looked so bleak and bare when I went to see it last year after it had been taken over. I sat down on one of the chests to write something and one of the attendants told me to get up at once as it was very precious.

(What about early transport memories?)

Well, we had a trap when I was a girl. I was at the Girls' High School in Manchester and remember the first electric tram after the horse trams. It was all lit up. I saw my first car in Manchester too.

(Had it a red flag in front?)

No, that was for the trains! But I learned to drive in York and people would stop and say, 'Look, there's a woman driving!'

(Can you remember your Grandfather?)

No because my father's father was a sea captain and he died at sea the month my father was born. My mother's father was an architect and surveyor in Leeds and he died before my mother married. We have a tradition of the sea. My brother was on sailing ships and the tramps with Runcemans. He was apprenticed to them and it was very expensive. It cost fifty pounds to become a midwife. It was always three years to become a nurse and then get to be a midwife six months after that.

I went to Leeds as a sister when there was a matron, two day sisters and one night sister. I was one of the day sisters at Leeds Maternity. I went visiting to St. James's (as it is now). It was the Workhouse then - Beckett Street Workhouse. It was a great big, horrible, gaunt place to visit and still is, and they were looking for a blood donor. They couldn't get anyone with the right blood and when I rang up the next day the patient had died. I thought, 'This is dreadful. I wonder what sort of blood I've got.' Mostly men gave blood then, so I went to a session at Leeds Infirmary to see if I was suitable. You got a thorough check and asked lots of questions. Eventually I was given a card and I was Group O (there was no Rhesus factor then), which meant a universal donor. There are still only four kinds of blood.

The first immunising against diphtheria was done at Swillington in August 1933 and if you look in Swillington church-yard at the graves of young children it was bad there, but we didn't have a case for another ten years. Miss Brice ran the isolation hospital at Longwood. Doctor Ratcliffe and Doctor Hill were the doctors. The one at Lennerton was only for smallpox. Garforth Cliff was the other. When Doctor Harold (Ratcliffe) died the McCandlishes took over, and you can't beat the McCandlishes. I don't care who sends for them, a gypsy, anybody, they are there, one or the other! I also remember Doctors Pickersgill, Thirkill and Ashmore at Sherburn and George Metcalfe.

I used to visit the old people as well as the babies, the crippled and the gassed. There were a lot of gas cases at Garforth. Also I visited pumps and wells, everything. I went to Newthorpe Barracks one day. They were in great trouble because there were two dead cats and a dog in their well. It was their only drinking water. In the bad time in the twenties we ran soup kitchens which were really the start of school dinners. They found the children were much healthier with a good midday meal, which was provided by ex-soldiers, who had a sort of set pot that everything went into. Currants, ham, cabbage, carrots, potatoes, anything they could collect was washed and went in and was boiled. The net result was very palatable. They used to go to the Council School at Garforth or Great Preston and help to cut up chunks of bread to feed the children. They used to shout, "I've got a sprout." It was a lucky dip. People would line up to take a jugful home.

They had to work to get any dole. Six weeks they had to do and that road from Tadcaster to York was done by men who managed to get signed on to do it. It was terrible in Selby and the surrounding villages. I used to take a packed lunch, but I never ate it myself because there was always some starving family. This was before the First World War. The poverty was terrible. I could very often get a family a chit for a pennyworth of yeast and a stone of flour, which cost about eight-pence, to make bread. I never got a penny myself and I was only getting eighty pounds a year and I'd to live you know. I paid a pound a week to lodge in Selby as most of my area was at the other side.

When I trained in midwifery, when you got a typhoid case in an ordinary surgical ward that bed was a barrier case. A gown was thrown over the bottom and when a nurse attended that case she would put the gown on, scrub her hands thoroughly, do what she had to do, scrub her hands again and leave the gown on the bed. Woe betide if anyone else got typhoid in that ward. It was a terrible epidemic. Hundreds died. You couldn't go out without meeting a funeral.

In the 'flu epidemic after WW1, I was abroad to start with but I didn't miss it as it was all over Europe and into Greece and Salonika. We had fourteen deaths from 'flu when I was on night duties on Armistice night. It was bitterly cold and freezing and you couldn't bury anyone, it was too hard. Of course we were under canvas.

On marriage I'd say, "Yes you can have a separation if you want," but we very rarely had a divorce in my district. I was very much against it. Sometimes they did separate, but they always got together again. I used to say, "If you've loved them enough to marry them and live with them for a year or two, you should stick together."

(Let's get back to the big private houses you got into and from one extreme to the other. What about Lotherton and Parlington?)

I only remember Parlington as a ruin because of course they'd built Lotherton. Monk Fryston was a beautiful place. I remember Mrs Hemsworth and her sister Nurse Duke. She was a marvellous nurse and did it in a voluntary capacity, just like Miss Alice Maxwell Stuart up to a few years ago. She manned the hospital at Easingwold - St. Monica's. She didn't get paid either.

Monk Fryston was beautiful, but ordinary compared with Scarthingwell and the Fielden's at Grimston Park. The old Colonel Gascoigne had been an envoy in China and Japan like Sir Alvary was later, and they brought the vases and treasures back with them. Temple Newsam of course was massive and when you went in the pictures and the statues were out of this world.

Now at Hazlewood the Vavasours were still there when I first knew it, and there's still a Miss Vavasour who is a nun at Thickett Priory outside York. She's in her nineties and the last of the Vavasours to be born there. Only a few years ago she made another foundation at Wood Hall near Wetherby which was another Catholic stronghold. Hazlewood was unique. If you went in from the far side you went through an enormous archway into a great courtyard. Of course half of it is pulled down now but there was a long wing out there, the main hall this way and the chapel and then another wing of buildings which I think were the servant's quarters. Two men could ride through the archway side by side, but what fascinated me was a gallows slung out next to the church bell, and a veranda thing that the victim would go on and then they'd be pushed off. It's gone now.

I retired a long time ago and my district at Garforth collected a hundred quid and I wouldn't have it. I'd been paid a wage and they could give it to the poor. Doctor Taylor came to see me at the clinic and he said, "Look here, you'd be mad if you wanted to give someone a present and they wouldn't take it. We want to give you this and you've got to come," So I went and was given a bouquet of flowers and they'd bought a television set, and I enjoyed it for a bit.

It was Christmas and I was busy with school parties and I watched it with my supper. One night somebody used some very foul language, and I thought, "I must be going nuts. I'd never let anyone talk like that in my house." So the next morning I gave it away. Oh yes, just like that!

172

CHAPTER 9

SPORT

THIS SPORTING LIFE?

(Milford Messenger 1996)

The ending of the cricket season was never too sad an occasion for me, as my favourite sport, rugby, soon took over. But this year is different. Big money, and bitter public arguments, are not the build up to a new season that I am used to or like.

When my parents sent me off to school to Drax, I am sure they had not checked what games were played there. I had never heard or seen anything of the game of rugby till then. I wasn't to know that it was to become a major religion in my life.

Rugby Union at that time was more stops than starts, not spectacular to watch and not much better to play. In May 1946, while watching a cricket match, I listened to Wakefield Trinity beat Wigan 13-12 in the Cup Final, on the first and only portable radio in the school. I became a Trinity supporter, and had discovered Rugby League.

Wakefield Trinity, Rugby League Cup Winners 1946

To while away the time, some of us used to write off for autographs, enclosing stamped addressed envelopes, photographs and bits of paper. Rhodes and Sutcliffe, Hutton and Washbrook and the great Jim Sullivan are amongst my best, and really date me. But the 18-year-old Wakefield Wembley winger I wrote to was tops for me. Ron Rylance was a ball player, had attended QUEGS and could actually write his name in a letter saying he had played at Drax, and later had cycled to Sherburn. Our school day boredom was relieved somewhat by his Claire Rayner style answers to our rugby queries, and for me, autographed programmes, and once a famous claret and gold Huddersfield jersey, came my way.

Ron Rylance - Pin up, collar up

Eventually he played for Yorkshire and England at stand off and was in the British squad that won the world cup in France in 1954, but didn't play. When everything else was frosted off, I once met him outside the players' entrance at Headingley to watch the only game on, and finished up on the long field side bench with half the Leeds United players around me — and paying nothing!

Before going back to school in September I would travel to any game, going by bus, train and tram if father was too busy to chauffeur. After these ventures, my best tries were scored in the dark whilst fastening the hens up.

At Hull by train (a long trip) to watch Other Nationalities play France, I saw the great Arthur Clues carried off cold in the first few minutes with a broken jaw, from the best punch I have ever seen in any sport. Christmas Day derby games at Featherstone or Cas were extra friendly, with nips from miniatures, and the changed aroma from Woodbines to Whiffs was unique on that day.

With my father and friends I went on a supporters' special from Pontefract to cheer on Freddie Miller's adopted Featherstone against Workington - but in vain. We still had time to see 'Quo Vadis' before making a sober return in the early hours.

We were there in '54 to see Halifax draw with Warrington and then went off innocently mid-week to be in a crowd officially logged at 102,000! Hundreds got in free in the crush, including Sherburn butcher Walter Wainwright, who was hauled over the top of the turnstiles with many others.

Also in 1954 I was involved in the amalgamation of Old Draxonians and Selby and played until 1962. My wife, Pat, and her two sisters, Joyce and Nina, all married into the club and it was a special thrill to see three cousins play together in the first team at Pontefract on 1st December 2001, with another in reserve!

Selby Old Boys Rugby Union Side - first game 11th September 1954

Standing - F. Mellor ref., P. W. Mumby, N. Shaw, P. Bramley, R. W. Lister, G. M. Hanson, D. R. Liddle, G. W. Woodall, I. A. McGrath

Seated - C. Broadhurst, E. Burn, J. D. Bramley, S. Bramley, A. Mooney, S. M. Swift, V. Macgill

Playing and watching Union since those youthful, hero-worshipping days has seen my affair with Rugby League almost wear off, and Sky is now my limit.

When our accountant was chairman at Castleford about 1983, he invited my then eleven-year-old son and me as his guests to the Wakefield game and to see Australian Wally Lewis earn his astronomical £1000 for the game. I was amazed to find more discrimination there than in any union clubhouse I have ever known, with directors, players and children kept well apart. The Leeds United element and crudities were beginning to creep in even then.

It was still a big thrill a few years ago to meet Bert Cook, the little New Zealander who played for Leeds in their big spending days after the war. He had the smallest boots and the biggest smile! Shooting had become a big interest, and he was with us when we shot over the land where Drax power station now is. To eat lunch in his car, talk rugby, and listen to Winston Churchill's funeral was a mixed experience. He died too young of skin cancer. At his funeral at Boston Spa I still got a kick from saying good morning and walking into church with the great Lewis Jones. Sadly, Ken Trail and other just recognisable heroes, bent and limping from many old war wounds, and wrapped up from the cold in scarves and gloves, gave as much food for thought as the sermon!

I have been to Twickenham many times too, and once took a New Zealand young farmer, with two seven-shillings standing tickets, to watch his country play at the Arms Park. We stayed bed and breakfast for two nights with a farming family; amazingly their eleven-year-old son eventually played for Wales, and of course we still keep in touch.

Last February was the ultimate when I was invited to the Welsh game as the guest of our England Committee member, Oliver Grievson. A train journey, two nights near Green Park, a special bus to Twickers by 11.30, an empty new museum to savour, drinks, lunch, the game and more drinks (cola), bussed back to change to evening suit before strolling to the London Hilton for dinner with the teams!!

Any time during the next week or two I could have died quite happily, but since then the rugby world has degenerated into a shambles of wrangles over money. Where to get it, whom to give it to, and who controls the game is the problem. Shortly the two codes will probably merge and, like Headingley Cricket ground, these memories will fade into history, and me with them.

I apologise to cricket lovers about this article and its length. I have enjoyed putting it together and I know at least two or three people who will be interested and sympathise. I really have to thank my parents for sending me to a rugby playing school and giving me a religion that has been a lot of fun.

— But roll on next CRICKET season in Division 1 of the Wetherby League.

My Best Photo of My Big Three at Selby Rugby Dinner March 15th 1967 - Douglas Bader, Ken Holden and Johnnie Johnson

England Versus Wales at Twickenham
February 3rd 1996

I WAS THERE

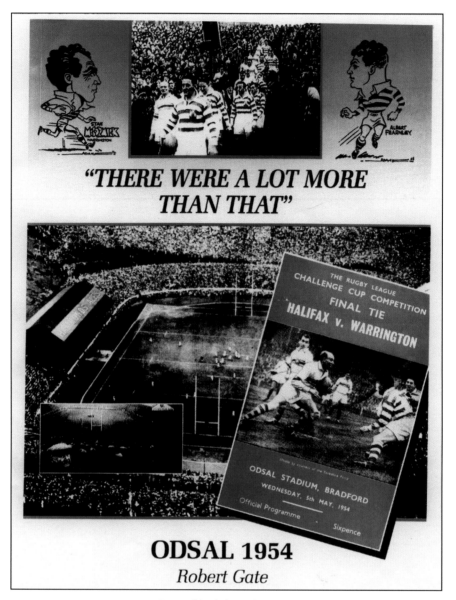

Cover of book by Robert Gate

Mr Gate got this book written on the cheap. The following advert in the 'Yorkshire Post' for survivors of the event got a lot of replies: -

<u>Search is on for faces in the crowd</u>

Were you there on May 5, 1954? If you were one of more than 102,000 spectators crammed into Odsal Stadium, then rugby league historian Robert Gate wants to hear from you. He is writing a book to mark the 40th anniversary of that dank evening when all roads for miles around were blocked by traffic heading for the RL Challenge Cup replay between Halifax and Warrington.

It was an extraordinary happening that was beyond the wildest expectations. The replay followed a 4-4 draw, which is still regarded as one of Wembley's biggest bores watched by a crowd of 81,841. Yet it seemed everyone wanted to see only the second peacetime final played in the North since the move to Wembley in 1929.

'I want to hear from those people, either by telephone or letter,' says Mr Gates. 'Everyone must have an interesting tale to tell, even those who didn't get there because they were prevented by the traffic congestion. Whether you were there as a spectator, gateman or programme seller I am interested in retelling your experiences.'

The replay turned out to be a much better match than the first with Warrington gaining a thrilling 8-4 victory. Those with a tale to tell should write to:

Robert Gate, Mount Pleasant Cottage, Ripponden Bank, Sowerby Bridge, HX6 4JL or telephone 422-823074

I wrote saying I hadn't as much as expected, but he replied and said it was just what he wanted and I am honoured to be in such company. The following is my contribution to the book:-

I am a sixty-year-old farmer who played Rugby Union for Selby. I was a great Rugby League fan in my young days but now only see it on TV. I have kept a diary since 1946 and thought I could go straight to the date for details of the Odsal Replay but I am disappointed at my offering – I think I have improved since.

We had travelled to the Wembley Final in a Ford Prefect, three big lads and a Drax schoolmaster, an ex-Hessle prop, H. E. Hopper (Harry), who was the driver. My diary entries for that day read:

April 24th

Dinner in Leicester Square

To Wembley in car

HALIFAX 4 WARRINGTON 4

Dull but even game

Tea at Maxim's Chinese Restaurant

Then saw Arthur Askey - 'Love Match'

Bed 12

I have to say I have had more hectic times since! The match ticket (3/-) is stuck in as is the signed serviette from Maxim's (my first Chinese meal). We decided to go to the replay, as we did not think there would be a big crowd. Times were hard then!

My diary says:

May 5th

Zoz came on 4.10 bus

Tea and off by 5

Jim, Wilf Earless. Uncle Walter, Kay and me

Terrible traffic and crowd

Very good game

HALIFAX 4 WARRINGTON 8

Rain after. Waited, then home OK

My father was away in France or he would have been with us and driven, so I must have driven. What a mixed bunch we were. Jim Bellwood was our foreman. Wilf Earless was the son-in-law of the lady who cleaned for my mother. He was a railwayman. Uncle Walter was the local butcher who stood about 5'8" and didn't see a thing. They hoisted him over the top of the turnstile to get him in so he was one who was not counted in the official attendance. He was a marine in the First World War. Zoz (Peter Mumby) went to school with me and hooked for Old Draxonians before we amalgamated with Selby in 1954. He could dribble a rugby ball like a soccer player. Kay was my younger sister.

If my father had not promised me a pound for a full diary in 1946, I would have sworn black and blue that I never took Wilf Earless anywhere, never mind Odsal in 1954!

Aerial view of Odsal Stadium

WARV UP AND GEE BACK
November 8th 1998

I forgot to ask yesterday whether horse ploughmen call their pastime sport. If they do yesterday's competition in our field bore no comparison to present day-overblown hype and posturing, and was a most pleasant experience with no losers. Nearly half an inch of rain overnight made car parking a worry but soil conditions were near perfect for a shiny finish.

Tom Cliffe at Camblesforth in 1997

Eleven pairs of various sorts of horses turned up from as far afield as Lincolnshire, Leicestershire, Lancashire and North Wales. 'Cardigan Jim' Reynolds, the eventual winner, travelled up the day before and his horses acclimatised in our stable of long ago which is now a casualty ward for pigs. Another Welsh couple came without their horses as their wagon had broken down. Not to worry, they borrowed those of an early finisher. Only a few horses work regularly and the others tend to be over keen and too frisky, especially those near to the static engines, which pop-popped at the end of the furrow.

I expressed my disappointment at the green wellies worn by sixty-five year old Tom Cliffe from Gainsborough. I had photographed him last year at Camblesforth in his brown boots, leather leggings, knee britches and a red and white spotted neckerchief and battered trilby. His acceptable excuse was that a gate at market had fallen on his foot and crushed his toe, making it painful to get into his boots. Tom had brought a spare plough for Sue Day, the only lady competitor to try, and she more than held her own.

Fred Stainthorpe and George Goodchild were the judges who had the task of putting them in order. All the work was of a very high standard; especially the high cut section. Here the ploughs have extra long mould boards to turn the soil gently without breaking it up. A weight boat presses the previous furrow to leave a nice pointed surface. In the old days oats would be broadcast and harrowing and rolling would complete the job; all very simple and uncomplicated.

There was no hurry yesterday as they only had to plough a tenth of an acre, but concentration and attention to detail was intense as the judges were looking for a level start and a shallow, even finish with no stubble showing. Cups and rosettes were the prizes, with every competitor receiving a horse brass and rosette as well as fifty pounds to help with travelling expenses.

Ploughing Match in progress

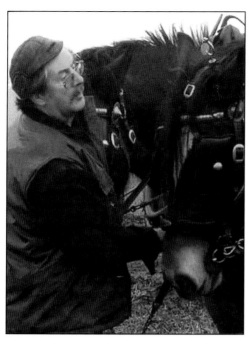
Warwick Romans with his horses

Starting with nothing, the hard working committee, fronted by Warwick Romans and his family, must be congratulated for a well-run event and a healthy profit. Over thirty local firms and stalwarts were sponsors to guarantee initial expenses. On the day a tombola and raffle also helped.

First prize, but not quite in keeping with the occasion, was nevertheless a much sought after Jordan Formula One yellow jacket. The Wheatsheaf delivered the lunchtime snap. The sun came out, the surface dried and people chatted and patiently watched the finishes eventually made, and passed their own judgement.

The event had been well advertised - even on Radio York - and I worried where we would put everyone that had expressed an interest and said they would come. In the end it was the old faithful that paid nearly five hundred pounds. Charlie Mytum hadn't come far. Harry Jackson and Roy travelled as usual by David Brown tractor and Brian Lockey rolled up on his bike. By 4.30 p.m. horses and folk had departed and a few piles here and there and some quality ploughing was all that was left.

It will be a pity to disc it up and plough it under with a four-wheeled hundred horsepower tractor and four furrow reversible plough doing more in an hour than they did all day!   But is it really Progress?   J.D.B.

IN TIME OF THE BREAKING OF NATIONS

Only a man harrowing clods
  In a slow silent walk
With an old horse that stumbles and nods
  Half asleep as they stalk.

Only thin smoke without flame
  From the heaps of couch grass;
Yet this will go onward the same
  Though Dynasties pass.

Yonder a maid and her wight
  Come whispering by;
War's annals will cloud into night
  Ere their story die.
                Thomas Hardy (1840 -1928)

A PLAIN COUNTRY FELLOW -

Is one who manures his ground well, but lets himself lie fallow and untilled. He has reason enough to do his business, and not enough to be idle or melancholy. He seems to have the judgement of Nebuchadnessar; for his conversation is among beasts, and his talons none of the shortest, only he eats not grass, because he loves not sallets. His hand guides the plough, and the plough his thoughts, and his meditations. He expostulates with his oxen very understandingly, and he speaks Gee and Ree better than English. His mind is not much distracted with objects: but if a good fat cow come in his way, he stands dumb and astonisht, and though his haste be never so great, will fix here half an hour's contemplation.

From Microcosmographie, 1628, a collection of character sketches chiefly written by John Earle (1601 - 65), Bishop of Salisbury.

Jim Elliot British Champion and 2002 Sherburn Winner

His finished work

THE FIRST WIN OF THE 1997 SEASON

This month I intended writing of the Old Mill Stream and George Watkinson's days at Low Mill, but lack of water again, time, and an inspirational cricket match yesterday, June 7th, compel me to bore you with that.

The Lions lost in South Africa, England lost in Argentina, Australia and Captain Taylor fought back in the Test and not many people backed Benny the Dip in the Derby. BUT behind the Swan, in front of a meagre crowd of about half a dozen, on a warm breezy afternoon with one vital shower, the real action took place.

Three Men and Proverbial Dog

Cocky Kirk Deighton arrived second from the top of Division 1 with their Australian who has three fast centuries to his credit. Milford, with one bad defeat and three honourable draws, languished at the other end — so a good game to win!

Captain Steve Hardacre, having won the toss, invited them to bat, as is the fashion. Peter Batty, Loz White and Dave Bramley shared the bowling and the wickets. The spinners had a rest day. The Oz man (name unknown) was nearly run out first ball, but proceeded to demonstrate his class until clean bowled by Peter Batty for 37 — one up to us!

Then down came the rain and out came the rule books. Half an hour lost for some reason or other, meant the team batting second lost five of their forty-five overs. After only forty-two of their forty-five Kirk Deighton declared. At least two of us (still from a crowd of six) and from a different era, thought this a noble gesture of Kirk Deighton's to give us an even chance. Not so however, their shrewd thinking was that their three unused overs would be added to the forty, so they had more time to bowl us out and gain full points. At 217 for 7 it evidently didn't occur to them that a few more runs might help avoid defeat.

James Liddle was disputedly caught for nought. Fellow opener Chris Allen was soon back for only 9, so not the best of starts. But Steve Korko, the in form man of the moment, held steady for his 26. Martin Bramley, 23, and Malcolm Chiltern, 24, contributed, but time was slipping away, and nearly ten runs an over became the required rate. Yet another epic innings was needed from captain Steve Hardacre and the crowd (like the Jazz Nite at church, disgracefully small) got it!! - 89 from 57 balls in 57 minutes, including six sixes and eight fours. The score book said his 50 came from 33 balls. In true village style Kirk Deighton (and their Ozy) had been smitten into Mike Elsworth's barley, nearly into some far off black sheep, and on to the tea hut roof. I have to admit that the Ozy did bowl him eventually, and when the final two overs came only five were needed, with wickets in hand. From the first, one of the most dramatic overs in the history of South Milford Cricket Club, with John Earless officiating at the bowlers end, came two runs and a man out, and still three needed.

First ball of the final over, another wicket down and doubts beginning to emerge, as did Peter Batty, crash hat on and bat swinging. Second ball a dot, as they say. Third ball an easy two to tie - but, calamity, in their hurry, they ran one short. So two still required to win from three balls. Easy but — a scampered single to tie at last, then another dot from a near (was) wide, and one ball to go in this absorbing game!! Either by accident or design, it was sadly too far for Mick Last to reach. The umpire said wide, and to their credit, at least Kirk Deighton didn't complain. An epic victory which took us from bottom up to nearly half way in the League.

TRIBUTE TO SKIPPER STEVE
Willow and cane, nothing but that —
O, but it's glorious, swinging the bat!
Leather and thread, there you have all —
O, but it's glorious gripping the ball!
Grass at our feet and the sun overhead,
Here let us play till the evening is red.
Then to the Swan and lustily sing,
Cricket's the king of games, CRICKET is KING!

E.V.Lucas

A weakened 2nd X1 arrived home from Shadwell in time to share in the celebrations. They had been out for 88 whilst chasing 175. Fourteen year old Justin, son of Clive, outshines his father on the cricket field having bowled nine overs and taken 2 for 17.

Other youngsters are performing well in the Thursday side two. Marital harmony and other dubious relationships have been severely tested in recent weeks as both sides remain undefeated in several cups. Playing four or five times a week is not unknown.   J.D.B.

Milford Seconds and Happy supporters after Winning Hare Cup at Spofforth August 26th 2001
Centre - Graham Hill and Son Jack with Cup, President K. P. Hammill, Scorer Sam O'Dell behind,
and Steve Hardacre Kneeling Right with Dog Odie

SEPTEMBER CRICKET

Yet another season approaches its finale with the AGM and post-mortems on 7th October and the dinner at Scarthingwell Golf Club on 8th November. So far there are no trophies to show off, although until the 2nds cracked last week to lowly Shadwell, they were riding high on top of Division Four, having knocked over two hundred in their previous three games to win. The 1st XI should just about avoid the drop after a reasonable season in Division One.

Saturday's away game at Fenton, so far avoiding the Princess Di blackout, will be a real derby as they are just below us.

Last Sunday, August 31st, was the one selected for our June coffee morning, with a lunch-time barbecue, bar, and six-a-side fun competition added on! Early rain cleared up and, although threatening and gloomy, the tombola, cakes and plant stalls etc. did steady business with many cricketers and relatives. The bouncy-castle kept our booming under fives happy for a while and Elizabeth Ransome's horse tiptoed round the boundary, with one or two unlikely Dettoris on board who had never been on a horse before. Katie White's human-fruit-bandit was a novelty, but soon owed me £9 before sorting out the rules. In his absence President Ken's shells were cleared twice, and the Wilkinson's father and son team won the egg throwing (and catching), with a record entry from local lads rolling up for the cricket.

Steaks, sausages and burgers were served, and beer and lager passed as adequate. The first team took to the field as rain began to fall. It accelerated gently all the time and everyone got wet except the umpires who were allowed brollies. Soon after the final, won by Peter Batty's side, the skies really opened up. Fortunately I had seen it coming and was back home reading the papers as over an inch came down. The rest were stranded in the pavilion trying to top up the profits by bottoming the barrels, and a good time, (as they say), was had by all. Luckily for the ducks, after recent dry summers and lack of water, their races had been abandoned earlier, otherwise they would have all been swept down to Cawood in the deluge.

Amongst the mayhem the intended Christmas Draw was postponed again until last night's committee meeting when it finally took place. One or two members did have trouble selling tickets past their draw by date in the 'Swan', and Shaun, the landlord, won the case of cider!!

Ambridge and the 'Bull' have nothing on us.

J.D.B.

Close of Play

How shall we live, now that summer's ended,
And bat and ball (too soon) are put aside,
And all our cricket deeds and dreams have blended –
The hit for six, the champion bowled for none,
The match we planned to win and never won?...
Only in the green-winged memory they abide.

How shall we live, who love our loveliest game
With such bright ardour that when stumps are drawn
We walk into the twilight, always the same
Old talk with laughter rounding off each tale –
Laughter of friends across a pint of ale
In the blue shade of the pavilion.

For the last batsman's out, the day
Like the drained glass and the dear sundown field
Is empty; what instead of summer's play
Can occupy these darkling months ere spring
Hails Willow once again the crowned king?
How shall we live so life may not be chilled?

Well, what's a crimson hearth for, and the lamp
Of winter nights, and those plump yellow books
That cherish Wisden's soul and bear his stamp –
Time's ever-changing, unalterable scoreboard,
Thick-clustered with a thousand names adorned;
Half the game's magic in their very looks!

And when we've learned those almanacs by heart,
And shared with Nyren...Cardus...the distant thrill
That cannot fade since they have had their part,
We'll trudge wet streets through fog and mire
And praise our heroes by the club-room fire:
O do not doubt the game will hold us still!

Thomas Moult

CHAPTER 10

WRITERS

J. L. CARR

I wouldn't think many people living in the humdrum sounding Carr Avenue will know much about the person their road is named after. Carr Avenue is a nice short address to write, but Joseph Carr, after whom it was named, and his family were something special. He came from farming stock and was the eldest of twelve. He and his wife had four children before they came to Sherburn in 1919. J. L. Carr, who I am pleased to see our splendid new magazine is taking an interest in, was the youngest.

Raymond (born 1905) still lives at Staintondale near Scarborough. He and his sister Kathleen married into the England family and the eldest of them, Ethel, married George Wright, a hard-working organiser and of Boys' Brigade fame. They were a clever, eloquent family. Ray has written his life story and called it 'The Journal', but sadly he won't see it deservedly published. Their mother wrote letters of advice and local gossip to them on their travels and all have been kept.

J. L. Carr

But J. L. Carr (known as Lloyd around here and Jim at Kettering) was two or three geniuses rolled into one. Sherburn Endowed Boys' School under Mr Thompson was a culture shock after Carleton Minniot near Thirsk and he twice failed his scholarship to Tadcaster Grammar so his parents paid for him to attend Castleford Secondary which entailed two rail journeys starting at South Milford.

He became a teacher mainly for the holidays, and taught in Birmingham for three years before the war. He became an intelligence officer in the RAF taking aerial photographs of Sherburn whilst passing by, but spending most of his war in Sierra Leone. He married Sally towards the end and their son Bob is an archaeologist. In 1967 he took a huge gamble by resigning his headship of Kettering Primary School to write full time and do a few other things.

Altogether he wrote eight novels as well as children's stories and poems. He was always doing something, and to wile away long boring days in Africa, he drew a large historic map of England, and later on, Yorkshire and other counties in the order that they might sell best. These and the sale of nearly a hundred little books of poems, quotations and dry humour helped to keep them afloat in the worrying early days.

Every one of his novels is on a different subject and in a different style. His last two he published himself and the long-winded title of 'Harpole, Foxberrow, General Publishers 1992' was about doing so.

The Harpole Report, 1972, must have been taken from his time at Sherburn School and was given a boost when Frank Muir selected it for his desert island. People go off and pop up later in other books like headmaster Harpole disappearing with gym mistress Foxberrow but turning up later as publishers.

A Season in Sinji, 1975, is a super officers versus men cricket novel from his time in Sierra Leone.

How Steeple Sinderby Won the FA Cup comes from his year as a pupil teacher back at South Milford and winning a Barkston Ash Cup Medal in the village side.

A Month in the Country, 1980, probably the best known and filmed with Kenneth Branagh, comes from his love of churches and has his usual unattainable woman. This time the vicar's wife.

The Battle of Pollocks Crossing relates to a year's teaching exchange at the far side of America. He came home from there the other way and walked across Japan!

What Hetty Did, 1989, was quite a challenge for a seventy-two year old - trying to get into the skin of sixteen-year-old Browning loving Hetty, searching for her real parents.

A Day in Summer, 1964, was partly filmed in Masham and I enjoyed a drink there earlier this summer in the King's Head where the action took place.

England according to J.L.Carr - all the history you need to remember

But novels, books and maps were not the end of this man's output. He had lived in Northamptonshire for over forty years, and in that time, mostly on Saturdays, he had painted churches, ancient buildings, windows, doorways and anything else that took his fancy. It amounted to seven huge volumes. They too were done in different styles and materials. He was an accomplished sculptor and in 1964 replaced two statues of Saint Peter and Saint Paul, destroyed at the Reformation, above the north door of Kettering Church.

Kettering Library holds a collection of his works and a day could be well spent there. It is a great pity he wasn't born in Sherburn.

Novels of J. L. Carr

- A Day in Summer (*Barrie & Rockliff, London, 1964*)

- A Season in Sinji (*Alan Ross Ltd., London, 1967*)

- The Harpole Report (*Secker & Warburg, London, 1972*)

- How Steeple Sinderby Wanderers won the FA Cup (*London Magazine Editions, 1975*)
  - '*It delivers with a kind of derisive gaiety some murderous blows at the fatheads who populate professional football.*' Benny Green, The Spectator

- A Month in the Country (*Harvester Press, Brighton, 1980*)
  - '*A Profoundly Affecting Tale.*' Auberon Waugh

- The Battle of Pollocks Crossing (*Viking, London, 1985*)
  - '*He is a wholly original writer and has written a book quite unlike any other.*' Nina Bawden

- What Hetty Did (*Quince Tree Press, Kettering, 1989*)
  - '*This book is generally so witty, so vivacious, and so original is a gem.*' Francis King, The Spectator

- Harpole and Foxberrow, General Publishers (*Quince Tree Press, Kettering, 1992*)
  - '*It's as accomplished, as entertaining and as outstanding as anything its author has done.*' D.J. Taylor

J. L. Carr's publications, novels and county maps are available from:- Quince Tree Press, 116 Hardwick Lane, Bury St. Edmunds, Suffolk, IP33 2LE. Phone 01284 753228; Fax 01284 765087

He died of leukaemia in February 1994 and left his huge collection of paintings in the hands of writer and friend Byron Rogers who has written his biography, 'The Last Englishman' published May 2003.

J.D.B.

Aerial view of Sherburn looking along Moor Lane towards Cross (Taken by J. L. Carr)

Aerial view from Milford to Sherburn showing New Lane to Highfield Villas, Bacon Factory Football Field and Eversley Park (Taken by J. L. Carr)

1940's

185

FRANK MUIR AND J.L.CARR

At this very uncricket time of year, except by satellite, this month's article was to be a tribute to the heroic deeds of Emley and to Dennis and Rod who try to do the same for South Milford.

I have written a little before of J.L.Carr's time as a student teacher under Captain Leggat and helping the local side win the Barkston Ash Cup in 1931. Mainly from these experiences he wrote his fourth novel in 1975, 'How Steeple Sinderby Won The F.F.Cup'. Three years before and from a less happy time at Sherburn School came The Harpole Report. This wasn't selling very well until Frank Muir chose it to take to his Desert Island and it got a tremendous boost.

Sadly Frank died early in the new year, just after I had bought his audio autobiography 'A Kentish lad' - so it wouldn't do him much good! This is his review of Steeple Sinderby, and it is nearly funnier than the book, which is dedicated to J.L.'s son Bob 'and for those others of my generation who have shivered into their kit behind hedgerows and in ditches'. - I suppose that includes Dennis and Rod.   J.D.B.

> Smart lad to slip betimes away
> From fields where glory does not stay
> And hold to the low lintel up
> The still defended challenge cup.

A.E.Houseman   The Shropshire Lad

The unedited view of 'How Steeple Sinderby Wanderers Won the F.A.Cup'

by J.L.Carr (London Magazine Editions, £2.50)

Daily Mail   Frank Muir

Happening upon this deeply funny and tremendously enjoyable book, by a writer unknown to me, produced mixed emotions. My first, unworthy thought was to hug the discovery to me, much the same as one does not go round yapping to everyone that you have found a pub in Wandsworth that does oysters, a tornedos steak and a glass of Medoc for 83p. But my second, more beautiful, Keats-like impulse was to spread the good word.

As the shrewd will gather from a hint in the title, 'How Steeple Sinderby Wanderers Won the F.A.Cup' is to do with football. This was not a favourable start for me as I am hard-pressed to tell the difference in a cup-tie between a bully-off and a leg bye, but this book is as much about football as 'Steptoe and Son' is about non-ferrous scrap-metal dealing, or 'The Tempest' is about adverse weather conditions off Corfu. The book is about people; the villagers of Steeple Sinderby who, due to certain people in their midst, won the F.A. Cup and were, in the main, little changed by it all.

The story is narrated by Mr Gidner, who writes verses for greetings cards, as a run-up to his Official History. This, he explains, 'will be much longer, bad taste will be expunged, its style is going to have more quality. It will also cost more'. We get to know the narrator well, and like him much, but are only given two tiny hints as to his past. One of the joys of J.L.'s style is his non-metropolitan economy of words. With a kind of Yorkshire abruptness he mentions a fact and leaves it to us to clothe it in theory. The two hints on Mr Gidner'g past are typical of J.L.'s tip-of-the-iceberg technique. The first, on page eight, goes, 'After I had this trouble and left theological college, I landed up in Sinderby...' The second, on page seventy-three, equally pregnant with implication, says, 'I couldn't give my mind to composing verses for Mother's Day (hard enough at the best of times because of the trouble I had with my own mother)...'

The countryside around Steeple Sinderby is lived in by people who could never conceivably live in a town so it is described without sentiment: 'People don't know about rural England between the last Mystery Autumn Foliage Coach Trip and the Mystery Blossom Journey into Spring. Mud, fog, dripping trees, blackness, floods, mighty rushing winds under doors that don't fit, sticking organ keys, stone floors and that dreadful smell of decay.'

Sinderby's giant-killing journey to Wembley is made possible by the headmaster of the village school, Dr Kossuth, an intelligent genius who escaped from Hungary, who formulates his Seven Postulations on the art of the possible in football, e.g. 'Postulation One: Surely it is possible to move a ball without staring down at your feet. Women don't watch their hands moving when knitting.' Other Sinderby non-players and players, who refuse to be forgotten once they have been read about, include Giles the vicar, who sprints along the wing like a reincarnation of the entire Greyfriars first eleven, meeting opposition with a good, old-fashioned shoulder-charge; Ginchy Trigger, girl-journalist, whose eccentric prose style recreates the games for readers of the 'Messenger'; Sid Swift, who was a First Division striker until he began to ask himself What It Was All About, whereupon, not being equipped to think, he wilted and took to his bed in his mother's house, his mother answering all enquiries with the statement that Sid was upstairs studying for the Open University; Maisie Twemlow, the last living fan of John Lennon; Corporal, who had a silver plate in his head from the battle of Alamein and could only answer the last question but one put to him. And Mr Fangfoss, Chairman of the Football Club, and everything else - a man much admired by the narrator - whose family had farmed their 800 acres since Agincourt, and was born with his mind made up.

Foreword to 'How Steeple Wanderers Won the F.A.Cup'

Book-writing can be a tedious job needing some incentive to keep one at it. The impulse here was 'Can this unbelievable feat be made to sound like the truth even though it didn't happen?'

So I stacked the cards - a foreigner with remarkable theories, two young men with good reasons for having quit top-class football, a Chairman of napoleonic ability.

Then I dredged up memories of 1930 when I was an unqualified teacher, 18 years old and playing that single season for South Milford White Rose when we won a final that never ended. (Pitch invasion and furious fighting are not new things.) I learnt much of rural life during that long-gone autumn, winter and early spring...But is this story believable? Ah, it all depends upon whether you want to believe it. J.L.Carr, 1992

Good Photo of J. L. Carr's South Milford AFC
Ernest Harrison in overcoat, Granville Hepp. arms folded left and Frank Poole behind towel man.

Back Row - Raymond Boston, Roy Boston, ?, Mr Boston, Bill Hodgson, Bill Anderson, ?, Granville Heptinstall, Ernest Harrison
Front Row - Clarry Cawood, ?, Frank Poole, Lloyd Carr, Fred Boston, Denis Laycock, Vince Gell

- A poor photo from a newspaper cutting of 1931 Barkston Ash Cup Winning Team who played 'A glorious game against Boston Spa in the Cup Semi-Finals at Tadcaster on Saturday'.

A.G. STREET

I have been collecting books by A.G. Street for many years and a second-hand bookshop in Beverley has been my Mecca. A.G. Street was a Wiltshire farmer whose alternate enterprise in the depressed twenties and thirties was writing. Exasperated by the opinions expressed and solutions put forward in newspapers, his wife goaded him into writing to the 'Daily Mail' and to his surprise a cheque for three guineas came back and a request for more.

'Farmer's Glory' was his first, and the most famous of his novels and reminiscences. It vividly told of pre-mechanisation at the turn of the century when half the population was still involved in agriculture. He survived three years of prairie farming in Canada, which left him with tales to tell of ploughing virgin land and lonely survival for the rest of his life. He was lucky not to be fit enough for World War 1 and the book tells of his struggle to survive the hard times that followed when once again cheap food came in from all over the world.

In the days before the Milk Marketing Board he cut out his shooting, gardeners, his daughter's ponies and sacked most of his men, and went back to dog and stick farming. He came north to buy a new-fangled Hosier milking bail so he could milk the cows in the field to save walking them home. He then bought a bottling machine and went off delivering to his friends in the area. It is now called profit enhancement, so it isn't new.

Eventually AG must have written more than two dozen books. One, 'Wessex Wins', was about writing 'Farmers Glory' and getting into broadcasting and fame. His Wiltshire wit and wisdom was an asset for years on 'Any Questions', and his page in 'Farmers' Weekly' was always the first I read. His writings of the bad times in the twenties and thirties make present troubles seem par for the course. If he were alive today I'm sure he would quickly grasp the supermarket and the political situation but still be amazed at the changes since he died, just before harvest, July 21st 1966.

He wasn't happy with his life in 1939, as his writing, lecturing and broadcasting had made him a stranger to his farm and he was using home for the occasional bed and breakfast. He was fat, unfit and lazy, and forty-seven. With the outbreak of war his moneymaking engagements dried up. His only man was a reservist and soon went. AG was left with three pensioners and two lads to carry on.

In 1950 my father was in a similar position. I had just left school when Harold Barnet, who had lived in at Sherburn in the thirties as a lad, went off to work in the foundry at Avery's for more money. He earned every penny he got there and father had only me left to fall out with for a short time. The first Titan tractor had long since been replaced by two green Fordsons but we still had four horses and a cow to milk. We killed two pigs a year in the garage, salted them in the cellar and hung them from hooks in the kitchen ceiling. Mother sold eggs for pocket money, geese and ducks were fattened for Christmas.

The beginning of the end of those days came when father bought three grey Fergies at Otley show. Hydraulics, three point linkages and weight transference came with them, and later a muck loader and spreader, and the muck fork was almost redundant.

I have a black and white photo taken in the early fifties of drop drilling wheat after potatoes with a horse pulling a wooden drill that must have been old when it came from Fairburn in 1906. Soon after the shafts were replaced by a home made draw bar for the Fergy to take over yet again. The binder and grass reaper had been pulled by the old Fordsons for some time, and the hard graft of stooking, leading, stacking and later threshing went on with us until 1959 when an Allis Chalmbers combine was acquired from Tysons of Selby for £1750. Ninety thousand pounds wouldn't buy a very sophisticated machine today.

Only one and a half percent of the population are in agriculture now and the camaraderie of the pea-pulling, beet-bashing, tatty-scratting, hoeing and threshing teams are gone for ever, but life, though hectic, is a lot easier for those who are left. In Milford this week (17-7-00) the last three farms of around eight are reduced to two, as the tiles start to come off Michael Elsworth's barn. In Sherburn the last farm of thirty in 1906 awaits the same fate. People have to live somewhere, and smelly farms and noisy dryers are not happy bedfellows in modern villages.

I'm glad father put 'Farmer's Glory' in my way and wish I had the time to read more of AG Street's output, and three guineas to write an article for the Messenger at present day values would be tempting.

His daughter Pamela wrote an affectionate tribute to her much loved father.

'Tis hard to have to lie in bed
Dreamin',
Wi' all the summer's work ahead,
Screamin'
And callin' out fer such as I
To lend a hand 'afore I die,
But 'tis no use: my time be nigh,
Seemin'.

I've watched the barley up on hill
Growin';
I'm getting on but I be still
Knowin'.
And I do know as how fer me
There's only one more harvest, see?
My work be done; 'tis right I be
Goin'.

So when I'm took, don't let 'em bide
Weepin'
Wi' all the rest o' countryside
Reapin'.
Just mind thic barley field up yon,
You get 'un carried when I'm gone;
And leave me be to go right on
Sleepin'.

List of Books by A. G. Street
Farmer's Glory
Strawberry Roan
The Endless Furrow
The Gentlemen of the Party
A Crook in the Furrow
Already Walks Tomorrow
Holdfast
Shameful Harvest
Wessex Wins
Wheat and Chaff (Comprising Hedge trimmings, Country Days and Thinking Aloud)
Harvest by Lamplight
Feather-Bedding
Farming: How to Begin
Master of None
In His Own Country (Comprising Country Calendar, Moonraking, A Year of My Life, Hitler's Whistle and Ditchampton Farm)
Landmarks
Round the Year on a Farm
Kittle Kattle
Sweetacres
Bobby Bocker
From Dawn Till Dusk
Farming England
Land Everlasting
Cooper's Crossing
Fish & Chips
Johnny Cowslip

CHAPTER 11

MISCELLANEOUS

1933 AND ALL THAT

The second instalment of the OJS saga and all the high tech wizardry used, brings to mind the more basic detective work of the Saxton Grange Murder on 5 September 1933.

The villages of Saxton, Towton and Sherburn and the names Frederick Morton the deceased, his wife Dorothy, the maid Ann Houseman and the villain Ernest Brown were for a few months as famous as OJ.

It all happened on the patch of our very own PC Broadhead whose son I went to school with. Like the shooting of President Kennedy, everyone I talk to from that era can remember what exactly they were doing when they heard of it. Walter Wainwright says Morton, having moved from Huddersfield, was a Town supporter and had his buildings painted blue and white. They were both from moneyed families and had met on the hunting field, but as well as farming Morton dealt in cattle and many on Hire Purchase. He covered a wide area spending a lot of time away. Mrs Morton, to put it mildly, was flighty and bored and half frightened and probably threatened by Brown, the widower groom who also liked the opposite sex and as it later turned out had a record of violence.

On September 6th news went round that there had been a fire at Saxton Grange and later on Mr Morton had been found dead in his car in the burned out garage. He smoked and drank and occasionally slept in his car and at first an accident, as Brown had planned, seemed to be the case. Sadly for Mr Brown he hadn't the selection of TV whodunnits and video nasties to learn from as we have today. He was a real amateur, but it took the best people to prove him guilty.

He had taken the gun from the house ostensibly to shoot rats and had probably shot his boss in the car after he had arrived home at about 9 o'clock. He took the gun back, but took away one of two carving knives with which to cut the telephone wires. The two women were terrified of Brown's behaviour and goings on and dare not go to bed. At three in the morning they heard explosions and saw the glow of the garage fire at the other side of the buildings. They tried the useless phone and together with the two-year-old child, fled over the fields to Mr Hall's farm.

Brown outside Sherburn Police Station

Brown meanwhile, was dashing about letting out the horses and eventually went in the cattle wagon to the foreman's house in Towton to at last phone the fire brigade.

At the end of the day he had slipped up in many ways. Cutting the wires was to delay the fire engine as long as possible so that the body in the car would burn away. He forgot about a diamond ring, the keys and the grisly remains that the pathologist at first did not want to touch. Mr Churchill, the London gun expert, examined the gun, cartridges, pellets and wad which was found in the body and they all matched up. Methods used for the first time in this country came into their own when enlarged micro-photos of the telephone wire ends were compared with fresh cuts made by the same carving knife, and are still to be seen to this day on the wall.

Clumsily he had emptied petrol cans from both cars to get a good blaze, but had left the basin and moving spanner set to the appropriate size on the scene. He insisted he had been to bed but except for his slippers he was still dressed as the day before with collar and tie. The crafty foreman also peeped through his hut window to see an undisturbed bed.

Other things about Brown came to light during the enquiry. He had probably poisoned his wife but as a man can't hang twice, they didn't exhume the body. He must have been held at Sherburn police station as I have a box brownie snap of him taking the air outside with a pot of tea in one hand and his flat cap in the other looking a bit like Errol Flynn. The jury took less than an hour to decide his fate, but although the public petitioned for his reprieve, he was executed at Armley Goal on 6th February 1934.

If you, dear reader, were around at that time you will probably remember it well. Sweet dreams!!

EVERY VILLAGE SHOULD HAVE ONE
- A LOCAL HISTORY SOCIETY (Oct '95)

Amazingly it is twenty-one years since Sherburn Local History Society was born and we are still going strong!

John Penty hosts Sherburn Local History Society at Bilborough Manor

I see from my diary that on a cold, wet night on 29th October 1974, seventeen people were interested enough to turn up at the library, and we have enjoyed summer outings and winter talks ever since. I still have my notes for that meeting and they will be used at our anniversary dinner at historic Monk Fryston Hall on 30th January. Guest of honour will be our first Chairman and present Brayton Vicar, Rev. David Reynolds.

Mr A.O. Elmhirst was an early speaker who told of being offered a horse and trap to meet him off the train when he first came to work in 1928. Sam Hood from Aberford and Saxton's Dick Pearson were our self-taught experts who were often more than a match for visiting speakers.

All Saints Church takes some beating, but Cawood, Stillingfleet, Birkin, Kellington, Lead, Bolton Percy and Bilborough with its restored Fairfax tomb are others we have enjoyed. York and its Minster and Selby Abbey are local treasures we have made full use of. We have explored the turrets of ruined Wressle Castle, and sampled the grim accommodation of Civil War prisoners deep below the lawns of Pontefract Castle.

I see also I suggested the Halls of Monk Fryston, Scarthingwell, Ledston, Grimston, Lotherton and Parlington for starters. One month we explored the attics of Huddleston where Italian prisoners lived in the war. Another occasion we were in the cellars of Hazlewood where mothers and newborn babies were taken for safety in those dangerous times. None of us present will forget our monk guide telling us with feeling what a glorious sight it was from there when the moon shone on John Smith's Brewery!!!

Sadly I think we have been content to be listeners rather than doers, and except for detailed minutes of our goings on, haven't produced much worthwhile. In a few more years there won't be much village history to record. Tragically Sherburn's historic Hungate School awaits a buyer who is brave enough to take on the preservation restrictions.

However I am proud to have helped start a now thriving Society at Fairburn in March 2001 and I am pleased that Hillam now has one too.

J.D.B.

SIGNING IN

I hope it never happens here, but occasionally I wonder what I would throw out of the window first if our house happened to catch fire. Pictures, photos, slides, old books, post cards, stamps, cigarette cards, scrapbooks, fifty years of diaries, our Visitors' Book or my wife Pat; would all have me in a dither deciding which to rescue. After much consideration I think the answer would be for Pat to get out with the Visitors' Book and leave me to jettison as many diaries and photo albums as possible.

Although not very well written, my diaries are a good record of the events of my life, starting when Wakefield Trinity beat Wigan 13 - 12 in 1946. Births, marriages and deaths of hundreds of other people and all sorts of Cup, Derby and Aintree winners are listed too, plus the last twenty-five years of rainfall. Unfortunately, on the odd time when I am approached to settle an argument, I sometimes find I'm not as efficient as I thought.

As an ex-autograph hunter, and someone prone to hero worship, our Visitors' Book is something special and was a wonderful present back in 1960, although not fully appreciated at the time. Many of those early names - friends of my parents and relations - are sadly long gone now, but it's good to see their neat, legible signatures and occasional message. Visitors from afar have dutifully signed in. Young Farmers starting their Christmas carol singing tours signed in en masse over the years, their writing often better than their singing.

These thoughts and many others were triggered off when the BBC announced that Kenneth Branagh was to play Shackleton on his doomed 1914 Antarctic Expedition and the epic return of all the party. On October 27th 1969 a C. J. Green of 11 Laurence Avenue, Hull had signed my book followed by "The Antarctic Chef 1914 -16 Endurance 1921-22 Quest".

Endurance stuck in the Ice

I had read in the Yorkshire Post that he was the last surviving member of the expedition and had shown his glass slides to four US Presidents. I wrote and invited him to come and show them to Church Fenton Young Farmers, which was quite a comedown, but he agreed. We booked the Church Hall and invited everyone and had a good crowd. Mr Green came on the train, had tea with us and stayed the night. We had a job getting him to bed, he was still going strong and must have been nearly eighty. Everyone there that night will never forget him telling us of their big mistake when stranded and starving. They had killed and buried the dogs, so they could live off their food - but without skinning them! Later and hungrier still they dug up the dogs to eat and enjoy, but had great trouble with the frozen skin and hair. My diary account says 'best slide lecture ever!' I look forward to the programme next week to see if they have a cook called Charlie.

Another treasured entry is ex Romanian POW, Otto Hann. On 6th August 1974 he had written, 'Back in England again, a free man, after twenty-five years'.

Man of the Moment

H. E. Cook - Happy Huntsman at Drax 1965

Bert Cook was a tiny, smiling Leeds Rugby League fullback just after the war. He had played with the New Zealand Army side, married a local girl and eventually settled in Boston Spa. I first met him when we shot over land on which Drax Power Station now stands. He was a director of Andrews of Leeds, tile people, and for the first time ever I hardly argued when our kitchen floor was wearing thin, and H. E. Cook's still stylish autograph was in my book as part of the contract!

Hannah Hauxwell's writing is so big that she takes one and a half pages on 22nd March 1995. The night before I had shown farming slides at Sherburn Church Hall and she had helped with the commentary. She still loves her cattle, and next day she was just in time to see the few we had left before calling it a day with them! She is a wonderful, calm, quiet lady who can't be hurried. Her writing is nearly an inch high, with every dot and comma in place. You have to be very patient in her autograph queue, but I had no opposition when next day she wrote as she talked – 'Thankyou for taking the time off in a busy day to show me your lovely bullocks, which I have enjoyed very much' (underlined). Try stopping me.

A Yorkshire Rose ....

GRANDPA WALKER OR FATHER-IN-LAW LES

(May 1st 2003)

Amazingly this book is at last being printed. My father-in-law Les Walker has been doing a good publicity job in recent weeks and deserves a late selection of his eventful life, which I taped back in April 1992. He now lives alone in a little bungalow and gets his weekly fix with his eldest daughter Patricia at Hambleton and Brayton whist drives. The hard bit is sorting the genuine story from his well-told, longish jokes. In courting days all three daughters dreaded him reaching for his joke book (all clean), but despite this they all successfully married into Selby Rugby Club and, together with golfer son Leslie, produced him twelve grandchildren.

His best achievement was marrying Jessie Swaine in 1940, daughter of Louis and Fanny. Grandma Swaine, who was the eldest of the Makin family at Fairburn, never really got over her youngest son Don going missing on his second flight laying mines, and Les is never far from tears when describing collecting his things with brother-in-law Eddie and riding his motor bike home from outside his hut. I have inherited Don's hairbrush with RAF insignia.

Les was born at Layfield, a small rented farm on the Gascoigne estate. His father enjoyed Whitkirk market and was not a good example of nose to the grindstone. Brother Henry was five years older and bigger and stronger and they didn't get on. In 1937 farming was really bad and his mother suggested an alternative enterprise. Serving as an apprentice at electricians R. F. Winders after leaving Aberford School at fifteen was not a happy experience, crawling through grimy false roofs and threading cables as Leeds changed over from gas. Twelve and sixpence a week with four and sixpence bus fare wasn't a road to riches either. He was soon back on the farm leading peas and potatoes in his new five ton Bedford lorry. But they were still arguing. Their father suggested that Henry took another farm, but he was not keen on leaving Les on Layfield. He had no liking for cows and weekend work either and later went into contracting and corn drying and had a garage at Barwick-in-Elmet.

Les in Leeds United Strip

Jessie Swaine

Les solved the problem by asking if he could go, and within two days took Hagg Farm at Gateforth. He was already courting Jessie, so with her fifty pounds or so of savings and his of sixty-two pounds they were married February 6th 1940. They splashed out at the York Station Hotel but only for one night of honeymoon.

His wife was a good tennis player and Les had played cricket for Aberford and football for Whitkirk until successful trials took him to Elland Road in the days of Tom Holley, brothers George and Jack Milburn and Con Martin. He couldn't get into the first team but played for three seasons in the reserves at their Altofts ground in the Yorkshire League. In later life he had a season ticket and was a big admirer of John Charles.

Dealing and a quick profit were his forte (and he is still keen to win at whist). After buying two cows at Wren Hall, Drax, for less than twenty pounds one night, the fed-up farmer offered him the whole farm for three thousand pounds. They shook hands on the deal but to make sure he insisted that Les signed over a sixpenny stamp. Next day it was the farmer who had second thoughts but couldn't back out, as the sixpenny stamp and nothing less had sealed the deal.

They converted a piggery into a milking parlour with an assortment of cows and were soon producing two hundred gallons a day. If an unfortunate cow dropped below one-and-a-half gallons it was soon out, sold as fat and replaced. It was called a milk and feed system and after a Ministry demonstration a man stayed behind and offered him nine thousand pounds after only fifteen months there. Not only that, he asked Les to look after it rent-free until he got married. Les was more than happy to do so.

Gathering early potatoes July 1943 at Hagg Farm. Patricia Age 2 and Father Les showing how it's done

All was going well. He'd rented another farm and had bought a hundred acres at the Maspins at Hambleton, near Selby where he later built a house with stone he had had given from two cottages at Bingley. Lionel King built it in 1948 and they moved in after six months. Sadly in the summer of 1947 Les had been struck down with Infantile Paralysis or Polio, as it has become known. His football chances had gone with the war but he was captain of Selby Londesborough cricket team. He didn't feel too well at an evening game at Hillam but set off next day to Headingley for the Test match against South Africa. Len Hutton scored a century (checked Wisden) but Les never got into the ground and came home feeling ill. That was a Tuesday and he was not diagnosed until Friday. He was in Seacroft for two weeks and wonders if he'd got penicillin sooner he'd have made a better recovery. He was determined to get well and made himself go, sometimes secretly, but had lost the strength in his legs and stomach muscles. Cricket had had it and later he took up golf and was mustard around the greens and became captain of Selby Golf Club.

May 20th 1960 - A young Leslie Walker Jnr. Gives demo to Leif Sylling and Fred Stoker at Common Farm, now under Gascoigne Wood Pit site

Sporting genes were passed on. Leslie Junior played one hundred and seventy-eight times at golf for Yorkshire and is now a Walker Cup selector. Daughter Nina when only seventeen won the North East England Ladies' foursomes with partner Jane Stringer and retired soon after. Four grandsons have played for Selby RUFC but sadly he's never got to see them play.

About this time, and for a bit of a holiday, Les joined a group of farmers on a trip to Ireland. They left him to rest in their Dublin hotel. Les read in a paper that there was a cattle sale at Ganleys just down the road. He got himself there, found them cheap and bought thirty-two. He seemed surprised that they wouldn't accept a cheque from an unknown Englishman. Luckily Selwyn Leake, a Whitkirk market man, came in, vouched for him and saved the day. Two weeks later he was back and proudly boasts that except for Christmases he attended Ganleys' Monday market every week for the next thirty-four years. Ganleys' market was run by brothers Will, Jim, David and Bobby. They were up and going by 4.30am, selling up to four thousand store cattle and walking them to the boats for England before the town got busy. Three hundred was the most Les bought on one trip.

Except for the first two years of travelling by boat the rest were by plane from Manchester with many other northern buyers. There was an on-going battle between traditional fairs and the auctions at that time and Les was even threatened once. The auctions won but it now seems unbelievable that the Irish cattle trade has almost come to an end. You can now drive miles and never see a field of decent bullocks of any sort, never mind Irish, and I only know two or three people fattening any inside. There is no doubt that Les Walker Snr. was there in its hey day and I'm glad I've got him taped.

Les and Jessie Walker at a Wedding in 1965

THE LAST ROUNDUP

There were mixed feelings as our last seven bullocks were loaded as usual, at 6.30 a.m., for Selby market on 16th August 1996, and Home Farm was without cattle for the first time in nearly one hundred years!!

The sons of my father's friends, who used to vie with each other for the biggest and best at Wetherby market, gave up years ago. I think we kept on for nostalgia and exercise, and for having something living on the place besides the cats and dogs. BSE, and all the form filling and hassle since, were the final straw, as well as feeding something for months that was not appreciated and enjoyed with a clear conscience any more.

Golden Pig Prospects

Instead, two yards that each held fifty fine animals, are now filled with six hundred pigs every three months, especially for Mr. Sainsbury – boars and gilts together with nothing to do but eat, sleep, etc.!! It's a great life for them, but I'm still filling up on beef. An uncle used to say, 'You never get tired of beef', and he's right. Harold Lunn (brother of bike shop man, Granville) used to buy the tops for Mrs. Wilson's shop at Crossgates, and that is where we still go for joints for special occasions!

Having pigs doesn't make the decision as drastic, and in spite of the flies and the smell, it is good to be involved with something that is wanted, and hopefully, pays better for the work undertaken. I won't miss the form filling, ear tag checking and the wild ones up the wall, the vet bills, the dead ones, doors and gates left open and wires cut. Over the years we have recovered cattle from out of Sherburn, Barkston and off South Milford station.

There is very little manual work left in farming, so the little bit of shovelling and carrying was a good warm up on a winter's morning and the weekend work was cheap therapy. It was always a special feeling leaving them on Christmas Eve, all bedded up and content, their holiday fodder handy for quick distribution later. Already we miss them in the fields and the evening stroll to count them, and check for lame ones.

Evening walk - Ch. Mills, Jim Bramley & Ken Millar

I cherish the friends made and the crack (jocular conversation), especially at Wetherby. Everyone knew each other, and what sort of cattle they bought. Butchers tended to buy from the same people. Afterwards it was either the pub or the teashop, and if the trade was exceptionally good, and being a Monday, the week was off to a good start!

Wetherby Cattle Market Christmas 1985 - Bidders and Spectators

J.L.Carr liked to quote, L.P. Hartley 'The past is a foreign country; they do things differently there.' Farming when I left school in 1950 seems a world away. We had four horses, two Fordson tractors, an old blue cow for milk, hens, ducks and geese, and we killed two pigs a year to share out with our neighbours. Ninety Irish bullocks averaged £55 then compared with £560 for forty-nine beasts last year.

Until the troubles started, and the trade eventually stopped, we bought all our store cattle in the West of Ireland around Galway and up into Connemara. There were aeroplanes then, but we can't have trusted them and went by train to Holyhead, by boat to Dublin, then north by train, with a view of the Mountains of Mourne, to where our buyer, Tom MacMahon lived in Clones. He hadn't a car so we travelled by train and bus, and stayed at the best hotels, where we put as much butter on soda bread as we fancied. Now cattle are sold in modern marts by the kilogram. Then it was fairs in the middle of town, or a handy field, with a lot of bartering and a final hand slap to seal the deal. Sheep and pigs were penned in front of shops, houses and hotels, and maybe up to two hundred cattle, of all ages, were kept in separate lots in the middle by drovers, without any pens at all. By daylight it was all over. The farmers were paid and cattle loaded on to lorries and trailers at the old railway yard, to catch the boat and on by rail to Milford Station, from where we walked them home, often very weary.

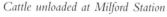

Cattle unloaded at Milford Station

Haggling for Cattle - Pat MacMahon & Charlie Maguire

The cattle business in Ireland is like a second religion to the people and everyone takes an interest. To travel about with people like Tom, and after him Charlie Maguire, was like being with royalty. Charlie had a Ford car and lived in Mullingar. If we hadn't bought enough at a fair we would then go off around the country, buying on the farms for the rest of the day. I was too young for the black stuff then but remember the mixed grills and steaks with awe!

I heard the other day, on the radio, that the last butcher's shop in Marlow had closed. The end of the road for the Milford shop, like so many others, just came quietly. The last farm in Sherburn awaits conversion to houses as Wainwright's Farm moves out on to the Tadcaster road (June 2003).In a few more years time, when everyone is mooching around supermarkets pushing their trolleys and hopefully buying our bacon, I'll be quite happy not to be around!

The Sun sets on Home Farm Beef

and on a wonderful dry harvest of 2003

ACKNOWLEDGEMENTS

At last this book has nearly come together. It has been quite a challenge for a humble farmer in his spare time and Pat and Suzanna have enjoyed the freedom of the TV controls.

I would like to thank again all those who have talked to me over the years, on tape or otherwise, and those too numerous to name who have given or lent me their old photos and information. Thanks also to my niece Joanna for her interest and advice, Ken and Joan Walker and latterly Julia Rankin for working overtime at proof reading, Norman Sykes and son Andrew of North Wolds Printers for their patience and Barbara Wilson for trying to set high standards of presentation.

Copyright I know is a delicate subject and I have tried my best to contact all whom it may concern. The following have been of great help in their different ways - Mavis Atkinson, Christine Bull, Raymond and Bob Carr, Stanley Cherry, Sgt. Ben Couchman, Peter Dawes, John Facer, Robert Gate, Brian Goulding, Sally Hall, Peter Halls, Marie Hartley, Vic and Irene Henry, Billy Hunter, Lincs. Aviation Centre, Byron Rodgers, Anthony Saddler, Thelma Tate, Joan Welbourn and Geoff Wilson.

I hope my selection of poems has added to the whole and I appreciate the skills and sentiments of the following on their various subjects - Margaret Barr , Henry George DFC, Omar Khayy·m, E.V. Lucas, Thomas Moult, Walter Scott, Colin Shakespeare, Pamela Street, Benny Wilkinson, , and Sam Wood.

Humble apologies to anyone I've missed. So far it has been a lot of fun.

J.D.B.

GENTLEMEN ALL! - & LADIES

Photo Gallery (pages ll & lll named left to right and top to bottom)
Grey Fergyites (back page of dust jacket)

Left Side	Right Side	Left to right and top to bottom
Digby Lamb	Frederik Frank	Ken White
June Denby	Roy Deighton	J.B.
Ken Hammill	Roy Liddle	Bob White
Bill Bramley	Suzanna Bramley	Sam Snowling
Geo & Charlie Mytum	Leif Styling	J.D.B.
J.D.B.	Steve Allen (Santa!) & Margaret Battle	Chris Bramley
Bernard Qualter	Snowy	Kay B.
Maurice & Rosmund Sissons	Jim Bellwood	Bob Winn
Henry Midgely	Roland Bradley	Bob White
Fred Sissons	Vern Midgley	David Heath
Bill Lyn	Laury Steele	J.D.B.
Jim Bramley	Norman Summers	J.D.B.
Walter Wainwright	Harry Jackson	Bob White
Walter Bramley	Charlie Mytum	Student
	Mick Birkley	Frank Downing
		J.D.B.
		Student
		J.D.B.